INDOMITABLE SPIRIT

Life in The Shadow of Death

INDOMITABLE SPIRIT

INDOMITABLE SPIRIT

Life in The Shadow of Death

Ziad Nassar

Edited By: Dr. Nadra Assaf

Published By
Ziad Nassar
2020

INDOMITABLE SPIRIT

Copyright © <2020v by Ziad Riad Nassar

All rights reserved. This book or any portion thereof may not be reproduced or used in any manner whatsoever without the express written permission of the publisher except for the use of brief quotations in a book review or scholarly journal.

First Printing: 2020

ISBN: 978-0-578-22995-9

Ziad Riad Nassar

INDOMITABLE SPIRIT

To all Lebanese from our generation who, like us, persevered and resisted the forces of evil and destruction

To all the living angles who proved the kindness of the human soul in the face of abject evil.

To all those indomitable spirits who rose above it all to shine a bright light unto the world.

To our children, especially my Alexander-Yari, Elyssa-Christina and Isabelle-Yara, and all youth to illustrate that our fate is not determined by the hardships we encounter, but rather by the attitude with which we face and conquer those hardships. All have the ability to overcome any obstacle in life, and succeed in spite of it. Let nothing stop your progress or ability to enjoy every moment of your life.

Last but not least.

To my parents who endured our reckless behavior with unconditional love and caring, enduring countless sleepless nights waiting for us and hoping we would return home safe, nurtured us and guided us from reckless teens to capable responsible adults.

INDOMITABLE SPIRIT

INDOMITABLE SPIRIT
LIFE IN THE SHADOW OF DEATH

Contents

FORWARD xiii
PREFACE xv
THE GOLDEN ERA 1
PEACEFUL COEXISTANCE 5
HISTORY AND IDENTITY - GETTING THERE ...11
   Marines and Sunbathers: 1958 15
   Imaginary War: 1967 17
   Jets Outside our Classroom Windows: 1973 18
PROPAGANDA AND MAYHEM 21
A KID IN PRE-WAR BEIRUT 27
   Abou Taleb 30
   Moving to Campus 31
   Abou El Abed 32
THE VILLAGE RETREAT- MONSEF 35
   Challenging The Sea, Befriending The Waves 38
   A Young Scout 41
HELL COMES TO PARADISE 47
   Civil War? 50
DEMONS AND ANGELS 55
SURVIVING THE STORM 61
   Changing Realities 62
   Jets Outside our Classroom Windows: 1973 63
OUT OF BEIRUT FOR THE SUMMER 67
   Our Own Beach Club House 67
   Idiots at Check Points - 1975 69
   Dead Man Floating 71
   Party Time Central 73

RETURNING TO BEIRUT: NEXT FALL 77
   Basketball and Missile Launchers 80
   Senseless Killings 82
FORCED SEGREGATION 85
THE NEW NORMAL 91
   The Teenage Mind 92
COLLEGE CAMPUS HAVENS 97
THE NEXT SUMMER 103
   The Ex-President's Body Guard 104
   Jet Fighters Within Reach 105
   Fire Fighting 109
DELAYED RETURN TO SCHOOL 113
   The Black Cave - 1976 114
   Return to Beirut: Branded 120
POLICE AND DISORDER 121
BREAKING FREE 127
A GREAT MISUNDERSTANDING 131
   The Aftermath - Mark and Joe 136
COMING OF AGE 141
STILL A TEENAGER 147
   Football with The Marines 149
SUMMER OF 1977 151
   Syrian Soldiers in Amchit 152
   Beach Camping 154
   Hiking across a Ravine 155
CLUBING IN OUR EARLY TEEN YEARS 157
   Late Night Swimming 160
SURVIVING A TSUNAMI 163
   Haske Flip 167
REFUGEES IN THE VILLAGE 169
   Flexing Their Muscles 171
   Fear of an Invasion: Night Swimming 173
FLIRTING WITH DEATH 175
ADAPTATION: REFUGEES AND LOCALS 181
   Floating Seat 181
   Shooting at Boats 183

Dynamite Fishing 184
STEVE AND OUR MOSLEM FRIEND 187
STRIP DARE.. 191
NOT YOUR STANDARD SCOUTS........................... 195
    Boy in the Nunnery... 196
    Scout Raid in Kour El Hawa 199
PARTY MAHEM.. 201
HIGH SCHOOL SENIOR YEAR 205
    Senior English-French Battle - 1980 210
    Senior Dance - 1980 212
SAND BAGS ON CLASS ROOM WINDOWS....... 215
SCOUT CAMPING IN CYPRUS -1980................... 223
COLLEGE YEARS.. 227
    Not a Morning Person 229
SNEAKING INTO THE GIRL'S DORMS........... 233
SKIING: CONQUERING THE MOUNTAIN......... 237
    Mountain Gypsy 239
    Dislocated Shoulder - 1981 240
DEFYING A 1981 SNOW STORM 243
PLAYS AND ACTING.. 251
    Palestinian Camp Late at Night 252
GREEN LINE CROSSINGS 257
STREET THUGS ON CAMPUS 261
WAR COMES TO THE MOUNTAIN 267
    Crossing Over 269
MISSILE WATCHING FROM A ROOFTOP......... 273
SUMMER OF 1981... 275
    Disrespecting the Sea... 277
LABNEH IN SHTAURA 281
FEDERATION SCOUT CAMP 285
CHALET 70.. 289
    A Check Point Near Us 294
THE OLD NAG 297
    Cast Party Car Overload 298
SPEED DEMONS 301
    Beyond Reason 303
    Foggy Lenses 304

FORGOING SNOW CHAINS 307
NEW YEARS PARTY – AT CHALET 70 311
   The Party 311
   The Morning After 315
A FOGGY TRIP TO THE MOUNTAINS 319
BLIZZARD OF '82 323
AUDITORIUM EXPLOSION 329
KILLER JOE 335
SKI RACE IN THE CEDARS 339
   The Way Up 339
   The Race 344
   The Drive Back 347
   Confiscated Car 349
SPRING SKIING 353
   My Best Friend's Girlfriend 353
   Refrigerator Ice 355
RALLY PAPER 359
A BAR-B-Q AND AN INVASION 363
   A hijacking 367
LAST SUMMER 371
   Yarze-Baabda: Into the Fire 372
LOSING MY BEST CHILDHOOD FRIEND 377
A FINAL FAREWELL 383

I would like to thank my life-long dear friend Dr. Nadra Assaf for her tireless effort in editing this book. Without her guidance and support, this would not be possible.

I would also like to thank my dear friend Kareen Nahas for her artistic expertise and vision in creating the book cover.

Not the least I would like to thank my three wonderful children Alexander-Yari, Elyssa-Christina and Isabelle-Yara, for inspiring me to write this book after sharing with them so many stories written herein as examples of how they could overcome any obstacle in life if they possessed the will and courage to do it. They also helped formulate and structure the book.

With all my love THANK YOU.

FORWARD

An *INDOMITABLE SPIRIT: LIFE IN THE SHADOW OF DEATH* by Ziad R Nassar, is a detailed journey of specific moments the author experienced during the Lebanese Civil war (1975-1991). This book is not just another book about the civil war, it is a story about the teenage spirit/rebellion of the time. The challenges Nassar faced in his young life were both difficult and interesting. He describes the incidents with enthusiasm, tenacity, and dedication to such a degree that the reader feels as if they are characters in the story too. In this new age of immediate documented expression, we sometimes forget what it was like to be a young person in the past. Thus, documentation of stories from war torn periods are necessary to provide an educational and entertaining look into the history of any region, nonetheless the Middle Eastern one. Thus, Nassar's book is a good jump in that direction.

He takes you on a journey that spans approximately 7 years (with some occasional flashbacks to an even earlier time) of the civil war period in Lebanon. The eloquence of delivery helps the reader to stay entertained. The short-story like format of the novel adds a level of engagement not often found in books of the same genre. His witty, sarcastic, honest and humble voice is very refreshing in the 21st century. Being someone who grew up during this war-torn period in Lebanon, while reading the book, I found myself crying at times and laughing at others. I was surely thrown into the past and relived many of my own personal experiences as if they were written on the pages themselves. It's Nassar's talent of retelling that allows for the reality of any reader to interact with his making the reader feel as if both stories existed in parallel.

In addition to the personal aspects of the book, there are interesting sections that highlight both political and economic aspects of the Lebanese civil war era. These nuances flavor the book in such a manner that any reader, regardless of cultural background or interest, would appreciate and find engrossing. Nassar also adds parts that reveal his astute political-historical insight and connect the present to the past with a little foreshadowing into the future. These are the most unique parts of the book and are the true gems that make the book highly exceptional.

In fact, Indomitable Spirit is a true narrative but also gives the reader the feel of fiction due to its vastly entertaining quality and astute details. As someone who lived in Lebanon during parts of the Lebanese Civil war, and currently resides there, I found the book very difficult to put down. The variety of emotions the reader feels, while exploring the book, cover the complete spectrum of feelings. As I mentioned before, I equally laughed and cried. Nassar does an admirable job in covering the necessary without embellishment while at the same time following the purpose he intended: to shine a light on the never-ending resilience of the Lebanese people.

Nadra Assaf

PREFACE

Too much has been written about the war in Lebanon. The conflict's political and military details have been discussed ad nausea. There are also volumes of descriptions of the suffering of people, death and destruction, etc. Yet, few, if any, have relayed the experience of a people who overcame a lifetime in the shadow of death and remained at the vanguard of civilization.

Little has been told about the people who continuously rebuilt their cities even as bombs were destroying them. Who made the most out of life, even when they knew it could end at any moment. Who fought valiantly to overcome the evils of war and sustain a civilized society that continues to produce leaders in every field of business and science and build global commercial enterprises. Who resisted the evil that came into their country and homes and defiantly hung onto their decency and moral values. A people who defied death and lived to tell a story of the indomitable human spirit capable of overcoming anything.

This book is about that unyielding spirit that, not only endured the horrors of a long vicious conflict, but shone through the darkest hours as testimony to human perseverance. This book is not intended to be a political analysis of the Lebanese war, nor an indictment or justification of the actions of the multitude of local and international actors in the war that tore a small country asunder and inflicted untold horrors on people.

This is a story of those who managed to overcome the most sever of conditions and still maintained their faith in a better future. It is said that "Hope reigns eternal." Nowhere is that truer than in Lebanon, where after almost four decades of brutality, people still retain their faith in tomorrow and strive valiantly to make it better.

INDOMITABLE SPIRIT

This is a story of people who, in the midst of the most horrible conflict, continued to conduct themselves in ways that defied the evils that befell their country and preserved a level of civilized behavior in spite of the chaos that surrounded them.

This is a true story. One of someone who survived the daily dangers in the shadow of that war during my teenage years and how people managed to retain a sense of normalcy and sanity while their world was blown to bits by forces so much greater than their capacity to influence, or even sometimes comprehend.

This is a story that highlights how instead of being crushed by the cruelty of war, the Lebanese became empowered by a determination to confront their fate and defy the evil that came upon them.

This is a story that clarifies how the horrors of war shaped our generation into a power that knows no bounds. We learned early that nothing could stop us if we possessed the determination to succeed. We survived the worst the world could throw at us and came out victorious. We looked the Devil in the eye, saw the depth of Hell, and resisted the temptation to be drawn into it. We threw a party in the face of evil and danced in defiance. We developed a toughness of character where no challenge is too daunting and no obstacle is insurmountable.

This is a story that clarifies how we gained a deep appreciation for life and a compassion for our fellow humans derived from our witnessing the horrors of war: learning that the joys of life can be found even in the most horrid of conditions. We defied the darkness, and not only lit a candle, but shone like a bright sun.

This is a testimony to humanity's resolve to persevere regardless of the circumstances.

THE GOLDEN ERA

The 60's and early 70's were the golden days of Lebanon in spite of its proximity to the regional conflict, and its effects. The country enjoyed tremendous prosperity and Beirut grew into a major international hub. Beirut was simultaneously the financial, commercial, educational, cultural and touristic center of the Middle East: A combination rarely found in another city.

Descendants of the Phoenicians – culturally at least - and ever the international traders and deal makers, the Lebanese formed the link between East, West, North and South. They intimately understood the cultures and mentality of all sides that made them best positioned to handle the trading and commercial interactions between diverse people. As such, they grew into major business brokers and a primary commercial hub, not only for the region, but internationally as well. They were also better educated and versed in international business than others; even most of the Western world at that time. It may come as a surprise to some people that even today the Lebanese still include more university graduates per capita than most countries or nationalities, if not all. That gave them an advantage in international business as well as made them the primary builders of the Middle East.

A high education level naturally comes with a plethora of higher education institutions that rank among the best in the world. Beirut became a major education center for the elite of the region. To this day, The American University in Beirut remains the only university whose medical degree is accredited in the United States. This is not true for other American universities around the world. The only Pharmacy degree accredited in the United States also comes from Lebanon – The Lebanese American University.

With education also came industry, development and innovation that put Lebanon on par with most industrialized countries by the mid-seventies. The per capita income in Lebanon exceeded many Western European countries at the time.

Many do not realize that cities like Dubai were little more than small towns with dirt roads in the early seventies. In fact, the Gulf States (Kuwait, Bahrain, Qatar, Oman and the United Arab Emirates) did not gain independence from Britain until then. There was a lot of oil in the ground, but little else. Many Lebanese from my parent's generation made fortunes building roads in the deserts to connect those small towns, and to this day, Lebanese own and manage an extensive amount of businesses in these countries.

The banks flowed with more money than they knew what to do with. Arabs, lacking any meaningful banking system and always fearful of their political establishment, stored their Petro-Dollars in Lebanon. The international communities conducting business in the Middle East used Lebanese banks for similar reasons. Furthermore, there was the banking secrecy that drew deposits from far and wide.

Regional instability and the rise of socialist regimes supported by the Soviets drove many of the wealthy capitalists out of countries like Syria and Iraq, and into Lebanon. Wealthy Palestinians similarly conglomerated in Beirut. All this further augmented the commercial stature of Beirut. As the only capitalistic free country in the region, Lebanon also attracted much of the region's intellectual and artistic talent, which turned the country into a main entertainment and cultural center.

Innovation and design lead in the late sixties a group of college students and their professor from a tiny college in Beirut to develop on their own missiles. They successfully tested the missiles to a range of four hundred kilometers and earned the support of the Government to develop a national missile industry. This was the era, when the US and the Soviet Union were still in the process of developing their own missile technology. However, global powers would not allow a small country like Lebanon to compete on such an important issue. Pressure came to bare, and the missile project was shut down. Some of those students became instrumental in programs like NASA and European space projects.

By the mid-seventies Lebanon had introduced its first locally designed and produced car, in addition to the company that locally assembled busses and trucks. Lebanese industry was on the rise, further bolstering Lebanon's economy and global position. Oil was also discovered in the ground and offshore with promise of wealth and prosperity. It has yet to be extracted.

Finally, tourism: A country made up of high mountains on the sea, in temperate Mediterranean weather replete with historical and cultural sites from time immemorial, was naturally destined to be a major touristic destination. The lively cultural and entertainment life was the icing on the cake in attracting large numbers of tourists to Lebanon.

It was in this Lebanon that I spent my early years. I was two years old when my parents decided to move back from Atlanta, Georgia. The booming economy and all the other perks of the country, including proximity to family and friends, was irresistible.

Our town of origin is on the coast, 7 kilometers north of the historic city of Byblos, and about 45 kilometers north of Beirut. Today, it is a distant suburb of Beirut and about to be engulfed by what will soon be a continuous urban sprawl from Beirut to Tripoli in the north. But, back in the 60's, life was still much more localized. It was considered a village an hour's drive from Beirut along a road that made its way through every town and village in between.

It was during this time period that my generation came into our teenage years and became aware of our future prospects. These were our defining years, when we started evaluating what we wanted to be when we grew up. We dreamt big. The economy was booming, the Lebanese were busy building the region and forming multi-national companies. Our parents were well connected. Our classmates were the children of the international business and diplomatic community working throughout the Middle East, as Lebanon had the best schools in the region. Many would place their kids in the dorms in Lebanon while working in the Arab world, which had not yet been developed enough for Western family life. Even the Arab elite sent their children to Beirut to study.

We had the world at our fingertips, and not even the sky was the limit. Or, so we thought.

PEACEFUL COEXISTANCE

People and cultures are products of their experiences, their history and geography. Lebanon is no different. Situated at the intersection of three continents – Asia, Europe and Africa, and located between the main population and political centers of the region - Lebanon and its people have been shaped by all the interactions, peaceful and antagonistic, of all those around them and beyond. Lebanon's location always put it in the path of every marching army in history. Even those as far away as the Vikings and Mongols, and more recently Americans and others, have come through the country at one point in time. The country withstood enumerable conflicts in its long history, pre-dating today's religions and even pre-dating written history.

However, Lebanon's location also made it the perfect meeting ground for all those seeking to trade with each other and interact in peaceful means. It made it the meeting ground for ideas and knowledge. It created the perfect melting pot for all who came in contact with it. Originally Canaanite/Phoenician, the Lebanese people eventually incorporated in their mix elements of every society they came in contact with. Travel in ancient times was an arduous and long process. People who came to Lebanon ended up staying for extended periods and naturally, some would settle, intermarry and become a part of the social fabric. Even armies who marched through the area left soldiers behind who eventually melted into the society.

The people of Lebanon, traders by nature, also travelled far and wide, spent time in the host countries and returned with spouses and children that further enhanced the mix. Natural disasters, wars and other historical events all contributed to the ethnic mix of people. Though this was not limited to ethnicity as it included varying religious beliefs and social traditions as well. People, cohabitated, interacted, and blended together resulting in an atmosphere of tolerance unmatched elsewhere in the world. This open interaction gave rise to a vibrant society that was capable of adapting quickly and effectively to change. It was a highly creative and productive society that absorbed the best from those around it and blended them into something even better. It is this cultural background that allows the Lebanese to migrate anywhere in the world and quickly integrate into the local society and become effective contributors to development and growth. The same factor is what also made anyone coming to Lebanon feel quite at home.

Over time, I have come to realize that this is an ancient trait of the Lebanese ancestors. The Phoenicians were so effective in their blending with the people around them, that some argue that they did not even exist. Even their temples were nondenominational with an obelisk at the alter representing the great God allowing anyone to pray to God as they viewed him. However, looking at the Lebanese today, one can attest with absolute certainty that the Phoenicians did exist. And through their descendants, they still exist in Lebanon and in every country they have been to. Those descendants continue to diligently bridge divides and bring the world together in peaceful means. Again, their complete integration makes their contribution almost ubiquitous. Almost, but not completely. A close look will clearly show a global network of individuals cooperating and working through their relations with others to keep the human race moving forward.

More than forty years hence, Lebanon and Beirut have become synonymous with war and mayhem. Few are those who still remember the pre-war Beirut; the Beirut known as The Jewel of the Middle East. And, to most of those who remember, the Jewel has long disappeared without a trace.

But, has it?

Four decades of propaganda, lies and misinformation is enough to twist any reality into an unrecognizable version of untruth. Yet, beneath the thick fog of lies is a different reality hiding in plain view for anyone who cares enough to see it.

Pre-war Beirut was the poster child of peaceful co-existence. People of all religions and national origins lived, worked and played together without much thought as to where they originally came from, how they prayed, or whether they prayed at all. By living together, I am not referring to simply adjacent neighborhoods, but rather living door to door in the same apartment buildings. So complete was the integration in some parts of the city and country that many times people did not even know the religions of each other. It was not until the age of thirteen when the war started, that other people's religion even began to have any significance to me.

Of course, prior to the beginning of the war, I knew about religion and knew the religion of many of the people around me, but it had no bearing on my interaction with them. To me, people were people. There were good people and bad people. There were those whose company I enjoyed and those who bored me to death. There were those with kind gentle hearts and those who were mean-spirited. But this could be said to exist in every religious and ethnic group. At least for me this held true because this was the society that I grew up in - the cosmopolitan society; and it was this segment which dominated the urban sectors, and even some parts of the rural areas.

The onset of the war made me realize that there was another society that was neither tolerant nor compromising, that, although small, was to become the tool for foreign intervention, and the means through which the war would obliterate that beautiful comradery and spirit which made Lebanon the unique Jewel it had been. The war robbed the people of the ability to coexist, the tolerant majority, being by nature peaceful, became the target of a conflict they had no part in creating, as segregation and fear of the other was a major objective of the war.

With time, the old saying "Lebanon's Strength is in its Weakness" has come to strangely make sense to me, although I am not sure that is what it meant then. A strong nation that is intent on asserting its dominance will either survive as a powerful state or die under attack. If it dies, its people will be hated and will either wither away or have to abandon their identity. Lebanon's very existence was based on tolerance and cooperation with others. It neither sought domination nor fought wars for supremacy. The Phoenician empire that once dominated much of the Mediterranean is the only empire in history that was not built by military force. The Phoenicians never invaded any other country or city. Instead, they reached out with trade deals and cooperative agreements that made integration in the best interest of all. To this day, the people of Lebanon may be the only nation that can honestly attest that they have never initiated war on others.

As such, Lebanon never posed an existential threat to other nations. Even when war came to Lebanon – and it always did, given the Geographic location - the antagonists were always willing to make deals with the Lebanese. Invaders tried to gain access to what the Lebanese had to offer and benefit from them, rather than eradicate them. The word victim is not one I will ever use when describing the Lebanese and what happened to them because the Lebanese refused to become victims. Furthermore, Lebanese immigrants were not deemed a threat, as they always came in peace. They never strove to change their host countries, but rather quickly assimilated into the society and became a part of it. That is not to say that they did not have any effect on the host society. On the contrary, they always ended up changing it, but it was never a forceful or threatening change. It has always been a gradual infusion of traits that the host society spontaneously adopts. The immigrants would always seek to integrate themselves in the economic and cultural life of the host and work hard to build and improve the society. Their contributions to their host country made them a welcome and beneficial intrusion – never a burden. As such, they were able to maintain their identity without fear of retribution. In fact, their contributions to their host made their identity a badge of honor – to those intelligent enough to recognize it - as there are always ignorant bigots everywhere.

This is the Lebanon I grew up in and knew intimately. This was a culture derived from millennia of history that existed in a large part of Lebanon, and it continues to represent the majority of the population. In the environment I knew, people of various religions lived together in harmony. They respected each other's religious beliefs and cultural traditions. They shared each other's holidays and celebrations. I recall so many Moslem families setting up Christmas trees and sharing gifts like their Christian neighbors, and Christians partook in Moslem festivities all the same.

This is the true essence of tolerance. Many Western societies today attempt to impose tolerance by banning people from exhibiting their beliefs, lest they offend others who are different. This is not tolerance, but mutual oppression. A tolerant society will not be offended at someone else's religious celebrations. Tolerance means accepting others and even enjoying their feasts.

Surely this was not the whole truth. There were demons lurking in the shadows, waiting for the opportune moment to undo the peace they so hated.

The war brought those demons out with a vengeance.

However, where Demons dare to offend, Angels are always there to defend.

INDOMITABLE SPIRIT

HISTORY AND IDENTITY- GETTING THERE

We are the products of our experiences – personally and nationally. Thirteen centuries of Islamic empires dominating the region created identities aligned with religious affiliation. The last several centuries, the eastern Mediterranean was the domain of the Sunni Ottoman empire which was ruled by a Sultan who referred to himself as the Khalifa – Heir to Mouhammad. Sunni Islam was the identity of the Empire with all others oppressed or tolerated depending on the whim of the sultan – but never accepted as equals. Furthermore, the Ottomans where central Asians who invaded the region centuries earlier with very little in common with the locals.

This meant the original communities, particularly non-Sunnis, maintained their identities which became closely aligned with their religion, whether Christian or Non-Sunni Moslems such as Shiites, Druze, Alawites, Suffis, etc. The division was less about religion than it was about identity, with religion being one of its manifestations.

In the nineteenth century, most of the Christians in the region still spoke Aramaic, or Armenian or Greek, not Arabic, and the term "Arab", as also defined in any Arabic dictionary, meant nomad. Nomadic people who camped on the outskirts of cities and towns where referred to as "Arabs" regardless of ethnicity, and they continue to be called Arabs in Lebanon to this day. As such, towards the end of the Ottoman Empire, and the rise of Arabism challenging them for leadership of the Sunni Moslem world and the title of "Khalifa," those with other identities - such as Phoenician, Syriac, Assyrian, Greek, Arminian, etc.- rejected Arabism. Sadly, the Ottoman Empire in its final years succeeded in annihilating much of those communities through a genocidal offensive that killed millions and displaced even more.

The years between 1860 and the end of WWI (1918) are known as the "Safar Barlik" in reference to the massive displacement of people from the eastern Mediterranean – today's Lebanon, Syria, Iraq and southern Turkey. By the end of the first World War, when the Ottoman Empire was finally dismembered, and the French and British empires took controlled of the Middle East, Mount Lebanon was the only place that still had a Christian majority. Everywhere else, they had been reduced to a small minority that had no choice but to adhere to the larger national identity around them.

Over time and given the pro-Soviet lean of the region in general, those minorities became instrumental in forming socialist movements that dominated many countries. Social National movements were ideal venues for the minorities to protect themselves as they promoted the interest of the majority, and championed the same causes, without the Islamic identity that would isolate and subjugate them.

Furthermore, the majority of Sunni Moslems in the region, fresh from under the most oppressive Ottoman Empire, aspired to improve their lives and emulate the economic success of Europe, and were not interested in another draconian Islamic Empire. The poorer countries viewed socialism as a more efficient means to build infra-structure and raise the lot of the people and Soviet support, and propaganda further enhanced those beliefs. Dominant political parties like the Baath in Syria and Iraq were founded by Christians.

Lebanon was different. Mount Lebanon had maintained its autonomy from the Ottomans for centuries, managing to also maintain a much higher education level and more prosperous society than its surroundings, as the Ottomans put a serious ban on education and writing. The birthplace of the Alphabet, and writing, Lebanon was also the home of the first Arabic printing press, and it was in Lebanon that ancient Aramaic and Arabic literature was preserved during the Ottoman Empire. This led the early missionary schools from the US and Europe at the end of the Ottoman Empire to take Beirut as their base, founding the American University of Beirut and Beirut College for Women, Jesuit Universities, etc. that educated much of the region's elites through most of the nineteenth and twentieth centuries.

The Lebanese have also always been capitalistic in nature throughout history. In fact, the whole principle of capitalism was born in Lebanon as the Phoenicians built their trade empire, and it remained a continuous core element in Lebanese culture. The Phoenician empire was effectively a series of multi-national corporations pooling resources for mutual profit and growth. They were the first to introduce the principle of money away from precious metals and the principle of banking. Those principles were later learned and adopted by the Knight Templers as they worked with the Lebanese in the Levant and transferred to Europe to form the basis for European enlightenment and subsequently the industrialization of Europe and the West.

Furthermore, Lebanon is the birthplace democracy, where Phoenician cities were the first to introduce the principle of "Free People" who voted for their leaders and participated in all decisions. Those principles were later adopted by the Greeks and Romans to form the basis for Western democracies. The Roman code of law at the core of all Western societies was written by Phoenician legal experts in the Beirut Law school, which the Romans referred to as the "Mother of Laws". Throughout history the Phoenicians and their Lebanese descendants held fast to their freedom beyond anything else. Lebanon has always been the haven for all oppressed people seeking freedom, contributing substantially to the diverse mixture of people living in this small country. With a Christian majority, most Lebanese were adamantly non-Arab. The delineation of modern Lebanon's borders was resisted by much of the Moslem population that viewed itself as Arab and wanted to remain a part of the larger Arab nation, even if that was limited to just Syria in the beginning. Eventually, most Lebanese

Moslems, particularly the educated and business elites, would see the freedoms they had in a democratic Lebanon as preferable to the state-controlled socialist structures in other countries.

Following two decades of discourse, the compromise was defining Lebanon in the constitution as a country with an Arab facet. That meant Lebanese Christians maintained their independent identity, while the Moslems claimed their Arab identity. Built on a concession on issues as essential as the very identity of the people, Lebanon's political structure was fragile and open to external manipulation from the beginning. The Syrians never acknowledged Lebanon as a distinct country and continued to manipulate the internal division for its political purposes. Most Arab countries whose nations are based on Islamic Sharia law equally opposed the non-Islamic nature of Lebanon and continued to work on undermining it.

Lebanon's contribution to the rise of the Arab league was driven primarily by economics, which is always at the core of political decisions. The Lebanese were deeply involved in building the region into a modern society, and Lebanon served as the region's economic, financial, and commercial hub meaning partnership with the surrounding countries was natural. However, with time, the Arab league became clearly an Islamic club as it expanded to include countries that had absolutely nothing in common with the original eight countries. Countries like Somalia, Djibouti, Mauritania, the Comoros Islands, etc. have no ethnic, linguistic, cultural, or historical link to the Middle East, but, they were Moslems.

Yet, the Lebanese took pride in being deal makers and peace brokers. The national self-image has always been of a people who build bridges between various places, peoples and cultures. This has been the history of the country and its people for thousands of years since the very first documentation of Phoenician traders who built a vast network of cities that cooperated in promoting progress. As such, Lebanon diligently tried to keep its distance from the confrontations in the region, be they local or global, and work for common ground. The closest was the Arab-Israeli confrontation, which had raged since 1947. In 1949, Lebanon signed an armistice agreement with Israel, which was abided by both sides for decades. Staying away from a conflict so close, though, when all involved were pushing the war into the country, was not an easy task.

The initial Israeli-Palestinian conflict brought a large number of Palestinian refugees into Lebanon. They were housed in camps set up near cities – easy access to supplies and services – and were supposed to be temporary. But, as it is so often said "Nothing lasts longer than the temporary." Those camps have since grown into permanent housing that have been there for more than 70 years and continue to expand as the population grows and more waves pf refugees arrived with every new conflict.

The war on Lebanon was effectively fought under the banner of "Defending Lebanon's Arab identity," and as in all wars, the truth is always the first casualty. It is true that the Lebanese were solidly divided on many issues, but that did not warrant the whole world partaking in the fight.

This is not a discourse in politics, but those details are necessary to explain the background for the reality under which we lived.

Marines and Sunbathers: 1958

The short lived United Arab Republic (Egypt and Syria) in 1958 along with Iraq threatened to invade Lebanon to incorporate it into their union. Jamal Abdel Naser had a dream of a united Arab Country that could take its place on the world stage and had people in Lebanon who shared that dream. But, it was more nationalistic than religious. The US deployed the Marines in Lebanon for a few days without incident, and it was all over.

INDOMITABLE SPIRIT

I have met some people who had been among the young Marines deployed to Lebanon then. They never tire of making jokes about the beer guzzling and hotdog eating sunbathers on Beirut's beaches as the Marines deployed. They clearly exaggerate when they tell of deploying straight in the midst of bewildered sunbathers. However, the crux of their statement is accurate - there was no war in Lebanon for the Marines to fight. Their deployment was a warning for Iraq and Jordan not to join Egypt and Syria in a United Arab Republic and to prevent the forceful takeover of Lebanon which had refused to join.

A good friend, and one of the new recruits in that deployment, tells us how they were given strict orders that there was no war going on. They were told that they are not to engage in any war like activity unless specifically ordered from the high command. Fresh from boot camp, he complained that he had come all this way to be told not to fight anyone. As he tells it, he was denied any ammunition and sent on shore with an empty gun. It appears the commanders felt he was too eager for a fire fight and that he may begin shooting the poor beer-drinking sunbathers. Based on my experience with the man, his commanders may have been correct in their fears. He is a good man, but full of spit fire, and always eager for a good show down.

Shortly, thereafter, Lebanon returned to its boisterous livelihood, and all was forgotten. At least it appeared that way. The politicians swept the problems under the carpet and pretended that nothing happened. People wanted to believe that it was all over and focus on making money and enjoying life. Egypt and Syria separated in 1961, and the Lebanese got seriously busy building the Oil-rich countries and handling all the financing and trade.

All seemed to be fine on the surface.

Imaginary War: 1967

I was five-years-old when the 1967 Arab-Israeli war erupted, yet I clearly recall some of the events. Even though Lebanon was not party to that war, it bordered Israel and Syria, and the airspace became part of the aerial confrontation between the two. As Lebanon was not part of the conflict and had a smaller military than either side, it did not try to limit incursions into its air space. I recall my parents scurrying to get us out of Beirut and northwards to the village, where we would be far away from any potential conflict should the war spill into Lebanon. Even though Abou Taleb had our backs, they clearly did not believe he could protect them from war damage.

They were discussing some conflict in south Lebanon with fighting on the Damour bridge, and in the mind of a five-year-old, images of war do not match reality. I must have watched some old movie with sword play and was imagining those soldiers dueling with swords on the bridge. I started to discuss this with my mother, who naturally had no tolerance for any such nonsense. She had three kids to get ready for the trip, including my seven-month-old sister, and just wanted me to shut up. I did not shut up, but was mostly talking to myself, as even my older sister was not interested and was freaking out from the tense demeanor of the adults.

In a world war II style, everyone painted lights and windows blue. Even car headlights were painted blue. There was still the belief that lights attracted aerial bombardment. Somehow blue was supposed to prevent detection. I am not really sure why a pilot would see a white light but not a blue light. But, who was I to argue. I was five.

The war did not last long, and nothing really happened in Lebanon. In spite of the fact that some elements of the population were seething about the Government's refusal to join the Arab ranks, it was all swept aside. However, that war brought another wave of Palestinian refugees into Lebanon, as many northern Palestinians crossed over, and many others were shuttled by Syria and Jordan into Lebanon.

INDOMITABLE SPIRIT

Jets Outside our Classroom Windows: 1973

In 1973, Lebanon -again- sat out the Arab-Israeli war, and the Lebanese went on with their lives as if nothing was happening, but Lebanon's airspace was part of the battlefield.

Our school overlooked the sea from atop a steep hill with no buildings to block the view. Our classroom windows in October 1973 faced the sea. Early afternoon, we would hear the deafening roars of jet engines that literally shook the building, and at age eleven, one could not help but rush to the windows to see what was happening.

There they were: A Syrian MIG jet chasing an Israel Phantom F-4 jet, close enough that it almost appeared the antenna on the front of the MIG was about to go through the Phantom's engine. No one was paying any attention to the teacher screaming at us to back away from the windows, as the jets were less than five hundred meters away. The excitement of watching a live aerial battle so close made us ignore all the potential danger.

As we watched, the Phantom went into a roll-and-brake move and lands right behind the MIG, which slipped under it when it slowed down. They just switched positions, and the Phantom fired a missile straight into the MIG's backburner, breaking left into the Mediterranean to avoid flying into the explosion. The building shook violently, and the teacher ducked, but the naïve kids, with no real appreciation for the danger, were cheering half way out the windows.

The Syrian pilot had given up upon switching positions with the Israeli and hit the eject button. As debris fell into the sea we watched the pilot slowly parachute down and was met by a couple of fishing boats from a nearby harbor. As they hauled him into the boat, the show was over and we finally responded to the teacher's pleas to get back to our seats.

No one could concentrate on anything other than discussing what we just watched regardless of how much the teacher tried to return the focus to the class material. The teacher relented and abandoned the scheduled lesson as she figured there was a life lesson there that was more important than the planned subject matter. She took the opportunity to explain to us the danger that we were in and that we should not have stayed at the windows. Jets fly really fast, and five hundred meters can be cleared in seconds. A wrong turn or a misfired missile could have brought havoc on our building. We agreed with the logic, but this was just too good of a show to miss. How many people get to see that?

As the Lebanese focused on the positive and worked towards building a better future, other forces were pushing in another direction. For the Lebanese, their world was about to change in a major way and most were not paying attention, as they were too busy enjoying their good lives.

PROPAGANDA AND MAYHEM
PRE-WAR YEARS

The early nineteen seventies witnessed massive socialist/communist movements around the world, with demonstrations and revolutions, from East Asia to South America, including Europe and America. Lebanon was certainly not spared those revolutionary forces, but, there, they took on added dimensions as they aligned with other divides.

The Arab-Israeli conflict with Israel supported by the West brought the Arab world into the lap of the Soviets, with the exception of Lebanon that remained a die-hard capitalist pro-Western. As such, Soviet supported socialist/communist movements were viewed as pro-Arab by large segments of the Lebanese Moslem population, with the poorer segments of the population also lured by promises of sharing someone else's money, as is always the case.

The majority of Christians on the other hand rejected those movements. Even some of those who believed in the socialist principles feared that they would become a front for a more cynical transformation of the country, correctly so.

The Armed Palestinians, with Arab backing, joined the left, and began transforming the movements into Arab/Islamic in an era of massive Arab money pouring into Islamic institutions. The movements morphed from the original objectives of social justice to a more destructive force for the transformation of Lebanon's national identity.

Initially, the Palestinian camps consisted of poor refugees needing basic humanitarian assistance. However, by the late-sixties, the Palestinians, with support from oil-rich Arab countries, began to organize and receive arms. The PLO was formally founded in 1967 following a resounding defeat of the Arabs at the hand of Israel and became the recognized fighting force to liberate Palestine. As

Palestinian military power grew, tension with the Lebanese Government festered, although, Lebanon did not wish to get embroiled in the fight. It provided all the humanitarian, political and diplomatic support for the Palestinians, but did not want a war on its border that would certainly destroy the country.

Eventually, the PLO grew large enough to threaten Lebanon's peaceful existence and had begun launching occasional cross border raids against Israel. When Lebanon attempted to stop the rapid advancement and power of the PLO on Lebanese soil, it found itself facing the wrath of the whole Arab world. Lebanon's refusal to participate in wars against Israel was already bad enough but preventing the Palestinians from waging their own war from Lebanon was deemed political heresy. Lebanon came under a lot of pressure to allow its territory to become the main battlefront against Israel.

The Arab league decided that the PLO should be granted free access to south Lebanon to fight Israel. Interestingly, Egypt, Syria and Jordan, all of whom share a longer border with Israel and possessed larger armies, were not willing to grant the PLO any operating rights from their territories. They tossed that bitter cup into Lebanon and when Lebanon refused, Arab armies threatened to invade unless Lebanon conceded parts of the country's southern border areas to the Palestinians. With the Soviets weighing in on the side of the Arabs, and the West backing away from confrontation, the Lebanese had no choice but to negotiate what they believed was the least painful solution – postponing the inevitable. In retrospect, it appears that maybe a conflict with the Arabs would have been the lesser of the evils. Maybe an attempted invasion would have forced the hand of the West and ended the ordeal early, but this is mere conjecture at this point.

The resulting 1969 Cairo Agreement gave the PLO freedom to act in parts of south Lebanon. The strict limits on its operations and the areas in which it could carry armed activity, negotiated by the Lebanese, were instantly disregarded by the PLO with the blessing of the Arab world. This was the seed of the problems that would haunt Lebanon to this day. The 1970 confrontation between the PLO and Jordan resulted in the Arab League transferring more PLO fighters and its leadership to Lebanon.

By the early 1970s, the PLO's activity spread throughout the country. With ample Arab and Soviet financing and support, they turned every refugee camp into a military fortress and began flexing their muscle beyond the camps and interfering in Lebanon's internal affairs. Most notably, they became the spearhead for efforts to undo the peaceful relations between Christians and Moslems in the country. Their activities were clearly branded in sectarian terms, pretending to champion the Moslem cause, and directing their venom against the Christians, whom they accused of being a Western beachhead in the region. That automatically brought the accusation of being pro-Israel. The Lebanese government tried to limit their power with several serious military confrontations between the Lebanese army and the PLO. I clearly remember Lebanese jet fighters flying overhead in bombing raids of Palestinian camps. However, those attempts to control the rise of the PLO were labeled as a defense of Israel, and an affront to Arabism, only deepening the rift. Gradually, national, regional, international and ideological dividing lines began to align. The internal split between left and right began to mirror the division between pro-Arab and Anti-Arab, which in turn fell almost along religious lines. The larger Soviet/NATA divide followed. The same aligned with the Syrian and Arab intent to undo Lebanon's political structure, and provided the Syrians with an opportunity to act. Furthermore, the Palestinians saw and were offered a venue to dominate the country and establish a base of operations against Israel.

To make things worse, the West, salivating over cheap oil, and lured by promises that Saudi-style hardline Islam is the most effective bulwark against the spread of Soviet communism, failed to see the monster in the making. Without much detail, that lead to an unspoken agreement to allow and support investing billions into Islamic movements and meant the West could not back the pro-Western capitalists in Lebanon against the Arabs. The destruction of Beirut would bring Petro-Dollars out of Lebanese banks to New York, London, etc., and the Israelis saw an opportunity to redirect the Palestinians elsewhere, and hopefully by taking over Lebanon they will forget about Palestine.

When all the fault lines align, a seismic break is a foregone conclusion. Lebanon was living on borrowed time as it strove to avoid the prefect political storm that was threatening the country in the early seventies.

Regional and global players at the height of the cold war had no tolerance for peaceful coexistence. Instead they saw Lebanon's conditions as ideal to fight their wars at the lowest cost to them – by proxy. Cosmopolitan Lebanon was in the eye of the storm. The constructive forces that transformed Beirut into a premier international city for business and pleasure were systematically overrun by destructive forces bent on war. Most did not want to see all this happening, and those who saw it, believed they could ride the storm to safety or simply surrendered to the fact that the forces were beyond their ability to confront or control.

It is said that we live life forward without knowing what is coming next; however, we analyze history backwards with the advantage of knowing all that has happened. Thus, we unfairly judge past actions through a prism of knowledge not available to those making the decisions.

Eventually, Islamization would spread to engulf the region and the world as we all witness today. What a different world we would be living in had the West confronted Islamic fundamentalist forces in their budding years in Lebanon.

Yet, the indomitable spirit of the Lebanese allowed them to survive this storm for more than four decades.

The Phoenix kept rising from the ashes and soaring ever higher.

INDOMITABLE SPIRIT

In spite of the open tolerant nature of the Lebanese people, history and geography simultaneously developed a very tough and resilient culture capable of overcoming challenges and obstacles. After centuries of stubborn resistance to successive Islamic empires, Lebanon's population, Christians in particular, had developed a level of toughness and resilient character almost unmatched anywhere else. They had taken refuge in rugged and at times inhospitable mountains to maintain their identity and beliefs. They built breathtaking terraces on sheer cliffs to plant the crops they needed and braved cold snowy mountains rather than surrender to invaders. Social evolution meant that only the toughest of the tough held on to their identity and heritage all those centuries. It was hard to recognize beneath the friendly hospitable demeanor of the cosmopolitan population. However, when push came to shove, there was always a solid line beyond which no compromise was possible.

We were raised with principle that if anyone can do something, we can. In the US they same "You are not better than anyone." In Lebanon the saying is reversed, and says "No one is better than you."

We were continuously challenged to go further and do better, which made it part of our character that we would always strive to outdo everyone and overcome any challenge we met.

This unrelenting and unyielding attitude became the main reason for the nation's survival.

INDOMITABLE SPIRIT

A KID IN PRE-WAR BEIRUT

By the 1960s, Beirut had risen to rival the most important international commercial centers. It was the place to be outside Western Europe and North America. With the massive oil wealth of the region, Beirut was destined for a great future. Or, so everyone in Lebanon believed.

The streets and side walk cafes teamed with people from all over the world conducting deals and enjoying this magnificent country. It almost appeared idealistic in some places. This was the era when Beirut came to be known as the Paris of the Middle East and the Jewel of the Mediterranean. It was extremely cosmopolitan and international. There was nothing in the world you could wish to have that you could not find in Lebanon.

Yet, in spite of being a densely populated large cosmopolitan city, at the time Beirut still retained a certain essence of a small town social and communal structure. I attribute that primarily to the Lebanese culture, which - like other Mediterranean cultures - values social connections and close family ties.

My family and I lived in the heart of Beirut and retreated to the village on weekends and summers. My father was a professor in what was then the Beirut College for Women in Ras Beirut. The college would grow into Beirut University College and then Lebanese American University as my father grew from Professor, to Dean, and then President. We went to school in the city.

We lived in Ras Beirut – literally the "Head of Beirut" – which was the newest part of the city at the time, including much of the city's banks and business headquarters, as well as a host of universities and top notch schools. As such, the residents included an exceptionally high rate of education and wealth. This confluence of wealth, education and international community turned Hamra street at the heart of Ras-Beirut into the Champs Elyse or Fifth Avenue of the Middle East, where you found all the high-end stores and merchandise.

Beirut was a walking city where most walked to school, work, shopping and entertainment. That did not mean there was not a massive amount of traffic caused by all the people that came from other parts of the country or across town. Traffic moved at a snail's pace during the day in the narrow city streets. Often, it was faster to walk than to drive, provided the distance is not too great. Traffic moved slow enough for us to roller skate between the cars as kids. We would slalom between them as we were actually moving faster than traffic. Concerned drivers and passengers would yell at us to get out of the street before we get run over. We would laugh and tell them they should worry about getting in our way as we sped past them.

Additionally, Beirut had a form of mass transportation I have yet to see anywhere else – the Service Cab. These were mostly older Mercedes Benz that roamed the streets picking up and dropping off passengers anywhere. They were not Taxis; – those were different. If you wanted a private Taxi, you would make a phone call for one. Service cars were not ridden alone. Others got on and off, as they would on a bus, but this was a car that could maneuver easily in the city streets and did not have a set route. The car would drive up a small alley or around a block to get you exactly where you wanted to go, if you had trouble walking or if there was rain. Each Service car usually serviced a limited part of the city providing transportation for short hops at a fixed rate.

Residential and business buildings were intermingled throughout the city. The ground floors of all the buildings had store fronts, cafes, restaurants, and theaters, which kept the streets full of people on the sidewalks and inside restaurants and shops. Many small sandwich and ice cream shops did not even have space inside for customers, where the counter sat just behind the shutter, which when open provided passersby with direct access to the store from the side walk. The inside consisted of little more than a small kitchen, and often they specialized in one type of sandwich: Falafel, Shawarma, Chicken, etc. There was even a store that only served French Fries in a paper plate or rolled up in a sandwich. Furthermore, there were also fresh juice stores where they would blend your choice of fruits in front of you.

Movie theaters were not clustered as they are today and almost every one doubled as an actual theater that often hosted live plays. They were scattered all over Ras-Beirut below ground under high rises. For the younger reader, my early years predated the internet and all the electronic gadgets that allow communications without ever leaving your seat. I was sixteen when Attari introduced the first TV video game - Pong - and it was not much of a game. People walked out their door to conduct business and interact with others. We were outside all day, and in doing so, we got to know a lot more people than the ones we were directly interacting with. Beirut was a real city, where the streets were lined with shops, restaurants, cafes and other business establishment. Most shopkeepers lingered outside the door unless they were tending to a customer, and they often were socializing with friends that simply dropped by for a chat. Many shops had chairs outside just for that purpose.

Thus, people knew each other intimately, and that was not limited to close friends and relatives. The shopkeepers in the neighborhood knew where everyone lived and knew who every kid belonged to. They kept an eye on everyone and acted like guardians for the neighborhood creating a truly secure environment in what otherwise would have felt like a harsh city.

Nevertheless, Beirut was still a big city with all that comes with it. Growing up there meant learning early how to deal with strangers and the street hustle. We quickly acquired street smarts at a very early age.

Abou Taleb

Each neighborhood had at least one person who was a sort of neighborhood watchman. He usually owned a store on a strategic corner and knew everyone. He felt, in an old-style fashion, that he was responsible for everyone around him. The neighborhood I lived in until the age of 10 had Abou Taleb. He stood about 190 cm tall with a shaved head and a large, reddish curled moustache. He owned a small flower shop on the corner of two main streets – Hamra and Sadat - the type of store that you cannot walk into with barely enough space to store things at night while the flowers sat on the side walk during the day. He was not married, and spent his days and evenings socializing with everyone. I rarely saw him without beautiful women on his side. He watched and knew everyone. He was a kind and friendly man, but fiercely protective of the neighborhood, and could be tough as nails when necessary.

I recall a story my parents told me about an incident with my younger sister when she was a few months old in the spring of 1966. My father's aunt came by and took my sister for a walk in her stroller. She did not live in the immediate neighborhood; a stranger to Abou Taleb at that time. As she walked past him, he looked in the stroller and saw my sister, whom he recognized. He begged my great aunt's pardon – he was always very polite, in spite of his tough demeanor – to inquire about her relationship to the girl. She told him the girl was her nephew's daughter. He proceeded to interrogate her, asking her how many brothers and sisters the girl has, her father's name, mother's name, and grandparents, whom he also knew. Finally, satisfied that she was really related to my sister he apologized for the inconvenience and stepped aside. When my mother asked him about the incident the next day, he told her with all honesty "Madam, I did not know who had your daughter, what if she was kidnapping her!" That was the type of neighborhood you would feel safe in letting your kids walk to school without worrying about what will happen to them on the way.

Moving to Campus

By 1972, as my father became the Dean of the Beirut University College, we moved to an apartment on campus that was more convenient and economical for him. It was barely half a kilometer from our earlier apartment, and generally still in the same part of the city.

It was a small college with less than two thousand students at the time, with a compact campus consisting of seven building and a gymnasium, with an open treed area between the buildings. One of the buildings was faculty residence, where we lived, another was a girls' dorm with more than 200 residents, most of whose parents lived abroad, with a few from outlying areas of Lebanon.

My bedroom balcony looked straight at the tennis courts, which were on the roof of the Gymnasium, putting them at the same level as our third story balcony, less than 5 meters away. Although protected by a high chain link fence, tennis balls regularly landed on our balcony and it is amazing that none broke a window in all those years. At the other end of the courts was the Fine Arts building, connected to the gym underground. In front of the building was the main campus open space and hangout place for students.

At the age of ten, the campus provided a wonderful playground, with trees and open space, in contrast to the concrete jungle outside. My friends and I would spend hours climbing the large trees and swinging on the dangling vines, pretending to be Tarzan. We would wonder through the buildings exploring everything, particularly the theater storage areas that had every type of prop one could imagine. The gymnasium next door, with a pool beneath it, just made our playground complete.

INDOMITABLE SPIRIT

Abou El Abed

Our building was at the edge of campus and had an entrance from campus and an entrance from the street outside. Across the street from our building lived one of the real Abou Al Abeds, a tough man in his seventies who had taken it upon himself to look after the neighborhood, like Abou Taleb did in our old neighborhood.

Like so many of the original inhabitants of Ras Beirut he had sold part of his land and used the proceeds to build an apartment building on the remaining parcel. He rented out the building and opened a grocery store on the street front, managed by his son Abed. He hung around the building all day keeping an eye on things. He knew everyone and was very keen on defending the neighborhood and everyone in it and treated all the kids as his own.

I had a friend who grew up in that building and would like to tease him and play games with him. He would come up to him and tell him he had a headache or some other minor ailment and ask for advice. Abou El Abed was old school and would prescribe a hot cup of tea for almost any simple ailment. Then my friend would cynically ask if he ever heard of Aspirin.

That would rile him off his chair to chase my friend down the side walk yelling "Come back here. let me pull your ears and teach you some respect." He knew it was a joke that he fell for and was not really angry, but just upset that he fell for that trick again. Occasionally he would grab him by the ear as he passed by and reprimand him for being a naughty kid. But, he did so in a fatherly manner, trying to help raise a decent human being.

He even acted as a traffic controller sometimes. On one occasion a car was speeding by as he was crossing the narrow street and almost hit him. He smacked the top of the car with the palm of his hand and yelled at the driver to slow down. The car had slowed down to avoid hitting him, and now came to a stop. A young man with a large Afro and a heavy Palestinian accent stuck his head out the window and told him "If you were not an old man, I would teach you a lesson."

That did not sit well with Abou El Abed who yelled back at him as he starts to move "Who is an old man? Come back here and I will teach you a lesson in respect."

The Palestinian made the mistake of backing up at him. He was still in the middle of the street and did not run, but just side stepped the car and reached in the open window as the car passed him grabbing the driver by his hair. He takes a few steps as the car came to a stop and pulled the driver's head out the window and began to slap him. "WHO IS AN OLD MAN YOU BASTARD! WHO IS AN OLD MAN!" The driver at this point just wanted to get out of there, apologizing profusely and screaming for help as others came to support Abou El Abed.

They finally pulled him off the driver and he sped off. Abou El Abed looked at his hand that was tangled in the driver's hair and it looked like half the man's hair was wrapped around his fingers. He spent some time getting the hair off his hands muttering about the lack of respect these Palestinians have.

"Who sent these people here? Who do they think they are, coming here and disrespecting everyone!"

The war did not change Abou El Abed across the street from us, and he did not care if people had guns as he really hated those outsiders causing trouble and stood his ground. He was a Sunni Moslem who had lived all his life in peace with his Christian neighbors, his renters where at least half Christian, as were the clients of the grocery store. He cared equally about all and did not appreciate one bit anyone trying to convince him that suddenly those people he cared so much about are now the enemy.

Often, he would come out with arm raised ready to strike someone who would dare offend his neighbors. I was the subject of his defense on many occasions when some Palestinians would come at us for being

INDOMITABLE SPIRIT

Christians. He would yell and threaten them "These are our neighbors and friends. Who are you to get between us? GET OUT. Leave the neighborhood."

THE VILLAGE RETREAT- MONSEF

We almost always headed north to the "village" on the weekends, were the kids could play in open space and adults could relax away from the din of the city. Our village – Monsef - was on the coast, although much of the houses were about two kilometers inland and 200-300 meters above sea level. Our house was right on the water – literally. If one fell off the patio, one would hit the water, although it would be painful in the shallow rocky edge of the sea. On those exceptionally stormy winter days, the waves would get into the house, requiring a defensive wall to protect the house from the waves when my grandparents moved permanently into it in the early seventies.

The majority of the people from the village, like us, spent their week days in Beirut and came up for vacation. Many lived near us in Beirut and went to the same schools, so we saw them regularly. Others, we only saw in the village as there was a school there that they could attend.

Neighboring villages were not that far as each village barely covered more than two square kilometers, with houses clustered in one part and agricultural land scattered around the residential cluster. In our case, the next village up the hill actually merged with ours, as several houses of our people were technically in the next village. On the coast, the first houses in villages to the north and south, were a few hundred meters from the last house in ours. This allowed us to easily walk back and forth between them and made our playground much bigger. There were about 80 kids in my age group in my village – from two years older to two years younger than me. There were even more in the neighboring villages, many of whom also resided in the same part of Beirut, and some were related to people in our village. That was a lot of kids to play with, and we only came into the house to eat and sleep.

Even though these were villages, there was a very high level of education, and barely anyone from my parent's generation and younger worked the land. My generation actually all graduated college with more than half acquiring postgraduate degrees. Agricultural land consisted mainly of Olive, Almond and Fig trees, and those are cared for and cultivated by hired labor. The only agricultural work we did is picking some fruits for personal consumption. Ah, and green small almonds before the shells harden right off the tree in early spring is something I really missed all these years.

In the summers, we spent more than three months in the village, from the day after school ended to the day before school started. Those who worked in Beirut would drive in every day and spend the afternoons on the beach. Lebanon continues to have a summer work schedule for people with office jobs. While regular schedules are generally 8-5 with a lunch break, summers are 7-2 without a lunch break, so people can spend the afternoons enjoying the summer weather with their families. It could not get any better than having a house right on the Mediterranean in summer time. Every morning, I got out of my pajamas and straight into a bathing suit, and I was on the beach. I came in for some food at lunch time, and then I was back to frolicking on the beach with friends until sunset. When we got tired of swimming, we would play some ball game or other children's games on shore. Then it was back into the water. As little kids, that would be the end of the day, until we grew a little older.

It was there that we developed the other facet of our character growing up. We could say it was the alter ego of the cosmopolitan city kids we were in Beirut. In the village we learned how to deal with nature and all its facets. We challenged the mountains and the sea and built a strong daring character that always confronted its fears and conquered them.

Hunting was a major part of village life, and almost every house had guns. Kids were introduced to guns early and instructed in their safe use. I got my first BB gun when I was ten, but I had used my friend's guns before. We would spend hours practicing with that gun until we became expert marksmen and could hit a BB with another BB from twenty meters away. We actually hunted small birds with those guns and got quite a few, and, as we practiced, we got to the point of being able to shoot a bird in mid-flight with a BB gun. However, for us there was much more to it, we would chase lizards and other small creatures trying our marksmanship and improving our abilities.

Bats were a real challenge. Although night creatures, they would often come out after sunset but just before dark. They could barely be seen in the twilight, and they moved fast and erratically, but most importantly bats have sonar sensors to navigate in the dark. We learned that they can actually sense the BB heading their way and evade it. It was just amazing how fast they shifted directions when we fired, they just bobbed up or down and avoided being hit. We had to get one., and the challenge became an obsession. We would wait for them at dusk and try over and over again. Eventually, we figured we need to double and then triple team a bat to get it. One would aim at the bat, another just over and the third just below it and we fired simultaneously.

The principle was sound, but execution was not that easy. First, we were shooting a very fast-moving object, which was hard enough without sonar evasion. Second, we needed to actually fire at the same time, which took many tries before we got that right. Finally, we had to know how high or low the bat would bop to know where to aim. We must have wasted a thousand BBs before we got a bat, but we finally got one.

For an eleven-year-old, that was a euphoric moment like climbing mount Everest, and we celebrated that event and spoke about it for years. Some simply did not believe it was possible and challenged us to prove it. We did not care. We knew what we had accomplished and were satisfied. We were not about to spend that much time and ammo trying to duplicate our feat. Actually, we were not sure we could. It probably was a simple law of probabilities.

INDOMITABLE SPIRIT

Challenging The Sea, Befriending The Waves

Challenging the rough seas on our rocky beach was amongst our favorite pastimes, and the higher the wave the better. It was a constant test of our abilities and toughness, but it was not about strength in any way. There is no human being alive who is strong enough to withstanding a crashing four-meter-high wave with shear strength. During my lifetime, the sea has broken pieces of the rocks that weigh more than ten tons and tumbled them to different location. That is not a force anyone should disrespect, or ever attempt to confront with shear force.

As I had come to explain to all my uninitiated friends, a cubic meter of water weighs one ton, and salt water is even heavier. The average person provides a roughly one square meter frontal area if squarely facing the wave, which means a wave that is five meters deep would exert the force of five tons against a person in a frontal strike. Moving at thirty to forty kilometers per hour the wave would hit you like a moving small truck and you are gone.

Furthermore, as I explained to my kids when I introduced them to this game. The waves could be your best friends or your worst nightmare, depending on how much respect you offer the sea and its might. Disrespect it, and the sea would quickly remind you who is really boss.

Finally, never, ever, let your guard down, as even relatively calm seas still produce odd waves that come out of nowhere and knock you over.

In light of all this, challenging the waves was a game of skill, agility and determination. We started at a young age and worked our way to progressively larger waves. We learned to read the movement of the sea and anticipate each wave's course and strike pattern. No two waves act the same, as the direction, spin and the rocks beneath the surface give each its own character and pattern. We learned how to counter the effect of the waves and how to use their forces and the rocks' effects on them to our advantage and developed the skill to confront four and five-meter-high waves while on the edge of the rocks and remain standing.

The small lagoon we regularly swam in was formed by a rocky outcrop that circled around from south to north creating an enclosure with just a small opening to the north. The encircling rock is over three meters high, making it perfect for diving, but also diverted waves from the main swimming area. At the mouth of the lagoon the mainland rock at sea level jutted out to sea to partially close the opening. However, the corner created by the outcrop had worn out from waves through the ages to become a slope into the water. The waves would curl around the outer rocks and crash into the slope, and that is where we went to play with the waves. There was no water behind us to fall into – only rocks to be dragged on if we failed. It took a lot of skill, agility and knowledge of the sea to confront those mighty waves, and we got good enough that we would head to the Blata when waves were high enough to come over the three-meter rock. The trick lies in the fact that as powerful as the waves were, they were still liquid water – not a solid. Tackled properly, we could allow the waves to slip around us and divert much of the force. However, there would still be enough force that required countering and agility to remain on our feet as we were pulled back by the waves. We would wedge our bodies into the incoming waves with the elbows and knees forming frontal points that split the wave, thrust ourselves into the incoming waves as hard as we could to penetrate as much of the wave as possible, and then back track with the remainder, resisting and maintaining the wedge until the whole wave passed us. We walked up the slope and along the rocks until we emerged from the back of the wave, and then ran back to the slope before the next wave arrived and started the process again.

From experience, we could tell which way a wave would behave before it hit us and be prepared. Some simply pushed straight through with extreme force, while others would crest and then slam into us with a harder downward force. Yet others, the hardest to handle, would spin against the rock and literally twist our legs from under us. Each wave required a different strategy and dictated confrontation at a different level of the slope. Some were just too monstrous to handle and required diving into, and would literally slice all the way through the back side. But, as we gained more experience we could manage to dive in and then break the dive just short of the back side to allow the wave to bring us back to the rock standing.

Tannour was another place to test our prowess against the waves. This was a narrow slit in the flat rocks at sea level that ended in a roundish opening. As the waves receded the water in the tannour would drop precipitously and then blow out with the incoming wave. Large waves could drop more than two meters down and then blow out another two meters above the rock level. If the wave lifted, you above the rocks and you lost your grip you would be floating sideways and onto some seriously jagged rocks. Sounds crazy to go there in rough seas, but it was the challenge that counted. The waves had eroded the rocks over time so that the walls of the tannour were not vertical anymore, but rather slant inwards below the surface. That allowed us to push our bodies against them where the water just pins us against the rocks instead of lifting us over. When the waves receded we just hung from the edge of the rock waiting for the next one. The slit from the sea was curved and the water had hollowed the rocks below the surface on the inward side of the curve. We could swim under the rocks and pop up in the tannour, and did that often when we swam in during really rough seas to avoid being slammed against the rocks. However, it was not that simple, as the water beneath is still subject to the ebb and flow of the waves, and although a short distance, it could take too long if not handled properly. The waves could keep pulling and pushing us back and forth forever. We would swim forward with incoming waves and then cling to the bottom of the rocks as the waves recedes and repeat again until we cleared the rocks.

The continuous challenging of ourselves and each other helped develop a "can do" attitude towards life. We developed a resilient and in ways defiant character that viewed every obstacle in life as a challenge to overcome, instead of a deterrent that prevents progress. We cherished every opportunity we got to prove our abilities and skills. We lived in a culture that valued daring and boldness.

Furthermore, we developed strategic and tactical ability as well as planning and awareness of events around us.

A Young Scout

I joined the scouts at age six, when a troupe was first formed in Monsef. I was the youngest kid to join and spent my first year as a Mowgli. As I got older I moved up the ranks until I made it to leadership and I remained active in that position until I left the country at age twenty. Let me explain how that worked:

The scout troupe had both boys and girls, each divided into three age groups, under twelve, twelve to sixteen, above sixteen. Leadership roles could be attained before reaching eighteen, and the troupe was led by people who are generally under twenty-five. The troupe met regularly throughout the year, at least once a month. However, the summer was the most active season, as we would be out of school and mostly in the village. Summer included several camping trips, numerous day trips, and many other activities. As little kids, we were primarily playing and learning about scouting, but, as we grew older, those activities took on a new life. It was much more than scouting, as those activities became social events in their own right.

Aside from several camping trips and day trips, the scouts performed a lot of social work. For example, one day each summer we took to cleaning the road from the top of the village to the beach. We would gather early in the morning and then walk all the way down picking up any trash along the road. Upon reaching the beach, we hopped in the water to clean off all the dirt, and then enjoyed a hearty breakfast supplied by the leaders.

One summer, we undertook the project to expand the concrete pad near the beach that we all used. There was one concrete contractor who knew what needed to be done, but the work was performed by about fifty teenagers. We moved stones to fill in the depressions in the rocks, mixed the concrete by hand, poured it in place and then smoothed it over. It was hard work, but very satisfying. The end product was not perfect, but it was ours. This was the concrete we would sit on for years to come. We owned it as we built it with our own hands. Unlike most troupes that operated in cities, with members that mostly only knew each other during scouting activities, ours was based in a village and consisted primarily of kids from that village. That meant we all knew each other intimately outside scouts, and many were related, which created a more relaxed and informal atmosphere. We were more like a big family than a scout troupe. Some activities were limited to one of the six groups, and others included the whole troupe. There were also federation events where all the troupes in the country got together for major competitions. The troupe also manned the volley ball tournament in the village, which included building an entry way from sticks and ropes – no nails. We would spend a couple of days tying all the sticks and lumber together, and always took pride in building a bigger and better structure every year. Those were really works of art, as the towers and bridges could hold several adults walking on them. We would camp out near the court and work through the night, and then man the tournament itself while sleeping on site.

Those events left us with so many beautiful memories. We challenged each other and pushed ourselves to the limit. The tough work, creativity and cooperation, built character like nothing else. One of the earliest full troupe camping trips I remember was in late September and near the highest village in Lebanon – Hadath El Jibbeh – at almost 1,800 meters above sea level. In late September, temperatures at that altitude dip below freezing at night, and it was a cold camping trip. It was the apple picking season, and there was a lot of apple orchards nearby. The locals met us when we arrive with several crates of apples, welcomed us and specifically instruct us not to touch the apple trees. They told us that they would deliver crates of apples to us every day, but insisted we do not touch the trees. Apples are very fragile and can bruise easily, and they also worried that we would damage the trees as we yanked on apples randomly. We agreed but did not think they would actually know if anyone picked an apple somewhere. We were wrong. The next day they come fuming, telling us we were not supposed to touch the trees. It appeared one of the older girls had picked an apple, and they could tell from the way the apple was removed from the tree. Just amazing how attuned the farmers are to their trees, and how oblivious we were to their relationship with their crops.

In the morning, we would head out to the local spring to wash up. This was an actual spring from the ground that filled a small pool for watering the fields, and the water was barely above freezing temperature and would numb our fingers and faces as we washed. None of us even contemplated washing more than our faces with it.

While we washed and rubbed our hands to keep the blood circulating, we heard heavy foot stomping and "HUH, HUH…" We turned around to find a platoon of army commandos in nothing but shorts and bare feet, in freezing temperatures jogging towards us. They passed us and hopped straight into the half-frozen pond, and let out a loud scream as they landed in the icy water. We shivered just watching them. That was part of their rugged training – enduring cold and extreme conditions, and they would do that every morning as we struggled just to get our hands in the water. These young men earned my respect and admiration, and. At that young age, all I wanted was to become that tough and able to withstand anything.

As we grew older camping trips became more intricate. However, with war starting, our camps were limited geographically, as we did not wish to take any chances in Syrian or Palestinian controlled areas, particularly since we came from 'the other side' of the dividing lines, and there were plenty of mountains and valleys to choose from in our area.

In those days, there were no prepared camp grounds. We would look for a nice pine forest with enough flat areas for our tents and close enough to a water source. Usually it would be land belonging to a monastery that allows us to camp on their grounds on condition we cleaned up after ourselves. Of course, we would clean up. We were scouts, and one of the teachings of scouts is respect for nature – leave no trace.

We would park near the monastery and walk a kilometer or so to the site. We had to clear the ground for each tent as this was raw forest, and we often missed a stone or two that ended up poking us in the back as we slept. We built our own camp fire pits with stones and then dismantled them before we left. We carried our water in twenty-liter jugs from hundreds of meters away for cooking and drinking. We each had a flashlight, but the main lighting came from kerosene lamps and the camp fire.

In the very early days we still had the old army style tents where the floor piece was separate from the top piece. The tent tops were pegged and supported separately with nothing connecting the top to the floor, and one could slide out from the side of the tent. Those were donated to the troupe to get us started. We later replaced them with newer one-piece tents that zipped down and provided better warmth and water resistance.

On one of our early trips, one of the younger kids – about seven - in my tent crawled through the gap while he slept and had actually slid his head completely outside the tent. An older kid walking outside in the dark did not see him and kicked his head. The kid instinctively reached for his head as he felt the pain from the boot, but his hand hit the tent and no head. He felt around and did not find his achy head. We were woken to his screaming: "I LOST MY HEAD. WHERE IS MY HEAD." It took a few seconds to realize what was happening. We found him pounding the flap of the tent top with his hands and not finding his head. He was flailing and screaming for his head. When we finally stopped laughing, we lifted the tent off his head so he could find it. He felt his whole head all around, making satisfied noises as he calmed down and fell back to sleep. He never really woke up and was actually screaming in his sleep. We pulled him in so his head was not stuck outside anymore and we all tried to go back to sleep but it was just too funny to let go. We kept re-enacting his screaming and flailing for a while that night and we still occasionally tease him about his lost head to this day.

Scout life taught us about team work and mutual reliance on each other. We learned the value of cooperation and coordination.

Life was good by any measure. We lived in a vibrant prosperous society in a country that was blessed with some of the best weather and natural beauty anyone could hope to find. In spite of the few tense incidents related to the Arab-Israeli conflict and the Palestinian camps, Lebanon was a safe place with a seemingly very bright future.

INDOMITABLE SPIRIT

HELL COMES TO PARADISE

I had not reached thirteen years of age when the shots that came to define the official beginning of the war in Lebanon rang through Beirut on April 13, 1975. As usual, when the antagonists are chafing for war a relatively minor incident became the excuse for a larger conflict with ulterior motives. I was yet too young to fully comprehend the gravity of what had happened, even though the tension filled the air and fear of things to come was evident on the face of every adult I knew.

Sadly, I later came to realize that it was not just my young age that prevented me from comprehending the full gravity of the events. No one in Lebanon had a clue as to what was in store for the country. It took a long time for the public to begin to realize some of what had been planned for their paradise on Earth.

I clearly recall lamentations of adults about a potential repeat of 1958, but that was a walk in the park compared to what was about to unfold in Lebanon. The 1958 conflict was confined to a few people with hand guns and a few small bombs in garbage cans. It was hard to imagine what was to come. Perhaps people did not want to see the demons in the shadows. People's wish for good things to last forever always manages to prevent them from recognizing impending problems. Our wish for things to remain as they are, tends to obscure our vision and we simply fail to see what we do not wish to see until it is too late.

Clearly, problems had been brewing behind the scenes. The demons of hell were descending on Lebanon with a vengeance and, the joy ride was coming to a sudden and cruel end.

The war officially began when the Palestinians, armed and financed by the Arabs, launched their offensive against Lebanese Christians. This launch served as a perfect pretext for Syria to invade and occupy two thirds of the country under the guise of an Arab league "Deterrent

Force", which in turn brought Israel into the country to "protect" itself from the Palestinians and Syrians.

Moslem Fundamentalists found their arena for Jihad, with Arab financing, particularly from Libya, Saudi Arabia and the Gulf states recruiting Fanatics from all corners of the globe and shipping them to Lebanon by the tens of thousands to "Liberate Lebanon from the Crusader Infidels." All operated under the tutelage of the Syrian government acting on behalf of the Arabs.

Soon after came the Iranian revolution, which was in part brewed within the chaos created in Lebanon by a host of Western intelligence agencies intent on deposing the Shah. That created a strong nexus between Iran and the Shiites of Lebanon, which led to the rise of Hizbullah.

Christians, feeling threatened by the hordes of Islamic fanatics shipped to Lebanon from around the world, formed their own militia to defend themselves. Ironically, the same regional and international players bringing the Islamic hordes into Lebanon provided support for the Christians to defend themselves from them. It was all designed to wreak havoc and destroy the county. Many knew it but had no choice but to play along for survival.

All of this was conducted under the watchful eyes and participation of the international community, with the Soviets, Americans, Europeans, Israelis and Arabs all fueling and extinguishing fires as their interests dictated. The East-West divide, North-South divide, Moslem-Christian divide, The Arab-Israeli divide, the Shiite-Sunni divide, and every other international divide passed through Lebanon. Add global economic warfare to that and the West's need for cheap oil and to siphon Petro-Dollars into Western Banks, you begin to see the tip of the iceberg. Only the very tip. The full story is yet to be completely defined.

In addition, there was the untold number of groups that would emerge out of nowhere and disappear just as fast. You would see the local grocery delivery boy suddenly open up shop with a few of his equally destitute friends in some basement room with a few guns and declare themselves a militia. They always came with fancy romantic names like the 'The armies of the Islamic World,' 'The Brigades of the Oppressed on Earth,' 'The Socialist Union of Arabs and Moslems,' etc. Armies or Brigades in plural not singular, even when their members were in single digits. The fate of billions of oppressed and the whole Arab and Moslem world rested in the hand of illiterate Hammoudi and his idiotic friends. It made for nice headlines in international press, but it did not fool the locals who knew better.

All these international players and the multitude of foreign-funded rag-tag groups created a chaotic situation with absolute unpredictability. The small fleeting 'Brigades' were there to keep the pot stirring as they were the ones who often set up car bombs or kidnapped someone to start a conflict and then, disappeared, erasing all trace to who really gave the instructions. Sometimes they really disappeared, killed by the same people who hired them. It was generally known they had received a few bucks from some foreign intelligence agency, but most of the time, even they did not know who was funding them. All they knew was they were getting more money than they would performing their menial jobs, and they got to lounge around acting important.

In brief, what had allowed Lebanon to rise to prominence – its existence at the cross roads of the world – had become its bane. The poor and uneducated from all sides were recruited to wreak havoc on the country with promises of grandeur or the illusion of defending a cause. Tens of thousands of marauding hordes from all over the world would attack and destroy outlying Christian villages and towns killing thousands to scare the population into segregation and make it easier to propagate the war. People would be picked up and executed based on religion in random road blocks designed to instill the same fear. The general public was being mercilessly terrorized into segregation and submission.

The beautiful dream world that was Lebanon had suddenly turned into a nightmarish hell. Fear ruled the day. Uncertainty and unpredictability became the norm. Death was around every corner.

Civil War?

All this conflict with direct involvement of multiple states was called a "civil war". Before the internet and direct public access to news from around the globe, the rest of the world, was kept in the dark regarding who was doing what and this led them to simply believe that the Lebanese could not live together. But, anyone living in Lebanon could clearly see that foreign fighters (who came from around the globe) outnumbered the Lebanese participants by more than twenty to one.

There was nothing Civil about the war. There never is. All the talk about civilized war conduct is nothing but lies. Wars are killing fields where fighters aim to eliminate as many of the others as they possibly can. Nothing about that is civilized behavior.

The "civil war" label also fails on another front. The Lebanese public "the civil society" were by and large simply victims of other people's wars. If the Lebanese really disagreed on anything it was how to extract the country from all that mayhem. Endless debates from politicians down to the least educated revolved on who was at fault and how can it be brought to an end, and while disagreeing on almost everything, everyone agreed with certainty that foreign hands were deeply involved in everything.

What befell Beirut and the rest of Lebanon was a hellish conflict that included so many participants it can best be described as a compressed world war. It was not a civil war in any stretch of the imagination, and there was certainly nothing "civil" about it.

It is important to note that the Lebanese did not wish to kill each other, and never viewed each other as enemies. In spite of the long years of conflict with massive propaganda machines painting the Lebanese as enemies of each other, they continue to ardently view each other as parts of the same community. The Lebanese spent more effort helping and sheltering each other than they ever did fighting each other. In particularly harsh bombardment campaigns, people took refuge on the other side of the artificial dividing lines in areas populated by those of other religions and who are supposed to be the "enemy". Would this happen if this was truly a war between the religious sects? This did not happen once or twice - it was the norm. Sure, there were Lebanese fighting in the war, but they were almost always in defensive positions, mostly fighting against a foreign force of one kind or another. Occasionally, they turned on each other, as they disagreed on the means to extract Lebanon from the hell it had descended into. On other occasions, militias would fight over splitting the spoils of war, but that was a minor part of the conflict.

There was never a true segregation of the public in opposition to each other. At no time did the people at large turn on each other in an attempt to eliminate each other. Moslems and Christians continued to coexist and interact normally in their daily lives even as the war raged around them. The Lebanese had no control over the conflict, and all they could do was maneuver their way through the quagmire and hope to survive the day - one day at a time. Those who attempted to unite the Lebanese to bring back order to the country were summarily executed by massive bombs that destroyed whole neighborhoods. Those executions often were undertaken by several foreign powers cooperating in spite of their opposing agendas, as their interests coincided when someone tried to shut down their playing field. For the powers that be, Lebanon was the arena in which they confronted each other at minimal risk to themselves and the place they tossed their problems to avoid confronting them. The majority of the people were simply caught in the middle of a conflict they strained to understand. Their utopic existence gave way to a hellish nightmare. Making one's way to the office, school or store became a kind of Russian roulette. You never knew when, where or why fighting would erupt or where the next explosion would occur. Missiles and bombs could begin landing on any neighborhood randomly without warning. Random is an accurate description, as bombardments did not target military installations or formations, but fell in scatter form on residential and business neighborhoods. Random road blocks would emerge suddenly and disappear just as quickly. They would pick up a few people based on their sectarian affiliations and haul them away. Most were never seen again, and there are still more than 17,000 people unaccounted for, whose fates remain unclear. They left home one day and were never seen again. This is aside from the hundreds of thousands known to have died during the war even if bodies were not recovered.

By 1990, in 15 years, more than six percent of the population had been killed, another fifteen percent wounded, more than half the population displaced by the war, and a quarter of the population left the country. To put this in perspective, if we apply the percentages to the US population, these numbers compare to twenty million dead, fifty million wounded, more than a hundred and sixty million displaced, and about eighty million people leaving the country. Yet, people persisted in spite of all this mayhem in their belief in the future of a united Lebanon that would transcend the conflict and once again rise from its ashes, like the mythical Phoenix, to once again play a leading role on the world stage. It became a national challenge to overcome the war and retain their dignity and place in this world.

The Lebanese people survived the war one day at a time and embraced life in the midst of impending death. They defied the death machine by insisting on enjoying life in spite of the mayhem around them. Parties were held in bomb shelters and Christmas decorations were hung even on destroyed streets. Businesses and industries continued to operate and even expand against the odds. Rebuilding businesses and

INDOMITABLE SPIRIT

residences in the middle of war became the way to resist the war and prevent it from achieving its objective of destroying the country. Oh, and we all went to school daily.

It was our resistance. It was our way of yelling out to the world "YOU CANNOT KILL US. WE WILL STILL BE HERE LONG AFTER YOU MOVE ON."

Most of all, the Lebanese embodied the old saying: "Those who can laugh at their problems will never be defeated." And laugh they did. There are more jokes about the Lebanese wars than any other subject, and hundreds – maybe thousands - of comic plays, movies and TV shows made fun of every aspect of the war. Most of all the jokes targeted the foreign forces. Unable to stop them, demeaning them with jokes was a very effective way to psychologically deal with the invasions and minimize the pain and sense of helplessness.

It was and remains this unwavering faith and defiance that allowed the miraculous survival of Lebanon through all that befell this small country. The perseverance of the people, the commitment to continuously rebuild what is destroyed and add to it against all odds is the legacy of our generation, as is the ability to continue to laugh at all these problems and still find the GOOD in life.

Some may consider it insane to keep rebuilding while others are persisting in their destruction. Many would argue that it is better to move to safer ground, but where would that be? Will the devil that was attempting to devour Lebanon not then move on to greener pastures? Has that not already happened? Is the whole world not enduring the wrath of the fanatics and lunatics they nurtured in Lebanon and other places?

This is a legacy that I for one carry with honor. A legacy of persistent belief and working for unity and good to overcome the evil others do. The ability to lick our wounds, dust ourselves off and stand again and again in the face of unrelenting offensives. The tenacity to do so with a smile and throw a party in the face of the invading hordes.

INDOMITABLE SPIRIT

For every tear we shed, we diligently produced a thousand smiles to compensate.

For every structure they destroyed, we built a thousand others in Lebanon and throughout the world.

For every evil act committed against us, we delivered kindness to a thousand others.

We resisted an unrelenting offensive on our humanity and survived to deliver hope to the rest of humanity.

We maintained a legacy of the indomitable spirit.

DEMONS AND ANGELS

Living in war-torn Beirut became a surreal existence. The demons of Hell converged on Lebanon like moths to a fire: killing with a vengeance and turning life into a living nightmare. But, as is always the case where demons appear, angles step in to protect the innocent and Humanity is the price over which they fight.

When most people think of war, they imagine military configurations fighting each other. Even when the battles are fought in urban areas, they remain primarily amongst and between the armed forces. Civilians caught in the crossfire are simply at the wrong place at the wrong time. In such conflicts, civilians have the ability to identify safe havens and seek shelter away from the front lines. Safety is defined by the distance the civilians are from military locations. However, that was not the case in Lebanon because civilians were the primary target of the war. On their way to work, school or to even to buy food, they were pulled out of their cars or off the sidewalks and never seen again. Car Bombs were planted at school entrances and timed to detonate when students were leaving for the day. Market places were blown up without having any military value what so ever. Bombs and Missiles rained on residential neighborhoods and business districts indiscriminately and without warning. Often, bombing sprees were timed for maximum casualties when everyone was on the streets. Whole towns were wiped out by large military forces inflicting unspeakable horrors on the unarmed inhabitants. Upon the entry of the forces, everyone caught in the town was killed in a brutal and gruesome manner and their corpses displayed for the living to see.

The war brought onto Lebanon was designed to make life a literal living hell. The clear and present danger at all times was designed to terrorize the population into fleeing the country, or at least parts of it. It was not a war for political control as some would claim. It was not about territory. It was designed to annihilate a way of life that stood in contrast to regional norms. The open coexistence and peaceful cooperation of people presented an example to the world that many considered an anathema to their political philosophy and ambitions. Religion was a political tool used to gather Islamic radicals from around the world to converge on Lebanon and die fighting even though the war was not about religion and certainly was not about the Lebanese population arguing about how to pray. Lebanese Religious leaders never tired of expressing unity under God, speaking about tolerance and coexistence. No one ever debated anyone else's religious beliefs or prayer practices.

That being said, it is widely known that religion is a very powerful tool in mobilizing fanatics to commit the most evil of acts against humanity even when it is in contradiction to all religious teachings. Try as you may, you will not find a single passage in the Bible or the Koran that sanctifies the wholesale killing of innocent unarmed people. No holy man can justify the brutal inhumane acts committed against unarmed civilians. Armed men would tie people to two cars and drive in opposite directions, splitting them in half. Innocent people were crucified, hung alive on hooks, and chopped to pieces while still alive. these are just a few of the gruesome acts of torture attributed to the war. Such hellish assaults on humanity exposes the soul to the most evil demons one can imagine.

Religion often talks about angels and demons as if existing in an alternate and parallel universe, only occasionally encroaching upon the human realm. But, what if angels and demons actually dwell within us all, hiding behind a human façade, just waiting for the opportune moment to emerge? What if, angelic and demonic traits are an integral part of the human soul, exposed only by circumstances?

I do not have an answer to such ponderings.

But, what I know with certainty is that good and evil emerge in human form more often than most ever expect. I have seen them at work. I have experienced their presence in more ways than most can conceive. Demons live among us and within us, and they come in many shapes and forms. They dwell among us inflicting unspeakable evil upon innocent people.

I have had the opportunity of looking closely into the eyes of raving fanatics with a gun pointed at my head to see the depth of hell. There was no humanity left, at least none that was discernable. Those people were willing to kill a perfect stranger who has never done them any wrong. They were perfectly willing to inflict harm without remorse or a moment's hesitation, and they did so repeatedly; and this was the terror machine unleashed in Lebanon. One can point at the fact that these people were often drugged. One can point at religious zealotry as the driver behind such acts. However, no drugs or religious indoctrination can produce such hatred and heartless behavior if evil was not already present within.

I have known many religious zealots of all kinds who remained kind hearted and compassionate. In fact, the truly religious would never harm innocent people, but would step in to protect and defend them. The truly religious believe in the sanctity of life and in a compassionate loving God who would not command or condone a barbaric assault on his children.

This was not the hand of God in any stretch of the imagination.

Simultaneously, the war also brought out the best in people. The presence of evil always draws out the angels in those pure souls. Those were the people who would risk it all to save a stranger. They would step in front of a loaded gun to prevent a raving lunatic from killing an innocent they did not know. They would run out under fire to pull the wounded from the street and mend their wounds, keeping them alive until they could make it to the hospital. They would hide individuals targeted by the raving hordes, knowing the risk of getting caught. They would give them a place to hide and share what food they had until it was safe to make it home. They would even lend them clothes and money, if needed even when they did not know them or expect to see them again. They did not ask you what your religion was or where you were from before they offered to help. Often, they did not ask at all. It was enough that you were a fellow human being in need. They are the true "Good Samaritans" and much more. The biblical Good Samaritan did not risk his life to help the stranger but those living angles risked losing life and limb to help save a strange soul.

Perhaps it was their own soul that was being saved and brought closer to God.

During high school one of my closest friends was the son of the Grand Mufti of Lebanon – The highest Sunni Moslem religious authority in the country. They lived several miles outside the city, and he mostly hung out with us close to school where we all lived. We occasionally drove to his house on weekends in the hills south of Beirut. We were a mixed group of Moslems and Christians, and it never was an issues as the Mufti's wife would welcome us with open arms, and whenever the Mufti himself was at home, he would come in for a brief chat, not as a religious authority, but as a fatherly figure. He was a very kind and friendly man.

One Saturday afternoon, as we sat in the Mufti's family room, the Mufti walked up to the open door and leaned on the frame and just stared at us. He looked tired and distant and had a glaring gaze that felt like it was piercing through us. As it was somewhat unsettling, we asked if he was okay. He nodded, and said he was enjoying looking at us, even though it certainly did not seem that way to us. Realizing he was making us uncomfortable, he said "I am just enjoying the sight of your friendship without regard to religion or town of origin." He continued, "do not let anyone convince you of all the religious hatred thrown out all over the country." This was three years into the war, and he was under a lot of pressure to champion the fanatic Islamist cause. "Religion," he proceeded, "is not how many times you go to a Mosque or a Church, it is not how many times you pray and proclaim your belief in God." He posed for a few seconds as if letting that settle into our minds. "Religion is about how you treat others. Show the grace and compassion of God in your behavior. Treat others as you would want God to treat you. That is true religion." "We are all God's children." he said, waving his arm across the room as he turned around and left while his words hung in the air.

At seventeen, we understood the words he spoke and knew he was referring to our close friendship across sectarian lines. It took years to truly understand the full meaning of the words he uttered that day. So much evil is committed in the name of religion that God is innocent of.

This was religion as the Grand Mufti knew it, preached it and lived it. Sadly, he would be assassinated specifically for that belief in humanity and the sanctity of God's children. He refused to advocate war in the name of religion and stood fast in his beliefs even as he knew he would die for it. This was also the advice of so many priests, bishops and Moslem holy men over the years - the truly religious and pious were the ones who suffered the most.

Along those lines. resistance to false religious teachings meant maintaining our humanity in the presence of unspeakable evil. It meant sustaining decency amongst wretched acts. The Lebanese were simply not willing to surrender to evil. They insisted on living life to the fullest in spite of the shadow of death cast so ominously across the country. It became a national challenge.

It meant *living* in the shadow of death.

Maintaining our humanity and civility became the weapon of choice for most Lebanese in the face of the converging hordes of barbarians. These simple acts of kindness to all became the golden chain that bound people together providing hope against utter despair.

There is an old saying in Lebanon that translates as: "How constrained life would be, if not for the space provided by hope."

Hope reigned as an eternal flame in Lebanon, and it came through the faces of those living angles who would not hesitate to lend a hand to anyone in need.

SURVIVING THE STORM
EARLY DAYS OF WAR

As the bombs came crashing into the city and country side, the people's initial reaction was to flee for safety. Most of those who fled, migrated within the country. A large part of the inhabitants of Beirut originally hailed from towns and villages around the country, and even though they lived and worked in the city, many maintained residences in the countryside for weekend and summer retreats. Many who did not have their own retreat havens, had relatives and friends to take them in. As for those who were not as fortunate to have a safe place to escape, they left the country.

The fleeing, migration and immigration was supposed to be temporary. Everyone believed the conflict would end in weeks, and all would go back to normal. This belief remained throughout the war. People took up residence in hotels and/or with family or friends in other countries, and the war dragged on, degenerating day by day, with each day brining news of yet another atrocity that exposed an increasing level of human brutality.

Everyone knew that with time, a decision had to be made. People could not remain in temporary status for too long. Money was running out, adults had to go back to work, and children had to go back to school. Some made the decision to immigrate to other countries, particularly those with immediate opportunities, but a large demographic decided to stay and make the best of the horrid situation.

Those who remained came to realize that the battles came in spurts. The war was not continuous or logical in any fashion. Battles came and were won or lost. Calm could be broken at any point without warning. Something as simple as stepping outside was always a risk as you never knew what to expect. For one to call the early days of war pure chaos and mayhem would be an understatement, but there are really no words that can accurately describe the conditions we had to endure. It took more than a year before clear dividing lines were established. These lines were the one consistent, which allowed people to know what to expect. Prior to those clear demarcation lines, everything was fluctuating.

The whole country was religiously mixed, not only Beirut, and one could not throw a stone without hitting someone from another religion. As the powers that be strove to segregate and vied for territory and strategic positions the lines were ever shifting, inflicting untold harm on large segments of the population. Palestinian camps – military fortresses – were scattered all over the country, including three that were in what eventually became the Christian area. They dominated major highways and roads and became a target for removal to eliminate the permanent threat.

Changing Realities

Demographics changed substantially with movement of people, and that included the student body. We saw many of our classmates disappear to other schools that avoided risky trips through divides and danger zones. We suddenly had an influx of new students whose families moved to the area or who used to attend a school that fell on the other side of a divide.

Ours, the International College (IC) was a prestigious prep school for the American University of Beirut, and expensive. So, the bulk of the student body came from educated professional families that -in spite of different political views and affiliations- remained civilized and mostly tolerant of each other. The endless heated debates never turned violent among the educated, and friendships remained in spite of the utter disagreement on the situation. Often these disputes existed within the same home as brothers and sisters found themselves politically aligned

INDOMITABLE SPIRIT

with forces that were supposed to be killing each other. They would become each other's saviors, though, not killers.

Unfortunately, there are always exceptions, particularly in those early years of war when people moved into Beirut from other parts of the country and some uncivilized elements made it into our school. They did not last long as they truly did not fit in, nor did they have the intellectual rigor for the advanced learning.

The school had been expanding rapidly before the war and had built a huge campus on a hill top about 15 kilometers south of Beirut, which initially housed the high school students. However, these were older students and more likely to be politically engaged and active. The rise of the left-wing movements and demonstrations before the war were resulting in multiple incidents in the school. Within reach of the PLO and right-wing activists, the school was becoming a battle ground and being distant from the city it was hard to control.

Just before the war started, the Middle School classes were moved to the new campus and the older high schoolers were brought to Beirut. It was a beautiful and pristine location with a lot of land, but I did not get to enjoy it more than a portion of the year. By the end of April, a few days after the breakout of the war, the busses stopped heading there.

Jets Outside our Classroom Windows: 1973

In 1973, Lebanon -again- sat out the Arab-Israeli war, and the Lebanese went on with their lives as if nothing was happening, but Lebanon's airspace was part of the battlefield.

Our school overlooked the sea from atop a steep hill with no buildings to block the view. Our classroom windows in October 1973 faced the sea. Early afternoon, we would hear the deafening roars of jet engines that literally shook the building, and at age eleven, one could not help but rush to the windows to see what was happening.

INDOMITABLE SPIRIT

There they were: A Syrian MIG jet chasing an Israel Phantom F-4 jet, close enough that it almost appeared the antenna on the front of the MIG was about to go through the Phantom's engine. No one was paying any attention to the teacher screaming at us to back away from the windows, as the jets were less than five hundred meters away. The excitement of watching a live aerial battle so close made us ignore all the potential danger.

As we watched, the Phantom went into a roll-and-brake move and lands right behind the MIG, which slipped under it when it slowed down. They just switched positions, and the Phantom fired a missile straight into the MIG's backburner, breaking left into the Mediterranean to avoid flying into the explosion. The building shook violently, and the teacher ducked, but the naïve kids, with no real appreciation for the danger, were cheering half way out the windows.

The Syrian pilot had given up upon switching positions with the Israeli and hit the eject button. As debris fell into the sea we watched the pilot slowly parachute down and was met by a couple of fishing boats from a nearby harbor. As they hauled him into the boat, the show was over and we finally responded to the teacher's pleas to get back to our seats.

No one could concentrate on anything other than discussing what we just watched regardless of how much the teacher tried to return the focus to the class material. The teacher relented and abandoned the scheduled lesson as she figured there was a life lesson there that was more important than the planned subject matter. She took the opportunity to explain to us the danger that we were in and that we should not have stayed at the windows. Jets fly really fast, and five hundred meters can be cleared in seconds. A wrong turn or a misfired missile could have brought havoc on our building. We agreed with the logic, but this was just too good of a show to miss. How many people get to see that?

The road from Beirut passed between Palestinian camps and cut across dangerous territory. It was too risky to bus hundreds of kids ten to fifteen years old through that every day, so we were moved back to the old campus inside Beirut. The accommodations would have been impossible had it not been for a major shift in the student body. Some of our classmates had simply left the country, others from the opposite side of the green line, headed to other schools that did not require crossing the city divide every day, which initially reduced the student numbers. Thus, we were able to all squeeze in the school for the remainder of the year.

OUT OF BEIRUT FOR THE SUMMER

We finished the school year and headed to Monsef for the summer as was our usual modus operandi, but this time proved to be certainly different due to two issues: one, we were entering our teen years and life was constant rollercoaster of hormonal and physical change and two, the country had entered an era of war that made daily life a constant kaleidoscope.

Our Own Beach Club House

By the time war came, my Grandfather had long shut down his chicken farm by the beach and converted the building into six one-bedroom chalets for rent. The building was right off the water and perfect for beach chalets. By the summer of 1975, five of the chalets were rented out and the sixth one was left to become our own space as we were teenagers in need of our own private space to hang out and be whoever we wanted to be.

Due to the rectangular nature of the building the center chalets, including ours, had two entrances on either side of the building making it perfect for gatherings where the overflow of people can migrate in both directions. A Ping Pong table brought into the space by a friend, occupied the main living space and was used by all. Regardless of what was happening in the space, most important was the fact that we had our own place to hang out in and be away from the adults. That space became our party room, sleep over house, and much more. But, we only managed to keep the space for three summers, until it was occupied by displaced Christians from North Lebanon in 1978. For those three summers, the keys were left outside for anyone to use at any time. There was not much to steal, and it was in the middle of the village and extremely safe, but we locked the doors when no one was there just in case.

Those were the summers of our early-teens with hormones raging and sexual discovery being a main issue in our lives. The chalet saw a lot of action from teens seeking a private hideout. Whenever a couple had to be alone, they always had a place to be and it especially came in real handy during those summer beach parties. It was about 50 meters away from our swim and party area, but sufficiently secluded behind some rocks. Yet, occasionally, the hiding duo would become the show for those younger kids eager to see what sex was all about. Of course, since the chalet belonged to my family I always had first rights, but being that we were all close friends everyone used it almost equally.

We really missed our club house when it got occupied. We could not replace it anywhere along the beach. So many memories were made in that place, and it was there that so many of us experienced first love, and even lost their virginity.

"Haskes" were another venue for intimate retreats from prying eyes. A "Haske" looks like a Kayak but without a hole in the middle. It has a flat surface and could easily seat three people although it was generally used by two. Our gang had acquired one the year before in addition to the several others in the village making the total ten. These were shared by everyone. Mostly they were used for fun as people rowed around and enjoyed themselves and we used them to get to the next beach spot, about two kilometers away, to spend time with friends. However, they also had another use: SEX. We would row ourselves half a kilometer away from shore to where we could barely be seen as a dot in the water, and there we would do what we wanted without anyone seeing us. However, when we stopped rowing for a while, others generally knew what was going on, but at least we were not on public display.

The motion of the sea created a rocking motion that only enhanced the sexual sensation and the experience. There were, however, a few things we had to take into consideration. Bathing suits had to be secured to the oar to avoid losing them to the sea and then have to return naked to shore. We also had to head out and southward, as the Mediterranean

INDOMITABLE SPIRIT

drifts northward in a counterclockwise motion. If we headed straight out and stopped rowing, we would be several kilometers north by the time we finish.

In spite of the war, the party had to go on.

However, the war made that change ever so much more acute. There was no fighting or bombing in our village, but the war and its effects were never far away.

Idiots at Check Points - 1975

In the chaos of those early days of war, many young men joined the local forces out of concern for the safety of their communities, sometimes without much regard to political dogma. With fluid demarcation lines, and so many forces at play often wiping out whole towns or neighborhoods, it was an act of survival more than anything else. They would often man temporary check points when there was the risk of infiltration, or sneak attacks, to help ensure the safety of their families, and that included our village and its surroundings.

Many would wear face masks to hide their identity fearing retribution given the fluid and uncertain conditions before the permanent dividing lines took effect. However, when those men manned check points near their homes, many knew exactly who they were. Their looks, the way they walked and talked gave then away to those who knew them well and only strangers would be fooled. Yet, some acted like they were not known to anyone.

Most had enough sense to act intelligently and realize that their task was to protect the locals from outsiders. However, there were some serious idiots on the streets who did not deserve the air they breathed.

One of the most blatant examples was when a middle-aged man came across one of those check points at the edge of our village and one of the masked men seriously demanded "Uncle Phillip please show me your ID." Recognizing the young man, he called him out by name and said "Uncle Phillip! And you need my ID!" He continued without mincing his words "You fucking idiot. What do you need my ID for?"

The young man answered with all sincerity and stupidity. "We must verify the identity of everyone coming through here."

Phillip could not take that much stupidity and got out of his car yelling. "Since I am your uncle, what more identity verification do you need, you moron?"

The others who also knew Phillip well intervened to save the idiot from a beating on the street by his uncle. They calmed Phillip down and sent him on his way apologizing for the idiot's behavior.

Shortly thereafter the man who armed and deployed the young men at the check point came along to check on them. The same idiot who questioned his uncle was at the point and saluted his commander and then said, "Mr. Salah. ID please."

At first, Salah thought it was a joke and laughed it off, telling the idiot that his request was a good one, but the idiot did not back down, he insisted on being shown the ID. Salah asked "Are you serious!" The idiot confirmed that his orders were to check the identity of anyone passing through.

Salah said, "I know. I gave you those orders."

The idiot replied. "I know that Mr. Salah, but orders are orders. No one gets through without ID check."

At that point, Salah stepped out of his car and pulled his gun out to shoot the idiot. As others intervened, Salah kept telling them that this man was a waste of oxygen. Needless to say, the idiot was never at any check point again. He was just too dumb to be trusted with a gun, as were many others who manned the checkpoints throughout the country.

Dead Man Floating

The war caught up with us in the village in other forms as well. One afternoon in the summer of 1975 as we frolicked in the water, one of my friends spotted a large floating object approaching the shore. We climbed up on the rocks to get a better view from a few meters above water. It was hard to figure out what it was at first. It looked like tattered cloths attached to something as the shallow waves tossed it around. As we debated what it could be, someone on a Haske headed out towards it. As he got closer to the object, he shouted out "It is a dead person." The body was face down and the clothes were shredded and somewhat obscuring the shape from the distance. The Haske rider backed away as we, on the shore, discussed what to do about it. We were teenagers with no experience with handling dead people, but we knew enough to realize the dangers of rotting flesh and kept our distance until a workable plan was in place.

A couple of middle-aged men overheard us talking and planning and came out to check what was going on. The adults asserted that we had to get the body out of the water as soon as possible as the tide would soon push it onto the rocks and there was no way we could avoid dealing with it. We could not just leave a corpse to decompose and spread decease.

They got a rope and a hook and then got on the Haske at which time the body had gotten close enough for all of us to clearly see it from the rocks. They tried to hook the ropes that tied his hands behind his back, but the corpse had rotted to the point that the hands detached from the corpse and the ropes fell off.

They kept at it until they could catch the hook on a bone and dragged it to shore. But, now what? The corpse had decomposed and been nibbled on by fish beyond recognition. The smell was not that bad yet due to the embalming effect of the salt water but it was a nasty sight that caused many to throw up.

They called the police in Byblos to report the body. The police were not much help and simply stated that they have no way of identifying the body since it was floating at sea and could have come from anywhere. This was before DNA testing and in the middle of a war that was producing a lot of unidentified bodies, so the police just told them to bury it.

Having received no official support, the older men brought shovels and asked us to help dig a grave on the far edge of town to bury it before it began to stink up the place. We walked over to dig while they dragged it back to the sea for easier transportation and over to the edge of town for burial. We dug a shallow grave, dropped the body in it and covered it up. Someone said a brief prayer for the man's soul, whomever he might have been, and we walked off.

This body would never be found. Twenty-five years later a structure was built on that site that temporarily served as a USAID location. when they worked on the site to build the structure, no bones were reported. This body was simply another missing person in the war who has never been found. We had no way of knowing who he was, or even if he was Lebanese. We had no way of informing anyone who may care about him that their loved one was indeed buried in the ground.

At age thirteen, I had my first direct exposure to the nastiness of death and the fickleness of life. I found myself helping remove and bury a disfigured corpse, in a scene so gruesome that most adults could not handle. Those type of incidents became part of our lives, putting us in an ever-flirting situation with the possibility of death, and pretending it was not even there.

The adults would tell us to simply forget about it and return to our boisterous playing in the water. It was like it never happened.

Just put it behind you and move on.

And we did just that. The day was coming to an end, so we took a final swim to cleanse ourselves from the stench of the dead body, and then headed home to shower and get dressed. That night we had a party to attend and that would help in putting the whole ordeal behind us.

Party Time Central

Our teen years, had a rhythmic progression that consisted of our days spent on the beach to our evenings spent at a party. Before any of us acquired driver's licenses, we were either at dance parties (usually in people's homes) or at sports tournaments, which were partial parties in their own rights.

Volley Ball was the prevalent sport outside the cities at that time, but basketball was also popular. Almost every town and village had a team and a volleyball court and would hold a tournament for about 3-4 days each during the summer. Whether we were on the team or not, we were there whenever our village was playing or when the tournament was held in our village or the immediate neighboring villages. It was the place to be. There was music, food, and entertainment, and, above all, there were members of the opposite sex to chase, with hidden dark corners and tree stands for captured moments of intimacy.

These sports events were how we met and befriended people from other towns. We made good friends and occasionally had the misfortune of getting on the wrong side of the locals. Often, the conflict among young males had to do with a female. Fortunately, those conflicts rarely progressed beyond a shouting and shoving match, because everyone and their brother intervened to disengage the fight and send each of the fighting faction to a different side of the arena. There were many lessons on how to deal with people and behave in public that were learned from those conflicts. When there were no games, we held impromptu parties, which happened two or three times a week, where we danced the nights away. Everyone was invited, including the friends from neighboring villages. Other times we were at the neighboring villages' parties. We would hold the parties in empty basements or abandoned old stone structures consisting of one large room that were either once the home of someone who was no longer around, or used to serve as an animal barn when pack animals were still in use. They became our play houses. We would draw electricity from a house nearby, bring a stereo and drinks, and we had a party. We began attending these by the time we turned 11 or 12 years old. We would be the youngest in the crowd, watching the older kids, learning the tricks of the trade, and preparing for the coming years when we would be the ones slow dancing in the dark. The events were set up such that there would be barely any light inside, and certainly no lights outside, and that is how we liked it. We were teenagers with raging hormones, and the last thing we wanted was the peering eyes of the adults on us. Yet, as I found out years later, the adults knew what was happening. I have had my aunts recently tease me about relations I was certain they never knew about.

My brother-in-law, four years younger than me, never tires of telling the story of how I put him and others to work cleaning one of those barns. The place had never been used since it was an actual animal barn, and still had animal droppings all over the floor. I was their scout leader and turned it into a scout project. I got several kids to spend the day cleaning the barn. They thought they would be using it for some scout related event only to discover we had a party coming up and needed the place cleaned. Since all the village's teens and their out of town friends were invited, there was always someone or something new to keep things interesting. We made new friends and developed romantic relations, constantly expanding our social circle and experience.

Sometimes, the party was held at the beach, at night. We would come in bathing suits so we could swim at night while we partied. The music left much to be desired, as the sound from the small portable stereos was absorbed by the sea and drowned out by the sound of waves, but the sound quality was the least of our concerns. We had a great time dancing, swimming and mating on the beach.

The party continued in the shadow of death, as we thumbed our noses at the warring hordes, and danced the nights away.

INDOMITABLE SPIRIT

RETURNING TO BEIRUT: NEXT FALL

By the next school year in October of 1975, we returned to Beirut to find a host of new classmates had appeared who previously attended schools that became too risky to go to and had there not been a war circumstance there would have been no space to accommodate these newbies. However, across the street from the back of our school stood the American Community School, which was specifically designed with a US curriculum to accommodate the children of US expatriates as well as Europeans. There was a substantial American and European expatriate community in Beirut, including the likes of Sting who attended that school and started his first band there.

Those were the students who had fled the country in waves as the war came. While Lebanese were willing to tough it out, foreigners quickly moved their kids out, even if the parents needed to stay. As such, our school was able to expand into these buildings in the fall of 1975, shortly after we returned to the main campus. My classroom for the next two years would be there, where only a narrow side street separated my building from the basketball courts on the main campus

With a highly educated population and minimal number of poor people who populated the militias, Ras Beirut, where we lived, was spared the most brutal of attacks. Many of the inhabitants and the Universities and business that dominated the area included many who crossed over the green line regularly, which further reduced bombing attacks. Yet, no part of Beirut was safe, and Ras Beirut saw its share of war, albeit to a lesser extent than some other parts of the city. When fighting raged too intense that school was closed, our parents would try to take us out of the city to the village, away from the main frontlines, which spared it the brunt of the fighting. As kids, that meant freedom from school and time to play. When the conflict died down we returned to the city and back to school.

Nonetheless, it was not always that simple. Often fighting would pin us down where we were, and if we were in Beirut, it meant bomb shelters or any subterranean floors, even if not designed as shelters. Those early days also witnessed endless propaganda rallies intended to gain support from the population for some cause or another. That was particularly potent in schools and universities as militiamen would enter school grounds, demand classes be suspended, and begin to spew political speeches. They were boring at best, and mostly extremely annoying. Few, if any cared about what they had to say, particularly when the Palestinians and their supporters spoke. Those where the people who destroyed our little paradise in the name of causes that were alien to most of us. Many would simply walk off campus as soon as classes got suspended and go find a nice video arcade or pool hall to enjoy our time in peace, leaving behind those who already agreed with the propagandists.

Often, no school meant no homework and time for a party. We would gather at someone's house, run the music and party the evening away. This constant disruption of school meant the curriculum had to be crammed into much fewer days than planned, but there was only so much cramming that could be done. So, when necessary, the schools eliminated the non-essential classes like physical education and art and increased the number of hours we spent per week on the core subjects. We could always, they argued, play sports and music after school on our own time, but we could not learn math or science on our own.

Like every other aspect of life in Beirut, schools took on the approach of making the best of a bad situation. Students still needed the skills to make it into college and then the work force, and that was the main focus by any means possible. All else became secondary and irrelevant. Attendance became relevant to war conditions. When students were absent because of the war, they received the information by other means, and as long as they passed the tests, they were not penalized. Often, students from distant areas would attend school for a few days at a nearby school just to keep up and then return to their regular school. Education is highly prized in Lebanon, and everyone cooperated to overcome the negative effects of the war.

Yet, life had to go on, and, as teenagers, we wanted to enjoy it as much as we could. We learned to ignore the war raging around us and proceed to live a fun-filled life in spite of it. We gradually morphed from fretting the war to using it to our leisurely advantage, and we did our best to turn every eruption in fighting and any other interruption of school into an opportunity for fun and play. However, it was not without incidents that constantly reminded us of the world we lived in. There was no escaping it and its effects. We had to witness and experience what no teenager ever should. On so many occasions our friends who were connected to the local militias came to our rescue. They would hear about some misunderstanding or find out someone was planning to hurt us and would quickly find us and tell us to disappear.

We knew better than to argue or ask questions and when told to disappear, we did so quickly and quietly. They would then dispel the situation and find us later to explain the misunderstanding, or on occasion, simple malice from someone.

Yet, there were not always someone around to hide us or protect us. We had our share of chases down the streets by fanatics wishing to inflict harm. We were shot, thrown in dingy basements, and harassed in so many ways over the years, just because we were Christians from the other side of the divide. I even had a raving lunatic press a gun against my head and pull the trigger, but the gun jammed. As he tried to make his gun work, I bolted as fast as I could. He managed to get off a couple of shots before I cleared the corner, but missed, and he never gave chase. I guess my guardian angel was on full alert that day.

INDOMITABLE SPIRIT

Basketball and Missile Launchers

In addition to the local conflicts, and unhinged young men with guns, we had to contend with the constant possibility of bombs and missiles raining on us. Furthermore, as young teens, we brought more danger to ourselves than should have been.

One Saturday afternoon, we gathered for a pick-up basketball game at IC as we often did at that age, and when in Beirut. The school was situated on steep terrain, with the courts located at the lowest level. More than thirty steps up from the courts started an amphitheater that extended the equivalent of 60 steps before we reached the level of the lowest building in the school. A two-meter wall separated the courts from the street behind the school, topped with a chain link fence to keep balls from disappearing. Among us that day was the son of the Yugoslav ambassador, who spent that year in Lebanon. A few minutes into the game he gets hit with bird shit, which is a very rare occurrence given the probabilities. As he cursed his luck, we explain to him that it is considered good luck in Lebanon due to its rarity. Not only did he not appreciate his good luck, he was hit two more times within fifteen minutes as if the birds were targeting him. We kept telling him it was a sign of good luck, and we were correct.

Shortly after the bird shit raids, we began to hear a lot of chatter and metal clatter on the other side of the wall that was certainly not normal street traffic. We posed to listen closely and realized there was military activity just on the other side of a thin cinder block wall. We could not see them, but what we heard was unmistakable.

Shrugging it off, we proceeded with our game as if nothing was happening, but in no time, we started hearing the whooshing sounds of the rocket launchers they had apparently just set up on that street. There was clearly more than one launcher and a lot of missiles going out from just two meters from the edge of the court, just over the wall.

INDOMITABLE SPIRIT

We stopped to discuss this, as we all knew that a response from the other side would be forthcoming. Outgoing rockets and artillery always brought incoming responses, and while outgoing does not hurt us, the return fire will certainly do a lot of damage. No matter how accurate the artillerymen could be on the other side, two meters was well within the margin of error. We were within the kill zone of any return fire.

Nonetheless, we idiotically decided to finish the game, rationalizing that we just needed a few more minutes and would be gone before a response to the missiles materialized. God forbid we leave without finishing the game. So, we played on to the sound of rockets flying and men clamoring to refill the launchers.

Five minutes later we finished the game, calmly dried our sweat, put our sweat suits on, gathered our things and began climbing the stairs out of the court. We had not yet reached the top of the stairs, when the first incoming shell landed squarely in the middle of the court we were playing on. It only missed the launcher by about ten meters, which is extremely accurate for a first shot from ten kilometers away, but it was on the wrong side of the wall – our side – and would have killed or maimed all of us had we still been playing.

Shrapnel clattered all around us but miraculously none of us were hit. It was time to run. By the time we got to the top of the amphitheater, the next shell landed at the bottom of the theater, again barely missing us, with more shrapnel chipping at the concrete theater seats around us, but none of us were hit.

Maybe that bird shit myth is true after all, or maybe it was fools' luck.

We continued to run upwards and out of the school towards home.

The launchers we were hearing were clearly not the only ones active during our game and now the return fire was blanketing the city all the way home. As we ran more than a kilometer home bombs and rockets were landing everywhere. Shrapnel, glass and concrete pieces were dropping from buildings all around us. Still they all missed us.

We scattered, each towards their own home. One guy lived in the same direction as me and was falling behind as I ran much faster and he kept calling for me to wait. "Why?" I would ask him. "Will my proximity protect you?"

I managed to make it home in one piece and found my father waiting for me on the lower level of our building. My mother had already taken my sisters to the bomb shelter and he wanted to insure I headed that way also and not up to the apartment. He did not let me get up to shower, arguing I could shower in the Gym, which is connected to the bomb shelter and well below ground. I ran up to grab a towel and a change of clothes and managed to call one of the guys to tell him I got there OK.

One more close brush with death and one more confirmation of our invincibility that simply caused us to take more risks and become more brazen in our attitude to the war.

Senseless Killings

The war brought chaotic behavior and death into the most mundane activities of our lives, as militiamen and foreign fighters roamed the streets wreaking havoc.

The war would often disrupt supplies and create a temporary shortage of certain items necessitating rationing to insure all are served and no one is left without. This included flour to bakeries, or gasoline, etc. When flour deliveries were disrupted, bakeries would limit each household to one kilo per day of bread to avoid hoarding as people tended to buy more bread than they need when they feared they could not get more and then threw it away when it got old, while someone may not get any.

To insure against any problems, militias assigned a man to guard the bakery and prevent any conflicts. This included the bakery attached to our building. But our neighborhood was all professionals and college professors who did not need much control. They understood the need for everyone to get some bread and worked together.

The young man assigned to the bakery was a local and knew this very well. He even left his gun inside the bakery and spent his time socializing with anyone coming to the bakery. The place was small and any clients exceeding three would wait their turn outside to avoid crowding, particularly in nice weather.

One day as I waited with half a dozen people outside for our bread, four young Palestinian teenagers – not from the neighborhood – show up and demand fifteen kilos of bread. The guard explained that they can only get one kilo and they start to pull rank claiming they needed the bread for the militia center. The Palestinians really did not look like representatives of any center, and he told them to bring a note from the center and they can have their bread. That set them off as they clearly were not there on behalf of anyone but themselves and they began to yell and pull out a hand grenade.

Abou El Abed saw the grenade from across the streets and came running, hand raised ready to hit them, yelling "WHAT ARE YOU DOING! YOU WILL KILL THESE GOOD PEOPLE."

Amazingly these armed teenagers took off running away from him, but they do not go too far. From the end of the block they opened fire in the direction of the bakery. The buyers had already dispersed anticipating trouble. The guard had retrieved his gun to try to defend the neighbors, but the poor man was too late. He took several bullets and died before he got to the hospital.

The very next day, the Palestinians came to hang his picture on the walls with the caption "He died so we can live. The martyr of Israeli aggression." Seriously! Right there were everyone watched it happen.

Abou El Abed walked over as they were hanging the pictures and tore them up. He told them they were adding insult to injury. It is not enough that they killed this young man over a few loafs of bread, and they were now selling us this crap.

He told them to let his family morn in peace. "This is not Israel. Why don't you bastards go fight the Israelis in Israel if you can find it."

FORCED SEGREGATION IMPOSED DIVIDING LINES

The country became divided into cantons controlled by various armed groups and foreign forces. Beirut was divided into East and West, with the old Downtown abandoned and demolished forming a clear separation between the two sides. Permanent roadblocks and check points were installed on roads leading from one canton into another, establishing a visible separation, even while some lines were still shifting.

The religious nomenclature for the various cantons were intentionally misleading but did not really fool anyone in the country. The reality on the ground was far from clear cut. The plethora of militias that popped up everywhere were rarely religious in nature and often included people of all faiths. Most were small rag-tag groups of thugs taking advantage of the chaos.

In the mid 1970's Islamic movements had not yet organized into what they are today. Politics in the Middle East split primarily along the lines of Capitalism vs. Socialism/Communism, with the majority in the region falling within the scope of socialism/communism. Lebanon was the only purely capitalistic country, and was the only country not constitutionally based on Islamic law, and all religions had equal rights.

The war brought much of the country under the direct control of the Palestinians or the Syrians, with dozens of local militias and warlords operating under their supervision. While labeled the "Moslem" part of the country, neither the people nor the armed operatives fully reflected that reality. The Syrian Government and Military were secular Socialist Baathists and included officers and soldiers of all faiths. They were the foot soldiers of the Arab league, and thus operated under the "Islamic" and "Arabist" umbrella.

Nonetheless, Syria had its own agenda, and it did not include Islamization. In North Lebanon, a segment of the Christians actually become one of the closest allies of Syria against other Christians, a couple of years into the war.

The Palestinians were also similarly mixed, and nationalistic in nature. The PLO and its offshoots were formed for the purpose of liberating Palestine from Israel, with no religious dogma. Their top leadership included many Christians, but again, their interests in gaining support from Oil-rich Arab states lead to the adoption of the "Islamic" and "Arabist" brand and attacking Lebanese Christians. They once declared that they were willing to fight until the last Moslem in Lebanon, as if Lebanese Moslems where theirs to dispense with as they wished. Most of the militias operating under those umbrellas, and direct supervision of the Syrians and Palestinians where secularists – Socialists, Communists, Arabists, Syrian Nationalists, etc. They opposed the Lebanese Government and Christian core of the population for being pro-Western and Capitalistic as for them the West was the enemy as they operated within the Soviet sphere, which itself was atheist.

In 1978, after the first Israeli invasion of Lebanon, elements of the Lebanese army from South Lebanon, along with other locals opposed to the PLO takeover of the south, formed the South Lebanon Army to keep the PLO from returning and began coordinating with Israel. It was called a Christian militia even though almost eighty percent of its members were Moslem as was the population that supported them. Similarly, the population remained mixed throughout the war, albeit to a lesser extent as the war dragged on. The segregation was slow and never absolute in spite of all the propaganda and atrocities committed intentionally to segregate people.

The Christian Militias were the most religiously monolithic as they defended themselves against the global Islamic onslaught, yet they too included a sizeable Moslem contingent. The population in their areas also remained mixed, and in places like Byblos no Moslem ever felt threatened or had the need to leave.

Primarily, people who had immediate relatives involved in politics or any of the militias and found themselves on the opposite side of their relatives' operations, found it safer to move. Even if they were not involved, there was always the risk of being harmed in an effort to pressure their relatives. Others simply feared being mistakenly harmed and decided to seek residence in areas that more closely reflected their political believes and affiliations.

Yet, the war and propaganda had a serious effect on everyone. While the general population did not exhibit any animosity towards people of different faiths, they became extremely leery of the militias that used them as pawns. This was particularly true if your family hailed from across the divide. Thus, even though there were many Christians in West Beirut, people like me, whose family came from the Christian heartland, were viewed differently and with suspicion by armed men.

Nevertheless, in Lebanon society is very intricately intertwined. We all had relatives, life-long friends and neighbors on every side and in every organization. Our classmates and childhood friends had their own connections as well that would come in handy way too often and save many lives. There were too many people who were involved by political conviction, but wholeheartedly opposed the war and the atrocities committed. Many remained engaged in hopes of lessening the violence and spent considerable effort trying to protect the innocent.

During the first year of the war, after enough foreign Moslem fanatics had been imported into the country, they gather on the southern edge of Beirut ready to cleanse West Beirut from Christians "Crusaders." The secularist militias rose to the occasion and even hung crosses around their necks – including the Moslems – in opposition to the religious cleansing threat. The attack never happened as even the Palestinians and the Syrians that dominated the military formations opposed it.

That reality meant that we could continue to live "normally", knowing that we could count on these connections. It also meant that many who escaped eventually returned to their old neighborhoods and settled back into their lives again. Most importantly people continued to travel and do business throughout the country. However, normal was truly relative, and Beirut had a new normal that included a lot of close calls with unhinged armed men or misunderstandings that could quickly spin out of control. As teenagers still learning how to cope with life, we were exposed to a higher dose of those misunderstandings and close calls.

In spite the continued mixture and interaction amongst people of all faiths, the conflict had a deep effect on our personal lives. Resist as we may, people's religion and identity became an important core element of who they were. Not that it defined whether they were good or bad. Having lived in a mixed society that included people from dozens of countries and all religious and political affiliations, we knew there was good and bad everywhere. However, it defined how we needed to deal with them, what one can and cannot do, where one should or should not go.

Taking the wrong person to the wrong place could be a death sentence.

Then there are the relatives and extended community, some of whom may not be so open minded.

Eventually, the geographic division of Lebanon set in with fortified lines slicing the country and Beirut into militia domains and areas occupied by Syrian and Palestinian Forces. People were branded by where they came from, what religion they belonged to, or their political affiliation. In spite of the fact that most of the population strove to ignore and refute those divisions, it had become a fact and even our own friends viewed us as coming from the other side. We were from another stock regardless of how close we were, almost like friends from another country.

This reality meant that our stay in West Beirut effectively placed us behind enemy lines, and viewed with extreme suspicion as potential spies or moles. That extended even to young high school students like us, and we were watched closely and monitored for any potentially insidious behavior.

Yet, the overwhelming majority of people effectively opted to look past the mayhem and strive to maintain normalcy and civility in the midst of chaos. In spite of the lack of any central authority to enforce laws, people stuck to a basic moral code of behavior that underlies them.

What was wrong was wrong regardless of the possibility of legal prosecution, and what was right was right even if no law was forcing you to do it.

In the fall of 1975, I had started dating a classmate, whose identity was never an issue. She was born and raised in Beirut but was Palestinian with a Jordanian passport. She was also a Moslem. Both of these were never even discussed by thirteen-year-old kids, but suddenly became important. Her parents, although educated professionals and not the least bit prejudiced, became very concerned about our relationship. They worried about what others would say and worried how it will affect the father's business as he dealt extensively with Arab countries and Palestinian officials. His little girl dating a Christian from Byblos could become a problem.

One day, while at her house, her father told me all this with no uncertain terms. He sat me down and explained: "You know we are not prejudiced. We have always known you were Christian (He knew my parents casually) and never had any problems with that. We like you. You are a good kid, and she is very happy with you. However, you understand the world we live in. Not everyone sees it that way. Some people around us are questioning me allowing her to be with you, and it is getting to be a problem." We both understood what we were up against. We stopped dating because the world around us had decided we should not. We remained friends, as that was perfectly acceptable, but dating was somehow a problem, at least in that case.

Every event or gathering had to take into consideration who could or could not come, and whether the venue should be changed to accommodate people. If you were driving and needed to change routes, you had to consider all those in the car and insure you are not putting anyone in undue danger.

This went beyond simple religion or origin. Even more important was the family relations. If someone is related to a leader in some political party or militia, they needed to be much more careful, even if they had nothing to do with what their relatives did. They were guilty by association and could become unwitting pawns and suffer the consequences. Yet, we persisted in befriending people of all walks. We partied together and helped each other out of jams when anyone was caught in the wrong place. We stood by each other and saved each other's lives on many occasions. It was our way – the country's way – of resisting the imposed divisions and surviving the ugliest attack on the people.

It was our act of defiance and resistance.

THE NEW NORMAL

It did not take long for people to adapt to this new reality. In a few months, a new normal emerged as people would pursue their daily lives in the shadow of war. Businesses and schools reopened. Alternate locations were found where necessary.

Dividing lines soon became another separation in the landscape almost similar to a deep ravine or a mountain. A divided city became a fact, and people would refer to East or West Beirut as if they were two separate cities.

People found ways to overcome and maneuver around the war, establishing new supply routes, and new means to survive. Those in other places check the weather and traffic before leaving home or work. The Lebanese began to check the status of the fighting instead. New personalities appeared on radios who would perpetually update everyone on the status of main roads. Every fifteen minutes they would rattle off the names of all crossings with status: "Passable and Safe," "Passable and not safe (meaning possible sniper fire)" or "Not Passable and Not Safe", etc. They would also provide information on any fighting outside the dividing lines, or any car bombs that just went off so people would plan accordingly and find a route around the problem areas.

To the outside world it appeared insane that people would adapt to such conditions and willingly choose to live through them. It would appear unthinkable that people would continue to rebuild and even erect new buildings and businesses under bombardment.

A shocked and surprised "WHY?" is almost always the question. Why not move somewhere else? Why put yourselves through all this?

Because this was their country, and the Lebanese were not abandoning it. People traced their roots thousands of years back. New studies indicate ninety-three percent of Lebanese are direct descendants of Phoenicians who inhabited Lebanese coastal cities more than 10,000 years ago. Their predecessors lived through extreme hardships and survived. They were not going to give up so easily.

The dean at Georgia Tech, who was a close friend of my father and had close relations with Beirut University College, once remarked to me that he believed the history of Lebanon resulted in their toughness. He believed that the repeated invasions of the country over millennia whittled the population down to the toughest of the tough. Today's Lebanese are the descendants of those who endured and survived the harshest of conditions. The weak had either died or left long ago. He may have a point. It may be social evolution and the survival of the fittest.

We learned to read the signs of impending danger and be alert to developments around us. Ironically the sight of armed men lingering on the streets would become a reassuring sign as it meant they were not on high alert and thus, a low probability of fighting.

Most importantly, we learned to always be aware of our escape route if the need arises. You needed to always have an escape plan. How do you get out of here if the main route is closed? Where would you hide if bombs came raining down? How would you get home? Those were the prevailing questions in our young minds.

The Teenage Mind

This would become our life at a very early age. We substantially skipped the teenage innocence phase. We were forced to grow up very fast and learn the harsh realities of life at age thirteen to survive. We became adults overnight.

We learned to be aware of all our surroundings and to negotiate our way out of a jam with armed militias and invading armies. We learned to survive on our own even if no adults were present and learned the intricacies of the political and military webs in the country.

But, deep inside, still resided teenagers that persisted in following our biological clocks. Although we were extremely aware of the dangers that surrounded us, and highly skilled in avoiding harm, we were still naïve kids on some level. We were young and, in our minds, indestructible. We pushed our luck at every possible opportunity that it is a miracle we even survived all the stupidities we committed. In a twisted way our crash course in life made us simultaneously more responsible and more dangerous. Our independence made us capable of taking more risks than any adult would be willing to. Our teenage brains had not yet fully developed to properly assess and appreciate the true nature of the risks we were taking or properly foresee the consequences of our actions.

In part, it was our eagerness to overcome the harsh reality of war and give our lives meaning and purpose. The ever-present risk of death became the impetus to take all risks to make the most out of life while it lasted. We saw too many people die prematurely and lost too many relatives and friends. Tomorrow was no longer promised or certain to come. Today was IT. If there was any fun to be had, it had to be NOW, regardless of the situation.

As young teenagers, we would hitchhike across the green line from West to East Beirut and then all the way north to our village and back, catching rides with anyone who would stop for us. Any of these rides could have been our last if the driver was intent on harm, but we did it anyway to make it to a party or scout camp on any other event that would seem trivial to the outside world.

The war resulted in many rules being skirted or ignored all together. Driving age was one of the most flaunted rules, as there were much more important issues to deal with for the police to worry about who has a driver's license. So almost all started driving their parent's cars, and some even got their own cars before the legal age of eighteen.

I had always been the youngest of my friends, with most being two to three years older than me and that meant that within a couple of years after the war began, many of my close friends were driving. With that came a freedom of movement that escalated our risky behavior to a new level. We could now go anywhere, whether we should or not, and often we should not have.

As a parent now, I sympathize with what our parents felt every time we left the house. If my teenagers are half an hour late, we hound them with calls and texts on their mobiles until they confirm they are fine. There were no mobile phones, internet or emails, and often no phones at all during the war, which meant a complete disconnect from our parents when away from home. They could only hope we were still alive and would be back, which is almost an unimaginable feeling in the age of connectivity. That was the world we lived in, and somehow our parents maintained their sanity while always wondering what has become of us.

To be sure, we strove to maintain communications and adhere to expectations. If we were supposed to be back home at a certain time and could not, we made every attempt to contact them to let them know we are still alive and well. Otherwise, we made every effort to be where we were expected to be, but that was not always possible. Consequently, our parents had their share of tense scary moments.

In addition, whenever we became aware of any flare-up in fighting or an explosion taking place, we found a way to contact our parents and inform them that we had survived whatever the event du jour was. HAM radios [an old-style walkie talkie of a sort] became ever so important. Absent access to a telephone, we could always find someone with a HAM radio to contact someone in our parent's neighborhood, who would relay the message.

Ironically, often those people would be militiamen who are technically at war with each other as we would be in a different part of the country than our parents. Yet, they would call their "enemies" to go tell our parents that we were OK. This humane act superseded any animosity they may have for each other.

Eventually, I developed a plan to minimize my parents' angst and any potential problems with them. When I left home, I would give them the latest time I could ever expect to return. If I returned earlier, they would not be concerned or fearful. That avoided them sitting up all night worrying if I was ever coming back and then having to deal with the effects of that fear and anger.

These were the years we spent just trying to be teenagers and attempting to ignore the war and all the political nuances it brought with it.

INDOMITABLE SPIRIT

COLLEGE CAMPUS HAVENS

In the midst of all the chaos of war, college campuses became a nice safe haven for people in the city to hangout. The park like campuses gave people an escape from the concrete jungles of Beirut, and had athletic facilities for those interested. BUC was one of those.

The crowd was mostly college students and their friends, but, as I lived on campus, I got to hang out with them even though I was much younger at the onset of the war. I always looked older than my age and most of my friends were older than me. I had a full beard when I was only thirteen and by age fourteen I could easily pass for a college student.

Furthermore, I was the dean's son and had keys to the gymnasium for us to get in even when it was not open to the public. In fact, I had a master key that allowed me access to any building on campus and that would often come in handy. The key also opened the dorm building for those occasions when girls were caught outside after lockdown and I could sneak them in.

Often, I did not need to go anywhere, since the world seemed to be coming to me. Yet, I went everywhere, as there was too much to do outside campus, and I was not about to miss out.

In the early days, I would play ball with everyone and occasionally hang out with the older crowd, but, looks aside, I was still too young and awkward to truly fit in with college students. When on campus, I mostly hung out with kids of the faculty and often had other friends come over. There were two guys and two girls my age, and in the same building and later two American girls, daughters of faculty, would briefly join the crowd.

However, hanging out with an older crowd seriously accelerates a teenager's maturing process. The college had just turned coed from an all women college a few years earlier so the student body was still almost eighty percent girls in 1975 and dorm residents were all girls. In part, many did not realize I was that much younger than they were, and, in part, some did not care. In any event some of the youngest college students were only seventeen and not that much older than me.

I found myself, a young attractive teen with raging hormones in the midst of a sea of captive pretty girls. There were no parents imposing curfews on the girls or waiting up for them or wondering when they were coming back. These were not the thirteen-year-old girls I hung out with before, but more experienced and many were sexually active.

Locked on campus with little to do, and a world disintegrating around us, there was little reason to hold back. These were the seventies with hippy style behavior, free love, miniskirts and no bras, which only added to the hormonal rage.

Below the Fine Arts Building and the Gymnasium lay a bomb shelter, which unlike many of the basements that people usually took refuge in, was a real bomb shelter, built for that purpose, with bathrooms and all. However, the shortage of space in the college meant the TV production studios occupied part of it.

During the war, several faculty from across the city took residence in those buildings with their families, along with four American professors and the families of two of them. Living on campus provided the safety of a gated community and avoided travel through dangerous crossings for those whose original residence was across the city divide.

The recurring usage of the shelter lead to permanent mattresses and other accommodations left there for regular usage. That way, when the bombs came crashing down at night, we only needed to get ourselves down there and not worry about carrying anything with us.

However, not everyone came down to the shelter. Many would prefer to rest in their own bed and take their chances, but my parents would have none of that. They refused to risk any harm coming to us and we were always there whenever there was even a hint of trouble.

Nonetheless, there would always be quite a few girls from the dorms in the shelter along with anyone caught on campus when trouble came. If it was too dangerous to go home, they simply spent the night. It was crowded, but lots of fun and the shelter became a hangout place. For a young teenager, sleeping in close proximity to so many pretty girls was one of the twisted perks of war.

Depending on security conditions we did not retreat to the village every weekend and spent many weekends in Beirut. By the time I turned sixteen, I would often stay in Beirut on my own when the family went to the village. There would be some concert or party that I wished to attend and stayed behind. I was already mature and capable enough to be left alone in a war zone.

Concerts with local bands were a big entertainment hit. Numerous bands including high school and college kids popped up all over town. It was a great venue to escape the war. Often a major festival would be arranged where several bands came together to play in the same venue. The concert would be held on a college campus or an open parking lot nearby.

Several of my friends formed their own band focusing on blues, and I helped them practice and set up for performances and thus always got into these concerts free. But I was not on stage so I got to enjoy the concert with the girls while they sweated their asses on stage. Not a bad arrangement, especially that I could get the girls in free as well.

The concerts would be held at night, with minimal lighting. We enjoyed the music, danced and had a grand time, forgetting the war-torn world around us and pretending that none of it existed. We created our own world separate from the ugliness that surrounded us and drowned out the sound of war with sweet music.

At one point the band decided that I had a strong deep voice that is ideally suited for Blues singing. They pressed me to try, and I did. The first attempt I managed to blow out the woofer speaker with my voice. My voice was and still is that deep and that strong. That was the end of my singing career. They decided they could not afford to keep replacing speakers and left me to play with the girls. Suited me well.

By my late teens, an American professor moved into the apartment below us with a teenage girl about my age – Tasha. She was really nice, and we would inevitably spend time together and get close, but she managed to antagonize me by comparing me to John Travolta. She claimed I looked like a hybrid of Travolta and a lion. I was ok with the lion, but Travolta at that time was Saturday Night Fever and disco and I hated disco with a passion. I wanted nothing to do with him. Yet she insisted.

We hung out and had a good time, but I would slowly learn how weird that family was. One day in early summer I dropped by to ask about Tasha and her mom told me she could leave her room because she was sun burnt. She had extremely light complexion, spent the whole day in the sun, and was lying in bed surrounded by ice to cool her down.

I turn to leave when her mom said "No. No. You can come in and see her. She just cannot leave."

I went in, said hello to the father as the mother knocked on Tasha's room to inform her that I was there, and then told me to go in.

As I walked into the bedroom, Tasha was laying on her back completely naked, rubbing herself with ice. I was never a prude, and nudity never bothered me, but I would have never imagined in my wildest dream that a mother would lead me into her teenage daughter's room while she was completely naked. It just did not feel right on any level.

I tried my best not to show how weird I thought they were. Poor Tasha was red as a tomato and looked like she was roasted on an open fire.

And, I maintained a cool nonchalant attitude, leaned over and gave her a kiss on the only part of her body not burned, and proper to kiss in the presence of her mom – her lips - and sat on the chair in the room.

If that was not strange enough, her mother and father began to come onto me afterwards. The father turned out to be homosexual and dated so many male students and other young men. He would pay the less financially fortunate for sex favors. His wife, who also taught a few courses in the college was set on young men as well, and I heard they had even shared some together.

That was just too messed up. There was no way I was going to have sex with the girl and her parents. I was certainly not going for Papa. No. No. No. I started keeping my distance from all of them, but as they lived just below us, they were not easy to avoid on the way up and down from my apartment.

INDOMITABLE SPIRIT

THE NEXT SUMMER

Again, we head to Monsef for summer in 1976, and by now the war had been raging for more than a year, and so many things had changed. In fact, we barely made it out of Beirut as the battles to remove the Palestinian camps from the Christian areas had started, and eventually engulfed the city with intense fighting throughout the summer.

Once in the village, we acted like the war was in a different country, most of the time. We proceeded with our lives as well as we could. Again, we spent our days at the beach, and our nights partying, and flirting with girls, night and day. What else were we to do with girls in skimpy bikinis during the day and short miniskirts at night.

However, that summer, at age of fourteen, I got my first shotgun, which was a five-shot automatic action, and I could hunt with the big boys. For a fourteen-year-old that was a big deal, and I felt all grown up. I was given the rules of fire arm usage and taken out for bird hunting with my dad. The rules were simple but strict. You never aimed a gun at anyone even when you knew it was empty. You never brought a loaded gun into the house – any house. And you always walked with your rifle pointed down in case of a misfire. Any violation of these rules would cost me my shotgun.

There was nothing other than birds to hunt in our neck of the country, with no large game to be found in an area that had been densely populated for thousands of years. At first, I enjoyed the experience of hunting with adults, however, the novelty soon wore off. Standing around waiting for migrating birds to pass over head was too boring for me. They would head out before dawn to catch the early birds, and by noon they are lucky to have come across a dozen birds they could shoot.

With that, my friends and I converted the hunting process into an exploration. We would roam the ravines and cliffs looking for anything interesting to do. If we came across migrating birds, we sure brought them down – we had mastered shooting flying birds with a BB gun and hitting them with shotguns was a breeze. However, we were more interested in what else we could find, and, as usual, we pushed our limits in how far we could walk and climb cliffs, etc. We removed the boring element from the hunting experience.

The Ex-President's Body Guard

An ex-President of Lebanon and by then one of the most powerful Christian figures in the country was friends with someone in our village and liked to come hunt there. One of his favorite spots was a narrow road that lead to an old church, which had no houses on it.

When he came to hunt, his body guards would block the road and make sure that no strangers would approach with guns. However, one of my closest friends lived next door to the ex-President's friend and we got to know the body guards so we could approach without a problem. As teen agers, we were not really interested in hobnobbing with the old ex-President, but the fact that we could go where others could not, made us feel important. We knew people who knew people.

One of those bodyguards was notorious for his shooting with a hand gun. We had heard the stories about him, including his ability to take out a match stick from a distance with his .45 caliber gun, but nothing compared to seeing it live.

The first time we met them there while hunting we were standing next to him when birds flew overhead. We shot and missed. He clicked his tongue, pulled out his .45 hand gun and took a small bird out of the sky with a single shot.

That hollow point tore the bird to pieces, but that was not the point. It was hard enough to hit a grown man with that hand gun at a closer range. The bird was at least fifty meters away and flying fast. I am not sure how many can duplicate that feat.

Jet Fighters Within Reach

The war included many skirmishes and battles between Israel and the Palestinian-Syrian-Leftist-Islamist alliance. Those conflicts extended beyond the border area in south Lebanon and included aerial strikes much farther north and in the Bekaa valley in the East.

When striking the northern Bekaa valley, to evade radar detection and air defenses, Israeli jets would fly low over the Mediterranean and turn inward where they needed to. They would ascend within a ravine, popping over the mountain right on top of their targets, strike and turn back to sea.

Our area was a prime route for many reasons. There was a deep ravine that lead all the way to the top of the mountain overlooking Baalbek where many of their targets were, which allowed the jets to remain below the ridges, Also, it was within the Christian area where they were not likely to take fire.

We all knew that, and heard the load roars of the jets as they turned on their afterburners to ascend the steep mountain, but nothing compares to being right in the path of a roaring jet with both engines in full blast.

We were on one of our hunting excursions on the northern edge of town, and had climbed up a steep ridge and gotten to about one hundred meters above the bottom of the ravine when we heard the distant roar from a kilometer away over the sea. We turned to see two jets heading straight towards us and really low. They passed us just slightly below our level that we could see the faces of the pilots and were close enough that we could have hit them with stones if we wanted to.

By the time they reach us, they had not changed elevation from their over water yet but began their climb right there. Those afterburners were deafening as they went into full throttle and turned upwards. They shook the ground we stood on and the heat from the engines almost singed us.

That was quite an experience that I would rather not repeat.

Target of a Night Raid

Our scout experiences also changed with age. We kept night watch two at a time for one-hour shifts, and this is where it got interesting at that age, as anyone who misbehaved could expect a raid during their watch. The raiders were people from our town but came disguised and meant to scare their targets. Psychiatrists today would claim this scars a young mind, but it actually made us tougher and more resilient.

We knew when a raid was coming as the leaders would collect all the hatchets and hunting knives. They really did not want a nervous kid to slice and dice the older scouts conducting the raid, but we never knew who the target was until it happened, although there were some who were regular targets as they always managed to annoy the leaders. The raiders were good at what they did, and we later learned to do the same. It was stealthy and designed to confuse the poor guards. Often the raid went beyond the guards and picked a few people straight from the tents. They would also steel the flag and demand breakfast to return it. Furthermore, all raids were followed by meeting to discuss the actions of all involved during breakfast, as they were supposed to be instructional and educational, not just for fun. They would tell everyone what they did right or wrong and explain how things could have been done better.

At age thirteen, I happen to be the target of one of those raids that could have gone seriously wrong. This camp was limited to a small group of the twelve to sixteen boys segment of the troupe with only four tents and the supply tent. The campground had a small clearing in the pine stand where we had our fire. The four tents were downhill from the clearing and the supply tent sat on the uphill side, where we needed to walk up a rocky slope to get to it. It sat about half a meter higher than the clearing, and we came into the campground from the monastery behind the supply tent. As we guarded the camp from within the clearing, where we could see in each direction, I heard noises from behind the supply tent. One of the leaders was up and instructed me to go check it out, but as I began to walk towards the noise I saw legs sticking out from behind a pine tree behind the supply tent. I backed off and told him, but he shrugged it off and said "Go." Nudging me in that direction.

At that time the man turned and now I saw a head sticking out from behind the trees. I told him that and backed off ready for a fight. The war had started and we were somewhat apprehensive of conditions, and they had not collected the knives and hatchets that night, so we were not anticipating any of our people. If our guys are not coming, then who the hell was this. I did not have time to finish the thought before he was up and rushing towards us. He was hopping over obstacles with his head fully wrapped and looked huge. He turned towards the leader who confronts him with his stick held out at head level, yet it ended up at the raider's waist level. I did not notice that he was at the top of the rocky rise, while the leader was at the bottom, where the difference in elevation along with their position made him look like a giant. I was a few meters away from them but the other guard had started approaching and was much closer and swung his one-and-a-half-meter solid oak five-centimeter stick at him, but the raider simply grabbed the stick and tossed it. That was it. We did not know anyone that size and that strong. This was not one of us and it was time to get serious. I rushed him with all I had and swung my big stick straight at his head. Luckily his reflexes allowed him to twist and take the hit in the shoulder, and equally lucky was that he was wearing very thick clothing that protected his shoulder, or it would have been shattered. It still hurt enough that he groaned like a gored bull. As I raised the stick to hit him again, another man grabbed me from behind and I redirect the stick downwards next to me and into his belly almost goring him. He let go of me and I turned around to find his bandana had fallen off his face and I recognized him. He tried to hide his face again, but I called him by name and said, "I know who you are we can stop now." Clutching his stomach with a stick still in my hands he did not want to push it, so he hushed me and said, "just come with me."

We walked off towards the Monastery where I found they had already brought the other guard. One of the stronger guys had actually thrown him over his shoulder and brought him there – he was thin and light weight. They sat us on the edge of a fountain pool, where I remember wondering if they planned to push us in it for fun. Then came another two guys. We did not see it happen but heard about it later. There were five in the raid, and while two brought us to the fountain the other three went after the tents. My tent had three other kids in it that they had expected to put up a fight, so they simply pulled the poles out and collapsed the tent on them as they slept. By the time they woke up disoriented and made their way out of the tent the raiders were gone.

One went into another tent to pick one kids up and woke up the whole tent. Not wanting to confront everyone and not wanting to leave him behind, he grabbed him by the ankle and ran, dragging him on the ground for about twenty meters before he picked him up and continued. This was too rough and he got chastised for it. The kid was in pain and crying. The third went into another tent, shoved his kid all the way into the sleeping bag and threw it over his shoulder and ran as the kid was balled up at the bottom of the sleeping bag, dazed and confuse. This kid was a coward to start with and he began to wail. They could not shut him up even after he knew who they were. Although the two of us were supposed to be the main targets of the raid, we ended up enjoying the show, watching the others plead and beg for mercy as the raiders pretended to be strangers.

In the discussion the next morning I was told they would never target me again. It was too painful as I had enough Tae Kwan Doo training including use of sticks to do some damage. Suited me fine.

Fire Fighting

Summer is a hot and dry season in Lebanon and prone to fires. Sometimes it is as simple as a broken bottle, where sunlight through the thick bottom acting like a magnifying glass sets fire to the dry grass beneath. The fire spreads to trees, and oaks and particularly olive trees burn quick and hot.

The disruption of the war limited what little firefighting crews were available outside the major cities. We may get a water truck out there with a crew of four or five, but if the fire in deep in a ravine, they could not get the water to it.

It was volunteer time. We could usually see the smoke billowing before anyone told us about it. However, when fires got large enough to require full intervention, church bells are rung as a call to all able-bodied individuals. Some tackled the fires directly while others supplied water and provided other support. On those long nights of firefighting, sandwiches are supplied to the ones on the front lines.

By then, I had already handled a dozen fires, mostly in support activity and had gotten myself to the front. Experience dictates that even through it was a hot summer day with the added heat of the fire, one dressed in clothes that protected the body - no shorts or T-shirts. We put on thick military style pants and jackets and a couple of bandanas, which were critical for surviving the thick smoke.

The water, in addition to hydration, was used as a fire shield. We would douse ourselves with water, including the bandana on our faces and charge into the burning shrubs beating the fire mostly with branches broken off other trees. Yet, you could only endure close proximity with the fire for about a minute before completely wet turned into crispy dry and we began to overheat. We took turns attacking the fire for a continuous fight that prevented the fire from re-establishing itself, while others rushed gallons of water to us to keep us alive. However, only the invisible teenagers were rash enough to do this.

INDOMITABLE SPIRIT

The older ones worked on establishing clearings wherever necessary to cut off the fire. The ground is rocky with many breaks in trees and stone walls that help limit the fire's progression, but not completely, as a raging fire, in stiff winds, could jump the walls or rocky clearings and catch the other side. That is where we stood our ground and killed the fire before it got hold of the next stand of trees. Without water supply, fires left ambers that could re-ignite the fields later, so sometimes we needed to fight the same fire multiple times before we were done. The worst were Carob trees, as they do not burn like other trees. They smoldered in a very strange way, and as they smoldered they would periodically explode shooting sparks and ambers in every direction, lighting other shrubs around them. We spent the whole night babysitting a carob tree one time just to keep it from re-igniting the valley, and every time it spewed sparks, we rushed to put them out. We stayed from two in the morning until seven before the Carob tree was finally done playing arsonist.

Later, one guy would come up with a better idea. He had an extermination business and used spray tanks that he carried on his back. The tanks could hold up to twenty liters of water, which may not sound like much, but when applied surgically in a controlled spray it went a long way. The smolder in the cracks of the Carob tree trunk, or in an olive tree trunk, was impossible to extinguish without water, as we could not beat the flame out of it. The sprayer allowed the water to be inserted in the cracks at the right location and put it out. Not only did he prevent the fire from spreading further, he often saved the tree itself, which would regenerate if not burnt too badly.

By the time we became adults we had become professional firefighters and learned precisely how to attack a fire and control it. Today, army helicopters arrive with large water scoops, lifting sea water to the fires and putting them out in minutes. I am not sure if I would have enjoyed that more than the challenge of confronting a raging fire with our bare hands. There is something greatly satisfying about doing the impossible.

Nevertheless, the war was never that far away and its effects were everywhere. Yet, we again ignored them and proceeded to live life as it should be lived. However, the war brought so many comic experiences as well as encounters with so many idiotic situations that became the base material for the thousands of plays, movies, and jokes about the conflict. Laughing at the problem is extremely therapeutic.

INDOMITABLE SPIRIT

DELAYED RETURN TO SCHOOL

Battles were still raging fiercely throughout Beirut by the time school was supposed to start in 1976, preventing us from returning to Beirut at the end of summer. We attended classes at the school in my village for almost a month before the roads opened and I could return to my regular school.

Even so, we did not start immediately. As was always the case, people hope the conflict will die down at any moment. As such, the first few days of school, we just had an extended summer. It was only when it appeared the roads will be closed for some time that our parents decided to place us in that school.

Interestingly, those free days in early October were the first time we were in the village during olive harvesting season. My grandfather owned a lot of olive groves as well as an olive oil press. A friend of mine and I decided we wanted to work the fields and earn some money. There were not a lot of field workers from our region, and the onset of war had seriously reduced the number of workers from other areas. So, our offer was welcome, and my grandfather offered us the same daily wage he paid other labor.

He quickly regretted that as he watched us work. The olive groves were scattered around the town, so he would dispatch us to a specific grove to pick the olives and return them to the press. While, regular laborers were bringing the equivalent of a hundred and fifty kilos per day, we were bringing in merely fifty kilos combined, because we spent most of the day hunting for caves in the ravines around town. He soon reworked his offer to pay per kilo we brought in based on the average rate others were getting per kilo. It did not change our behavior much, as we were not really in need for money, but simply filling time. We continued to search for caves for the next few days, until we had to go to school again.

That was however, a very interesting experience. We got to learn how the process works from picking to operating the oil press. We experienced something our city life would never have exposed us to and learned to appreciate what these laborers did. Most importantly, we learned to appreciate the easy life we had, where we did not need to carry huge heavy bags of olives uphill for a living.

The Black Cave - 1976

The cave hunting obsession resulted from our experience with the Black Cave earlier that summer, which was just too exhilarating.

Growing up, we heard many legendary stories about the "Black Cave" at the edge of town. No one alive had been in it or knew anyone from older generations who had been in it, and all attested that no one should ever go there. The stories came down through the generations and as all folklore, everything got eventually exaggerated as people tried to make the stories more interesting.

The cave was supposed to be deep and long with huge snakes, hyenas and other scary animals, and they even spoke of bottomless pits that one could fall through to never get out. The cave supposedly traversed large areas under the town and even reached the sea under water.

As teenagers, these stories were more than intriguing and we could not help wonder what was under our feet. All this mystery of the cave was gradually getting to us, and we began to ask questions from anyone who may actually know something about it. The more we talked about it, and the more people told us to stay away, the stronger our urge to explore grew. Eventually, we just had to find out for ourselves. Some of the stories were just too much to be true. Others were just intriguing and challenging.

We began to prepare for the excursion of our lives and we headed out to scout the area. The cave was on the edge of town in the middle of cliff behind an old small church and its mouth faced the other way and was not visible from any populated area. The topography there was so rugged and steep that no agricultural land faced the cave. We walked around, climbed up and down the cliffs we could climb without ropes and identified the best way to get to it. We returned home to prepare for the actual entry and four of us decided we were going to do it. With all the stories about large snakes and hyenas, guns were certainly a necessity. Not only shotguns, but hand guns as well, which were easier to handle in caves and on cliffs. Long ropes for the cliff and the cave were acquired from the scouts along with flash lights and candles. The candles are critical to insure enough oxygen remains in the cave, when the candles go out, the oxygen levels are getting low.

Even though it was summer time, we headed out in full cloth cover and thick jackets for protection from anything we may find inside. We descended about fifty meters of a sheer cliff wall to get to a landing close to the cave's mouth. Looking back at it, maybe we should have exercised a little bit more safety, but then we just grabbed onto the rope and climbed down. A slip of a hand and we would have fallen a hundred meters to solid rock bottom, but we were teenagers and fearless in everything we did. The entry to the cave looked benign enough. It was wide and we could see about thirty meters inside with nothing that looked concerning. We posed for pictures to memorialize our adventure in addition to pictures of us descending on ropes. In light of the stories about the bottomless pits we had decided we should tether ourselves to each other and to a rope tied at the mouth of the cave. We checked our weapons, turned on our flash, lit the candle and proceeded with caution. At the end of the thirty-meter open stretch was an opening on the left that was about one and a half meters in diameter. As we shone our lights into the opening we were met with a huge black swarm of screeching bats that were riled by the light. Hundreds came to us like bats out hell – excuse the pun. We took to the ground as they swarmed past us and disappeared - literally disappeared. We could not tell where they went.

INDOMITABLE SPIRIT

With the bats gone, we looked inside to find an enormous cavern the size of a small movie theater. It was rocky and uneven with a ceiling that was several meters high and could have very easily been a home for a small tribe in pre-historic times. Still not sure what we would find among the rocks, we proceeded carefully, checking every rock. There was nothing worth mentioning in that vast space, however, there were several serpentine narrow openings ranging from half a meter to one meter in diameter at the other end. We had to find out what was inside. I went out and untied our rope from the mouth of the cave as we were running out of length and knew that the area we traversed was safe. We found a place to tie it within the cavern and crawled inside the first opening, which would narrow and widen as we proceeded and turn left and right. The expectation was just exhilarating, but we were not finding anything. Then came a large bat out of nowhere, it crossed the lead guy and got stumped by the glaring light from the guy behind me and just hovers over me. I ducked and pulled my jacket over my head. Bats do not attack people, but they could be very dangerous, as their wings have claws at the ends of them that can do some serious damage if they strike while flying. It only took a few seconds for the bat to shred my jacket, and had I not had that thick sweltering jacket it would have shredded my skin. Then, it also disappeared as the others did.

We finally got to a point that was too narrow for anyone but me as I was the youngest and the thinnest in the group. We debated and then decided I will crawl through to see what lies beyond. I never got to a wide space but found shards of clay deep inside. Maybe this was once wider, or maybe they came there in another way? Maybe it was once a burial place deep inside the mountain? We would never know. We were already more than a hundred meters inside that narrow path and decided it was time to turn back. We could always come back another day to explore more now that we felt confident we would not be eaten alive. As we got back to the open cavern we noticed daylight shining through a thin horizontal crack in the rocks other than the opening we came through. The crack was just deep enough for me to slide through on my belly, and I decided to crawl through - A reckless move since it would be extremely hard to turn back if I needed to, but kids will be kids.

Both the top and bottom of the crack stepped down as I proceeded that I had to turn sideways to be able to slide down the steps. Four steps down and I came upon the opening to the outside. I was still wedged in the thin rock crack but staring at a hyena's lair, with bones and other remains of its last meal and the ground was extremely smooth and fit for sleeping. I really did not wish to step out into that, but there was no way for me to turn back. Dropping through the steps in the rocky crack was hard enough, and there was no way I was making it back up. I struggled to extract the hand gun out of its holster and pointed it forward and I began to bang my large metal flash light on the rocks. If there were any animals in or near the lair, the banging would spook them and I would not be surprised with an attack. Sensing no movement, I slithered out of the rocky crack into the lair and walked towards the cliff, heart pounding at three hundred beats a minute and a massive amount of adrenaline racing through my veins. The hyena was clearly out roaming the country side so I traverse the very narrow ledge back to the original cave opening where my friends had been waiting and tell them I found the hyena's lair everyone was talking about.

They cynically respond "Did it eat you!"

"No. I ate it." I snide back.

"No. Seriously. There is a hyena's lair over there." I assert.

One of them crossed the ledge to check it out, still not believing me. He confirms my claim and everyone is glad I was not eaten that day.

We were getting exhausted and still had a cliff to climb and a couple of kilometers of rugged terrain to cross, so we called it a day. We made it to the beach by mid-afternoon and just vegetated in the sun after a long soaking in the cool sea water. It was a good day. We dared the centuries-old legend and came out alive. We were not eaten by hyenas or large snakes, nor swallowed by bottomless pits. We were the champs.

We raved and ranted about our achievement and suddenly had so many who wanted to join the next excursion, and there was a next time, and a time after, until we explored all the narrow caves within the cave. We would learn much about that cave and the reasons for the legends in later years. We never found anything worth extracting but came across several places with clay pieces and other evidence of humans having been there before – long before.

I would much later have a lengthy discussion with someone almost as old as my grandfather whose own grandfather told him about that cave – not legends, but reality. The small church atop the hill dates back to the early days of Christianity, which has a well behind it cut into solid stone that no one from my grandfather's generation down has been in. There was never a need to, but older generations had been in it to clean it for use. The well has an opening in the side of it that leads to the cave, and water from the well also runs through another narrow opening out of the well. They threw some hey in it and then watched it emerge in the sea more than a kilometer away. There was clearly a direct path. He did not know much more than that, but we both figured, the paths may have been used as escape route for those early Christians, whether it was from the romans or Ottomans or anyone in between. The legends may have been developed to prevent anyone from exploring their escape routes.

That experience with the black cave set us up to seek other potential caves in the area. We spent a lot of time seeking them but found nothing that compared.

During my last summer we came across a very interesting opening in a mountain side. As we walked around a steep, heavily wooded area on one of our hunting excursions, we noticed an echo of our voices coming from the mountain and we began to investigate the cause of that echo.

We found several small openings in the rocks and eventually a site that looked like someone had intentionally closed an opening. Lacking the proper tools at that moment, we tried our best to remove the old stone and gypsum closure, and, eventually, removed enough to allow my reedy friend to crawl in. We only had a small ineffective flashlight and nothing else, other than our shut guns. I grabbed his feet as he stuck most of his body inside to check it out, as the cavern dropped down from the opening. He stated it was big enough to warrant further investigation and we agreed to return with the proper equipment to explore.

Sadly, a week late, and before we found the time to get to it, he was scheduled to depart the country and never made it. I left for the USA a couple of months later without ever finding out what those ancients had tried to seal in that cavern.

The next year after we explored the cave, we noticed a strange car drive through town every evening just after dark and turn onto the road to that church, and then return past midnight. No one lived down there, and there is no reason for anyone from out of town to head in that direction in the evening. By the third day, we followed them and secretly watched them to find then digging behind the church on the edge of the cliff. Even though we tried to be stealthy, they noticed they were being watched and took off. When the antiquities department was called, they found several Phoenician burial chambers with gold and many other artifacts inside. We are told they removed almost a ton of gold from those chambers. We would go later and scrounge around hoping they have missed a piece or two of gold, but found nothing.

Clearly that area had been inhabited for millennia, and possibly the legendary black cave played a role in that history.

Return to Beirut: Branded

By the end of October, the fighting died down, with the deployment of the Arab League Disengagement Forces, and we returned to Beirut to finish school.

However, a few days before our return I had developed a major inflammation in my left leg that had left me unable to even stand up. I had been treated by a doctor from Byblos, and then went through extensive testing in the American University Hospital in Beirut. They never really knew, scientifically, what was the cause of the inflammation, although all agreed that the most probable cause was my sitting on a cold concrete wall in a cool breeze when I was hot a sweaty. The sudden shock to the muscle causes contraction and inflammation.

Nonetheless, I ended up heading to school with serious limp which gradually healed. With that limp and, being from the other side, and having spent all the time there, many assumed I had been active on the front lines and had been shot. Denials and explanations never truly dispelled the accusations.

Thus, I was branded as a war participant and it stuck throughout my school years.

POLICE AND DISORDER

Chaos reigned supreme and the police were left with the untenable task of maintaining order in an increasingly disorderly situation.

The Syrian Military believed they owned the country and acted like it with total disregard and disrespect of all things Lebanese, particularly law enforcement.

A narrow street separated my school from AUB, which terminated at a gate on either side. At the end of the ally starts a long set of stairs descending towards the sea front at the back of both the school and the university. Faculty and staff drove into the school and parked along the side of the street, but the narrow nature of the street meant only one-way traffic at any time and certainly not suited for student pick up by parents. Any kids picked by their parents had to either walk up at Bliss street at the top of the narrow street or the other side of the school, where the bus parking lot was located and the road was wider and more accommodating.

The gate was always open, but an armed policeman stood guard at the gate making sure that only authorized personnel entered. A friendly fellow, always cheerful and chatty, but he always struck me as someone not to mess with. I was at the gate leaving when the policeman stepped out to check the reason for cars backing up and found the Syrian general and his goons yelling at everyone and waving guns between students. He intervened to inquire about the reason for all that and was told that the general was picking up his kids.

Apparently, the father showed up that day for pick up, instead of the mother, with his body guards and decided to drive down the narrow street while everyone was driving up. Since teachers often leave after students had already departed, traffic was light, but a few cars were pushed back anyway by his escorts pointing guns out the window. The policeman politely explained that the narrow street did not allow pick up there, and that he needed to wait for his kids at the main road or at the bus parking, where they probably were waiting for him anyway. But, the General would have none of that, insisted on going through and began to threaten the officer. The officer retrieved his AK-47 from his kiosk and told the general in no uncertain terms that he was not getting in and warned him that he would shoot his tires out if he tried. The general obviously did not believe that. After all, the Syrians controlled that part of the country and had very little consideration for Lebanese law. He could not believe that a mere policeman was imposing the law on him.

He dared him to shoot and ordered his driver to push forward and had his two left tires that were on the officer's side taken out while the officer screamed "Back up or the next bullet is directed at you".

The officer was determined to hold the line and forced him to back up the street on his bare rims as the General threatened retaliation screaming "I will be back…"

The policeman replied "I will be waiting."

It did not take long for a police contingent to arrive from the station two blocks away to try to defuse the situation. They wanted the officer to disappear while the higher ups negotiated with the Syrians to let the whole thing go, but he would not budge. He was adamant that "This was Lebanon" and no Syrian was going to supersede him.

Argue as they may, he stood his ground and was willing to die for his conviction. We took heart in seeing that the other policemen actually agreed with his conviction but did not want a battle on school grounds. Some had turned their attention to us, trying to disperse what had become a large gathering watching all this and cheering the policeman on. No one liked the Syrian army and their autocratic pompousness and we were all enjoying this policeman humiliating the general, which only emboldened him.

They eventually gave up trying to convince him and radioed the station for deployment at the main street to intercept any returning Syrians and negotiate at that point. The police and the Syrians arrived at about the same time, with about twenty policemen intercepting a much larger number of Syrians at the main road. The police had a small urban tank in the narrow street, which effectively prevented the Syrian jeeps and trucks from pushing down the street and forced them to negotiate there, while the early contingent held us back at the gate to keep us away from any possible gun fire.

The standoff lasted all afternoon as the General was very high ranking, which meant his insult required the involvement of much more than the station chief. Politicians got involved and the phone calls reach all the way to Damascus to end the standoff. Our school included children of powerful politicians that the Syrian Government needed, as their dominance over Lebanon was only possible through the active cooperation of local operatives.

Finally, everyone went away, but there was certainly a payoff somewhere for the General, which we never heard about. The next day we had a different policeman at the school, and we never saw the first one again. When we asked the new policeman about him, we were met with a look that said you know better than that and he said it is best for him anyway. We later found out he was transferred to East Beirut away from the Syrians. Everyone knew there was a high possibility that in spite of a deal, the General may still send someone to assassinate him. These people did not take lightly to insults.

These were the early years of the war when many policemen still held fast to their convictions and tried in their own way to maintain order through the increasing chaos. We heard about a lot of similar incidents, but I only directly witnessed one other as one had to be at the right place at the right time to see it. That one involved a traffic cop and a Palestinian. The Palestinians were just as disdainful of Lebanese police as the Syrians and they too believed they owned that part of the country.

INDOMITABLE SPIRIT

This policeman stood at a major intersection - Hamra and Piccadilly - insuring traffic obeyed the lights and maintained the flow. Both streets were one way with heavy traffic.

As we approached the intersection on foot we saw the policeman stop the traffic on Hamra street to allow the Piccadilly traffic through but the first car at the intersection continues to edge forward. He tapped his hood and asked him to stop as he turned his back to look at the other traffic.

The policeman was facing in our direction when this big burly man in an expensive Mercedes yelled with a heavy Palestinian accent "Fuck you and the Cedar on your head." Police caps have a cedar tree emblem on them that represents Lebanon and this was more than an insult to the man, but to the whole country. We stopped in our tracks and saw sparks coming from the policeman's eyes, who stood about 190cm tall with a thick moustache and a stern demeanor.

He stepped in front of the Palestinian's car and calmly waved the other traffic through, then turned around and reached into the open car window without saying a word. He pulled the man's head through the window by his hair, who was way too big to go through completely. Only his head came out and the policeman began to slap him while holding tight to the curly hair, repeating "You do not like the Cedar! You bastard! Huh!"

As it happened a special police car - division 16 - was coming down Piccadilly street. Those were the police elites who were specially selected and trained to deal with unruly individuals and riots. They rode three to a car in Chevy station wagons and you did not want to mess with them. The Palestinian idiot called for them to help him and cursed the policeman hitting him – big mistake. They stopped in front of his car and got out while the policeman told them what happened. They eased the policeman aside very calmly, opened the door and got the Palestinian out, then bounced him between then like a pinball machine.

They eventually tossed him in the back of the station wagon and sped off, asking the policeman to remove his car from the intersection.

By then the traffic had come to a stop and many people had gotten out of their cars to cheer that policemen. He took a small bow and told everyone, with all humility, he was just doing his job and begged them to proceed and unclog traffic.

Sadly, as the war dragged on, we saw fewer and fewer of those defiant acts, as policemen came to realize the futility of their efforts in the face of forces far too great for them to stop. Survival became the name the game. Too many of them were killed for upholding the law that they simply surrendered to the chaos and restricted their efforts to saving decent people whenever possible.

BREAKING FREE FROM PROPAGANDA RALLIES

Early on, tired of talking to themselves, the propagandists decided to lock all of us in the school and force us to listen to their speeches, as if that would somehow change our minds. Or, maybe it was just a power play to show us who was in control.

We put up with this at first, and locked in school, we would wonder to the basketball courts far away from the speeches and shoot some hoops, but, eventually, after two years of that, we had enough. These guys were cramping our style. If we were not studying, we needed to be doing something fun, or spending time with girls.

One day in early spring of 1977 I looked at the school gate as it closed for a rally and found it guarded by a young man from the SNP, which is secular in its principles born of the belief that all the countries from Iraq to Lebanon and even Cyprus are one people regardless of religion who should be united. Their principles developed in mid nineteenth century, when Arabs were challenging Ottoman rule and the population of the area was neither Turkish nor Arab. But, time passed, and the Turks managed to annihilate much of the population causing a major demographic shift that left the party out of touch with the reality on the ground. However, some held strong to their nostalgic and idealistic beliefs.

Ironically, even though Lebanon was the only country they could legally operate in, they still opposed its independence on account of their belief in a "Greater" united Levant, or Syria. The Syrian government banned them from operating in Syria but worked with them in Lebanon to undermine the Government. That location included mostly Christians from the local area and two relatives of mine where among the top leadership. Although we disagreed politically, blood was always thicker than water.

The video arcade near the school, which we frequented often, was across the street from the main offices of the Syrian Nationalist Party (SNP), and the people who ran the arcade were all active in the party and its militia. Nice guys on a personal level, and we got to know them intimately on account that we were regular patrons several times a week. We played the pinball machines, video games and pool, and most importantly, it was a hangout place where we were guaranteed to find other friends anytime we came.

I told my friends: "We are getting out of here." And started walking towards the gate.

They grabbed me and tried to stop me. "Are you crazy."

I said "Look up there. Who is manning the gate?"

They said: "Who cares! They are all the same."

"No. They are not. Leave this to me." And I kept walking towards the gate.

They followed muttering that I was going to get myself killed.

I got to the gate and demanded they open it and let us out. "You cannot force us to listen to this shit. We do not care about all this and want to leave."

The man I was addressing looked me in the eyes and said "I see you", which is a kind of threat that says, I know who you are and can hurt you. Clearly, he did not fully know who I was and only knew that he sees me at an arcade we frequent often and he was a member of the SNP. I had seen him there too, but he was not a regular and we did not closely know each other. However, I was related to his bosses by blood and had an advantage he was soon to discover.

I yanked the gate out of his hand and retorted "I SEE YOU TOO". He had not expected that from someone he deemed a Christian from the other side.

Before he could muster a response, I was pulling at him, telling him "COME WITH ME.".

Shocked he asked "where!!"

I said "To the SNP office. We need to talk to your bosses about you threatening me."

"What!!" he asked, still not quite believing what is happening.

I said "Who is there now, Habib or Norman? Let's go."

Worried that I was naming his superiors by their first names and dragging him to see them, he said "It is OK. We do not need to do that."

Now I felt really empowered, and in the true nature of a fifteen-year-old, I began to push my luck. That man had a loaded machine gun in hand along with other armed men and I was trying to drag him to be chastised by his superiors. Nonetheless, he was apologizing and telling me I could go wherever I want. He just wanted me to leave him alone.

I insisted that he keep the gate open for anyone to leave if they wished, in return for my dropping the issue, and he did. He just wanted what appeared to be a lunatic to leave him alone.

I walked off and a whole lot of kids scurried after me hoping he will not change his mind. They were not sure whether to cheer me as a hero or chastise me for potentially putting their lives in danger. But, they were glad to be out of there.

I headed straight to the SNP office, where I found both my relatives, and relayed the story. They laughed and then told me I was crazy and stupid to threaten an armed man. They were not there. What if he did not believe me? Anything they did after he shot me would be too late.

INDOMITABLE SPIRIT

Of course. But I was fifteen and did not think anything through. However, they reassured me that they would not allow the idiot to harass me. I asked that they not allow their goons to close the school so that Palestinians can numb our brains with speeches. They agreed and said they were not aware of that. Some of their guys get drawn into issues on their own.

The school gates were not closed again, at least not during the next two years I was there. The SNP would send their men down to make sure anyone wanting to leave could do so. The idiot became extremely friendly to me, now that he knew I was related to his bosses. The arcade managers, who certainly heard the story, never stopped teasing me about it and would jokingly call me "boss".

From then on, we went back to having our fun time whenever the propagandists wanted to make their speeches.

A GREAT MISUNDERSTANDING
ASSAULT IN THE STREETS

Several of us from Monsef went to the same school and were also all members of Monsef's scout troop, where the older amongst us had taken leadership roles in the troop and would often discuss upcoming meetings and activity. We were about to learn a very critical lesson regarding the dual meaning of words and phrases. What may be innocent and harmless can be very easily misinterpreted to mean something completely different.

As we spoke of training camps, leadership meetings, and troop activity, those listening were hearing something completely different. They assumed we were discussing military activity as we came from what had become the "Christian Area," Suspicion and monitoring intensified and the more we spoke the worse it got. It was not that hard to monitor us closely in school as they were everywhere in all our classes. And, since those listening and reporting were students, we had no idea we were being watched.

In early spring 1977, fighting had broken out in another part of Beirut, where two other guys from our town went to school, which meant they were not going to class for a few days. As they lived near us and our school, they would be waiting for us at the gate as we walked out for lunch, spend the lunch hour with us, and then met us at the gate again at the end of school at 2:20 to spend the afternoon with us, playing basketball, shooting pool or some other activity.

On the fourth day they were not at the gate, but rather farther up the street waiting for us. They had been pushed away by some militia men waiting at the gate just before we came out. One of the older guys and an older girl from our school met us up the street to warn the other two to disappear. They had heard the talk among their classmates and told us they would fill us in at the end of the school day and we agreed to meet further away from school, and out of sight of anyone monitoring the school entrance.

The remaining 2 hours of school were extremely tense and felt like they would never end. It was enough time for us to imagine every possible scenario and possibility. We were not far off in our assessment but had not expected the actions taken against us that afternoon.

There were six of us when we met – the girl and five guys – two others were absent from school that day. The girl and the older guy began to explain to us the misunderstanding of our scout talk and that these guys truly believed that we were plotting military action. They were telling the guys from the other school that they needed to stay away for a few days and that the rest of us need to lay low until the issue is explained to those people and the suspicion eliminated. It all sounded pretty straight forward, and we believed it will blow over very soon, but we were in for a surprise that day.

We were walking towards the home of the girl, as we spoke, with plans to go shoot some pool afterwards before heading home. The street narrowed in the last stretch on Makhoul street and the side walk became barely wide enough for two people. In some places we had to pass single file, as cars were parked partly on the sidewalk to keep enough room for other cars to pass. At that point we were chattering away about other subjects, teasing each other and acting like any bunch of teenagers, as if nothing had happened.

I was walking second behind the girl at one of the narrow side walk passes and walking almost backwards as I talked to those behind me, when I heard a load cursing scream that appeared to come from just above my head and the look on my friends' faces clearly indicated a serious danger associated with that voice. I spun around to find a guy dropping upon me swinging what turned out to be a belt with a half-kilo metal buckle.

He had been waiting for us in the small parking area behind a building and sprung out as soon as I cleared the corner. He had stepped onto a car and jumped off and was literally two meters in the air when I turned around. My Tae Kwon Do training came in very handy that day and spared me some serious injury as that buckle was aimed strait at my head with all the force from his jumping swing behind it. I managed to side step the buckle and block the swing, but the belt looped around my arm and struck with an even larger force (centrifugal force) at the back of my hand, doing enough damage that the hand still hurts every now and then.

He landed atop of me pushing me between two cars parked along the street and turned towards the next guy in line. He let go of the belt stilled looped around my arm as he kicked him in the groin and punched him in the face, dropping him to the ground. The third in line was the older guy telling us about what he heard and was the attacker's class mate and he began to call on him by name to calm down and talk to him, to no avail. This guy was intent to doing some damage.

As the mind races to find a way out of a dangerous situation, time seems to stand still. It will take ten minutes to explain all the thoughts that go through one's head in a split second. I looked around to assess the situation as I was sure this guy could not be attacking us alone. From behind us came another attacker, also a classmate of the upper classmen. The narrow side walk did not allow for more than one attacker from each side.

The last two in line had disappeared. I remember wondering what had happened to them. They had been there two seconds earlier. I found out later that they had been pulled into the store we were in front of by the owner, who hid them behind the counter. He did not know us, but this was Lebanon. People stepped into the line of fire to save strangers they have never seen. The shopkeeper saw teenagers in trouble and came to the rescue. He hid them in the store and then stood at the door inquiring about the situation.

I looked up further and saw armed men on both ends of the street blocking the street completely. The kids from the school where on the offensive, but they had armed militia backing, just in case.

From between the parallel parked cars and straight behind me came another upperclassman towering over me – he was a large fellow. I stepped back ready to defend myself, but he waved me down, saying: "Hold it, don't be stupid." Signaling with his head towards the armed men. I had dated this guy's younger sister earlier that school year, and, luckily, he liked me and was not so eager to fight, but he was still there with them. He was Palestinian and the attack came from the PLO and its student affiliates.

I turned back and helped my fallen friend up and. by now, the girl was nowhere to be seen. Being in front of my attacker, she had the opportunity to bolt the scene, and luckily the militiamen did not know who was who, so she made it past them and to her house a few meters away to call for help.

That is when my friend hobbling with his nuts crushed screamed "follow me" The big guy was still there staring at me but did not even try to stop us. We run down a narrow, crocked alley that connects to another street. We hear some of the men yelling at the big guy for letting us get away, and then start to chase us down the alley, but this was our neighborhood, not theirs. We knew people on every block that the attackers did not know we knew, and all we needed was to clear a corner and then slip into a building and into an apartment of a friend or relative.

They wandered up and down the streets for a while and then gave up. There were many high rises with hundreds of apartments, offices and stores into which we could have gone. They could not search all of them and knew their time was limited. Again, this was Lebanon, where everyone knew a lot of people and they knew that once any of us got to a phone there could be high ranking officials calling on them to back down.

They left.

We had gone into the apartment of a mutual relative of both of us. The 80-year-old lady who opened the door, and was all alone, was my Godfather's mother and the aunt of my friend's mother. Before we could explain anything, she had dialed my friend's home, and when his father picked up the phone, she said: "Do not worry, they are here, but you cannot recognize your son's face and they cut off Ziad's hand."

My friend quickly snatched the phone from her to explain things to his Dad before he had a heart attack. He told him we were ok and it is not that bad, but his father at first was not buying and seemed more concerned about my amputated hand and wanted him to rush me to the hospital.

That was the first I looked at my hand. In the massive adrenaline rush, I had not yet felt any real pain. The buckle had hit the back of my hand, and by then, a few minutes later, it was completely blue from the knuckles half way up my forearm. I was truly stunned at the sight and was standing there staring at my arm, wondering if it was broken. In retrospect, there was clearly fractures that did not heal correctly, which explains the recurring pain, but at that time, I could move it and use it and all was fine.

We now had the task of locating the rest of the group. We called the girl's home and found out that the others had made it there. Their Palestinian neighbors with the proper connections had gone down to the street and dispersed the mob.

It was over. For now.

We waited a bit and then were escorted home for our own protection.

The next day we naturally did not go to school, but our parents did. They had the task of clearing the air so we can go back. They met the principle and other school officials, who in turn called in the student attackers to talk to them. Other students came in as well, who were not party to the attack, but connected to the political factions and militias. Those were the good guys who would often forewarn us about the lunatics, and then work to prevent any harm from befalling us.

There was a lengthy and heated debate. The hardliners were not buying the scout explanation and insisted that we never return to school, while the others were arguing with them to back down and admit they simply misunderstood and let it go.

The next Monday we were back in school, with a compromise deal. They would leave us alone, if we promised not to talk to each other in school again. So, there we were, lifelong friends and in some cases relatives, and we had to pass each other on school grounds like strangers, or else.

Nonetheless, we did just that, and for the next two years we did not say a word to each other in school. After school was a different issue as we would meet just outside the school and head to the pool hall, the movies or each other's houses, but never in school.

I was not even 15 years old yet, when I learned this crucial lesson about minding my language. Words have many meanings and taken out of context could lead to a lot of trouble.

The Aftermath - Mark and Joe

A week later I entered the school bathrooms to find in waiting an old friend, whom I had not seen for two years. Mark lived on the other side of the Green line and stopped coming to school after the war broke out.

He snuck up on me and tapped me on the shoulder at the urinal. I turned around, and just stared at him in disbelief. I had heard he had joined the Christian militia and could not figure why he was standing there.

He placed his finger over his mouth signaling silence, handed me a small piece of paper and bolted out.

Bewildered I was left standing at the urinal, but not really urinating, as a classmate walked in before I got to read the note. It must have been a strange site, as my classmate broke out into a loud laugh and began to tease me about studying in the bathroom. His teasing was a perfect escape from having to explain what I was doing and I went along with the joke, pretending I was boning up for a quiz. I zipped up and walked out.

I read the note on the way up the stairs, which simply said "Pool 3 Joe". What on earth? I wondered. He was driven home after school to another neighborhood, when he went to school with us, and had never played pool with us before. In fact, we did not start playing pool there until after the war started. How does he know where we met? Was he spying on us also?

And, who the hell is Joe?

The pool hall we frequented was not exactly a well-known place. It did not even have a sign outside. It was a back room behind other stores, with a very narrow entry. It was a seedy place filled with low lives. We liked it because it was not crowded and we always found an empty table. We were polite with others and minded our own business, so they let us be. The locals had come to fondly call us "The Boys" as we were the only teens there while everyone else was older rough street type.

It is important to note, that in bad conditions, it is always helpful to know the "wrong" type of people and have a good relationship. You never know when you need their help. These were the kind of people with guns and militia connections who could get you out of trouble when necessary.

But, this made the note even stranger at first. Mark would want to avoid any militiamen from the wrong side. Why would he want to be there? It dawned on me later that day that the pool hall presented the perfect cover as no one would ever think a Christian militiaman would be there. Our presence there would not raise any suspicion either. Even if someone was watching they would drop the trail once we entered.

As we exited school, I told another guy, who was an even closer friend of Mark about that, and he decided to come along. He was one of the two who were missing from the action in Makhoul a week earlier. We drop our books at his home on the way and head to the pool hall.

Mark was not there, so we start to play pool as we waited. It was a tense time, as we wondered where all this is going. Shortly, after we started, one of the regulars, a seedy twenty something who was always there, came over and began to watch us play and made fun of us as we were unable to truly focus.

After a few minutes of teasing, he said "Clearly you are not in your game today. Why don't you stop and come let me show you another place you may enjoy?" We were seriously hesitant as that guy was a drug dealer and user and not the type of man we wanted to get any closer to. We looked at each other and start coming up with excuses about studying and tests.

He took a deep breath and shook his head with a grin. "Don't look so worried." He said and leaned over to whisper in my friend's ear, who was next to him, while winking at me. My friend looked perplexed, yet strangely relieved, with a hint of a smile on his face. "We can spare a few minutes" he said and pulled me along.

He had whispered "Joe" to my friend. As it turns out, Joe was the code word they used, and this druggy was a spy for the Christian militia. The seedy pool hall was a perfect setting for him to get close to the people he was spying on and find out all sort of things.

We walked along as he carries on with the charade, describing a fictitious place he was taking us to so that if anyone is listening they would see us with a man they believed was one of their own and would leave us alone.

A few blocks away, we were in a safe house used by undercover Christian militiamen, and Mark was front and center and this time he was not silent and stealthy. He hugged and kissed both of us, and began reminiscing about our school days, telling the other two men there all kind of stories. It was as if old friends had just coincidentally met, but we knew he did not go through all this just to reminisce.

It did not take long for him to get into the subject matter of his sudden appearance. They had found out about the attack and figured they had a perfect recruiting opportunity, and offered us all kinds of support, including weapons and logistics to work with them. They had reasoned that since we were already in trouble, we would be more open to working with them. After all, we were Christians from the other side and held the same political views as they did.

However, there was a major difference that they did not take into consideration - Our families. Their families lived on the other side of the Green line and they were only risking their own lives and could if lucky sneak out when discovered. We could not, as our families lived on the West side of Beirut, and even if we were lucky to get away, our families would pay a very heavy price, potentially being killed for our deeds.

We were still only 15, but the war had instilled a level of wisdom born from survival necessity, far exceeding our young age. We had the foresight to think about all these things as we had seen it happen to others.

We explained all this to them and told them how much we agree with them, which they already knew. We explained that we would like nothing more than seeing the Palestinians and Syrians removed from our neighborhoods, but we could not be active as they ask. We told them we would be glad to share any info we may have going forward, but on an informal basis. After all we would see Joe (as we came to refer to him between ourselves) all the time at the pool hall.

But, please no weapons.

We saw quite a bit of Mark after that as Joe would take us to the safe house occasionally when we had something to discuss. Joe gave people the impression he was taking us to a whore house, and it worked. He had access to a whore houses to take people to when they wanted that too.

But, soon it was getting ridiculous, so we opted to meet mark on the other side of the line, whenever we were there. It was much safer and there would be no suspicion. Meeting with an old classmate was not something people question. This was Lebanon and people were friends with others of completely different political convictions.

We quit the "whore house"

Later, Mark would come to AUB for his university studies next to our school, but he had not changed. He was just hiding in plain sight as a University student, while still collecting intelligence and recruiting people.

INDOMITABLE SPIRIT

COMING OF AGE

By the spring of 1977, I was still unsure of myself, as most kids in their early teens are, and even unsure of how attractive I came to find out I was to girls. I had my share of teenage kissing and petting and reaching into clothing early on. However, my first real sexual encounter was with a twenty-year-old college senior when I was not yet fifteen.

I was playing basketball by myself in the Gym. I had used my key to get in that afternoon after school and left the door open for anyone who would like to join me, and she did, tiny shorts and cutoff shirt, beautiful and horny. As it turns out, she was not really interested in basketball at all. She was all over me, constantly reaching for the ball and missing, touching and caressing me instead. When she had the ball, she would turn her back to me and come hard against me grinding into me. She would lean into me and climb over me in every possible way, and would trip and fall into my arms at every opportune moment. The ball was nothing more than an excuse for physical contact. I could no longer control my arousal at that age. In fact, it would be hard to control oneself under those conditions at any age. She finally reaches down and grabs me asking: "what do we have here." Lacking much experience, I was seriously embarrassed and tried to make excuses. She pulled me towards the bathrooms and came down on me, but the bathrooms were nasty from the game the night before. I told her I have access to the shelter through the door next to the bathrooms that was cleaner and more comfortable with all the bedding. We headed in that direction but did not make it there. We had to cut through a storage area on the way that included some spare mattresses, and she threw me on them and climbed on top.

I had no experience at that age, but she had enough for both of us. It did not feel like we were there long, but it was dark by the time we emerged from the storage area. I was worn out, but feeling exhilarated. We headed for the showers, together, and she is still all over me caressing and admiring my body. I was extremely athletic with slim well-toned muscles, but I had not, until then, realized how attractive that was to girls. She could not get enough. Women had complemented my physique before, but not that way, and it did not have the same effect on the way I saw myself. Maybe it was the fact that it was my first time going all the way.

That was a transformative experience that would repeat several times, but she stopped using basketball as an excuse. She would find me on campus and ask me to come help her with something in the Fine Arts build, which led to our mattresses in the storage basement. A few weeks later, she graduated, and I never saw her again. I cannot remember her name now, however, I can never forget the experience.

Word on campus got out amongst her friends who had not graduated yet, and by the time I returned from the summer in the village, I entered a whole new world. Sexually experienced college girls became a regular event.

In retrospect, I clearly was a safe outlet for their sexual needs, without commitments or complications. I was too young for considering any regular relationship or dating. I was not part of their group of friends and thus, nothing is known. They would not look like sluts having sex with anyone for the sake of pleasure, and my presence on campus was expected and would not raise any questions.

I was the ideal sex toy for a lot of horny college girls. Some may call that abuse. But, I enjoyed it and could not get enough of that abuse. One by one, they came. Some only once, others repeated often. At first, I was not picky as, at fifteen, having sex with an experienced partner was more than one would hope for. This was every teenage boy's fantasy. But, the novelty soon wore off and I became more discriminating in who I would indulge. There was a lot of really beautiful girls available. Why have sex with anyone who is not attractive?

Gradually, I gained experience that made me so much more desired. I was no longer the inexperienced awkward kid they handled as they wish. I learned how to really pleasure a woman and kept them coming back for more. With experience came confidence. Realizing the effect I had on women, and knowing that all I needed to do is be there to be able to have anyone I wanted was a very powerful boost to my confidence and self-image. Soon I began to initiate encounters with those I found attractive. First it was the college girls who were older and much more likely to go all the way, but then came the younger ones. Not much younger, as I grew older, but they were my age. Once I was set on such a path, the world became my oyster. I could have almost any girl I wanted with minimal effort and could not get enough. I became extremely flirtatious, even with girls I had no intention to date. It simply became my nature and I enjoyed luring women and watching their reactions.

Those were my coming of age years and were almost hedonistic. I would date more women than I could remember in the next few years.

However, there is always a flip side to everything. Multiple affairs with women I knew in advance I would never commit to or formally date brought a sense of detachment. Sex for its own sake with absolutely no commitment beyond the moment led to a kind of disengagement. I was always looking beyond the girl I was with for the next conquest, always scanning the field and assessing availability, and it became hard to establish a relationship that limited the scope. Furthermore, the confidence and experience showed through. The comfort I had with women produced a reputation of womanizer, even when few could point at specifically who I womanized. I did not talk, and most of those who would seek fleeting sexual encounters were not boasting about it either. Yet the moniker stuck, and, without specifics, people just said I looked and acted like a womanizer.

Honestly, I was never really a womanizer. Womanizers tend to view women as objects to be used and discarded, yet I never felt that way. I always treated women with the respect they deserved and never abused the power I had mastered. I only had sexual relations with those I felt certain wanted it and were looking for brief encounters. I admit I made a few mistakes in my assessments, but often it resulted from the women misrepresenting themselves. Sometimes emotions grow when they are least expected, and what started out as a few moments of pleasure develops into something more than they expected, but it was never intentional.

While I had many female friends and lovers, I never really had a girlfriend. It is not that I rejected the idea of having a girlfriend. I would not have minded a steady relationship, and a few almost became my girlfriends, however, none ever felt secure in a relationship with me. The reputation of womanizer makes women nervous that there is always someone else. They refused to believe that I would forego others for a stable relationship when they could see so much availability. Women can see through other women and see their interest. They saw the flirting and would never believe it did not lead to anything. The multitude of female friends only aggravated the situation, even when those were simply close friends. Equally important is the fact that I never tried to have sexual relations with those whose friendship I really cared about. Friendship is a critical part of a "Girlfriend". I feared that the insecurity they would feel would end the relationship and with it a wonderful friendship, so I drew a line and stuck to it. As much time as I spent with those female friends, I never crossed that line. There were times when we would be alone in an extremely intimate position. We even shared beds at times, sleeping against each other, but there was an unspoken understanding that our friendship was too valuable to allow a few moments of pleasure to ruin it.

No one believes that I never had sexual relations with those females I had been close to all these years. Most insist that it is human nature to cross the line when you really like people and opportunity presents itself. That may be true in general, but not with me. Maybe the fact that I had more than enough sexual outlets that helped maintain my control. However, I like to believe it is primarily a moral code that I developed. I hate users and abusers with a passion. I never wanted to become one. Just because I had the power and ability to use and discard people, I should never do so. It is plainly wrong and despicable.

Fleeting sexual encounters came with a mutual understanding of the temporary nature of the relationship. We enjoyed each other's company for a brief time, and then moved on. We remained friends after that and even had discussions that rarely happen across genders. We have discussed each other's relationships and provided advise and support where needed. It was a win-win situation.

INDOMITABLE SPIRIT

STILL A TEENAGER

Beneath all that, still lay a teenager that was not yet fully grown and needed to act his age. I needed to hang out with young kids and do what young kids do. My interests were varied during my high school years and I ended up with several circles of friends that rarely overlapped.

One group of high school friends I regularly played basketball with. We got together once or twice a week for a pickup game at our high school, but almost nothing else. Those were different from the ones I played with at the BUC campus. I do not recall having any other activity with these guys, even though they were really nice and we were close enough. It just never happened. We would finish basketball, have a nice fresh juice drink on the way to replenish our depleted systems, and then head our different ways.

Another group got together for cards in the evening on a regular basis. A couple of those were from my home town and we had other interests, including playing pool together and hanging out when in the village. But, the others were almost limited to those card sessions.

The pool players were another separate group that played several times a week. We had found our hidden pool hall, where we eventually met "Joe" and made it ours.

There were the musicians and associates. We got together for band practice or simply enjoying some music and hanging out. This group included one guy who lived in a small efficiency alone, while his mother lived in the adjacent efficiency. Whatever the reason for that arrangement, it suited us well as we had the place to ourselves when we got together. He was a music wiz. He was Google before it existed, and somehow knew every musical band, members, albums, etc, particularly American and British bands. He would consult for the music stores and tell them what to buy. Not surprisingly he became a disc jockey later in life. He had every kind of music one can imagine and it was here that we were introduced to so many of the great music we cherished.

Another member of this group has since turned into a full-time musician and composer. We would regularly hang out at his house. We never met his father, and never really knew if his parents were divorced. He would talk about his father working abroad but avoid that subject. and we did not push it. His mother and her sister, who often was at the house were both extremely sexy and always had some male French journalists around, whom we all believed were their boyfriends. It was just too obvious.

Interestingly their bathroom had no door. The door had broken off, and they just never bothered to replace it. That meant anyone using the bathroom was in full view of everyone as it opened directly to the main living area. It did not seem to bother the ladies, and as teenagers we were not complaining about the site of his beautiful mother and aunt. One time we even walked in on one of them stepping out of the shower. Hanging out there at that age was something.

Then there were my townies, with whom I spent the time in the village, and many lived in the same part of Beirut. However, although we ran into each other regularly at school and on the streets, we mostly got together in the village.

As I entered college and took up skiing, there would be another group that gathered at the ski resort and included almost none of the others. As much time as I spent on the ski slopes, I still maintained my contact with the other groups. That was a lot of friends to have, and even more friends of friends, and I had to squeeze my studying between all this action. Luckily, I did not need to study much, but I could have used more time. I had the ability to easily be a straight A student, but barely got by with enough grades to get into college. It always bothered my father, who was the Dean of a college and dedicated to education. He believed in hard work and achieving your potential and there I was doing the bare minimum required. I lost count of all the lectures I got on the subject.

Yet, I made it through and ended up gaining a graduate degree from Georgia Tech, one of the toughest and most prestigious universities to attend. I guess when you got it, you got it. So many hated me for cruising through school with such ease, while they worked their tails off day and night. Their ire did not bother me as I was too busy enjoying life to pay any attention to negative people. I spent all this time with so many people and yet I always felt alone. I never really felt I was an integral part of any of these groups. I am not sure if the fact that I hung out with so many different groups made me feel tangential to the core. Others did not view me that way, but I certainly felt that way. I spent my youth feeling that I was missing something. I always feared that something is happening somewhere else that I was missing. I was always on the move, trying to be in all places at all times, and, trying to be part of everything.

Maybe it was the ever-impending death in the air that drove me to want to do all things NOW before it is too late that always kept me anxious.

Nonetheless, looking back, I lived a charmed life in the shadow of death and destruction.

Football with The Marines

American football was not a sport played in Lebanon, but some of us with US connections would occasionally take to playing tag football in the fields at AUB, while in high school.

The US embassy was right next door to AUB, and the Marines would also come play football occasionally in those fields. We had seen them a lot and gotten to know many of them. After all they were mostly fresh recruits, under twenty.

On one occasion, they happen to arrive as we were playing tag football and decided they wanted to join us. We gladly accepted but told them they are much better at the game than we are and we needed to be mixed, as there was no way to make a fair and interesting game with us against them. So it was, but we had never seen them play before, and had assumed that they played tag football also, were a two-handed tap constituted a tackle. Not with these guys. We quickly found out they were playing full contact football without the gear, and, they were as rough as they come. They took pride in their toughness and would lift someone up and slam them on the ground with all they had.

We were extremely athletic and tough, but this was not fun at all. We tried to talk them into relaxing. "This is just a game, not world war," but they just did not know how to play any other way. They would ease up for a while and then someone gets excited and we found ourselves up in the air diving head first into the ground.

Finally, we had to apologize to these nice Marines and break off the game. We agreed to play separately from then on. No hard feelings. We got to know those guys well and started joining them for a few drinks in the evenings whenever they were on leave.

They were really happy to hang out with the locals and meet the girls we hung out with. They were a fun group of young men, but they drank like fish. It is a cultural difference. Lebanese drink to have fun and try not to get drunk, although not always successfully, while Americans aim to get drunk.

Eventually, one of those guys would get too drunk and fall off a tenth-floor balcony during a party we invited them to. Amazingly he survived the fall but had crushed his legs and pushed his pelvis into his torso. He would eventually die in the hospital from his injuries, but that night he was still awake as he was taken to the hospital. A nice guy. It is really a shame to have gone that way.

SUMMER OF 1977

Once again, we would spend the summer in the village. However, the summer of 1977 would be more memorable than the preceding ones.

That summer, following my encounter with the beautiful college nymph, I would have a similar encounter in the village. There were some older girls among those who hung out at the beach, and, while the older girls from our own village treated us as juniors not worthy of their time, those from other places were a different story. I will never know if it was pure coincidence or whether my experience on campus had altered my demeanor enough, however, I caught the fancy of a nineteen-year-old that summer.

The chalet became our retreat whenever she was around, and, again, she originated the affair. I was not yet confident enough from one experience to believe I could go after older girls, but there she was. It started at one of the many beach parties we had, and as we slow danced in the moonlight to our crappy music, she starts kissing my neck and grinding against me. I must say it is really hard to hide your excitement waring a tight speedo bathing suit, as was the norm in Lebanon those days. She whispered in my ear that we needed to take it somewhere else and asked if the chalet was available. I could not resist if I wanted to. She was not the most beautiful girl around, but was extremely sexy, and, at that age, any older women wanting to have sex with me was sexy enough.

To avoid embarrassment, we slow danced off the concrete landing until we could put everyone behind us where they cannot see me. We walk hugging and kissing to the chalet and found the mattress on the bedroom floor. We left the lights off to avoid attracting attention as there were no curtains on the windows, and we got busy. My experience was yet limited, but hers was not. It was heavenly.

I would find out later that several of my friends had followed and watched the whole thing through the open window. They could not say enough about it the next few days. None had yet had a full sexual encounter and this was the closest they had come.

That summer was quite different than those before it, as we grew older and developed different interests. It was certainly different for me, on many levels.

Syrian Soldiers in Amchit

Although the Syrians were involved in the war from the onset, under false banners, the Syrian Army first officially became active in fall 1976 under the auspices of an Arab League Deterrent Force, which was supposed to be a peace keeping force. They originally deployed throughout the country until they got into confrontation with the Christian forces and ended up retreating from the Christian heartland.

Their original deployment included a check point on the coastal road at the northern edge of Amchit about a kilometer and a half from our beach, and right above the beach that many of our friends from the next town frequented.

One day in early summer of 1977 we paddle our Haske to that beach to spend some time with friends. After a couple of hours, our friends decide they want to take the Haske back and spend some time at our beach, which meant we would walk back. This was not unusual as we had done it many times. We were used to walking barefoot all over creation, and they would end up heading back to their beach on foot at the end of the day. We never even gave any thought to the Syrian check point, which was supposed to be monitoring road traffic, not kids on the beach.

We would walk up towards the coastal road and then walk alongside it to our village. The foot bath lead straight to the check point and

INDOMITABLE SPIRIT

terminated just five meters south of it. That meant we would walk past the Syrian soldiers to get home.

That day we met what must be the stupidest soldier on earth. As we approached in speedos, barefoot and without even a towel, he stopped us and asked for IDs. We were only fifteen and clearly not armed in any way. We were still wet and had absolutely no place to store an ID or anything else. We pointed all this out to the soldier to no avail. He insisted that he needs IDs if we were to pass his check point. Furthermore, he was as mean as he was stupid and ordered us to stand on the asphalt. We walked barefoot all summer and had thick soles on the bottom of our feet, but asphalt in the middle of the afternoon sun is way too hot for more than a few seconds. We usually walked on the dirt next to the road to avoid burning our feet.

As we tried to reason with this moron, we kept stepping off the asphalt to avoid burning our feet and he kept yelling at us to get back on. We pointed to our village, which was visible from where we stood and pleaded with him to come with us and we would show him IDs. None of it was registering. The yelling woke up the officer from his afternoon nap, and he came out to inquire about the commotion. He watched with disdain as the soldier explained that we did not have any IDs. He was scanning us from head to toe as the soldier spoke, and then turns around and slaps him across the face.

"YOU IDIOT. Do you not see that these are kids on the beach?" he says. "Where would they put their IDs?"

He apologized for the stupidity and meanness of the soldier and sent us on our way. By that time our feet had gotten so hot from stepping on and off the asphalt that it felt like steam was about to come out our ears. However, we did not want to risk heading back to the beach to cool them off lest we end up having to explain our change of plans. We walked home steaming hot.

From then on, whenever we were walking back from that beach, we would leave the foot path and climb onto the road just north of the check point. The soldiers saw us, and we would say hello. But, technically we did not pass the check point and did not need to produce IDs. Yes, it was that idiotic, but we had to avoid that hot asphalt.

A year later the Syrians were gone from the area and we did not have to worry about them anymore.

Beach Camping

By that summer, I had grown to where I was co-leading small contingents of scouts on camp trips, by age fifteen. Our first camp was along the coast near a small fishing port in the next village over, which had too many underwater springs making the water freezing even in the middle of the day. The camp got raided as usual, and afterwards the raiders hung around with us. Around two in the morning a few of us headed to the port, stripped to our bathing suits and tried to swim, but it was just not worth it, so we decided to play games with the others following us. We wet our hair and splashed some water on ourselves and stood near the shore waiting. When the next guy showed up and saw us wet, he asked "You swam in this water?"

"Of course. Go for it." We said

He was hesitant, but we goaded him and shamed him until he took his clothes off and jumped in. He could not stop shaking for half an hour and kept looking at the full moon asking if it can provide some warmth.

By the fourth day, we had slept a total of no more than four hours. I was sitting on the concrete pier nodding off as others who were not camping with us were diving of the pier. The pier was more than five meters high and the water below is barely more than a meter deep, and we could stand on the rocky bottom, but we had learned to do these dives with ease.

As I dosed off, some friends kept pushing me to join them and perform my signature swan dive. My swan dive kicked me at least one and half meters above the pier and then I would float down to the water from an even higher level. In that shallow water, I would use my chest and open arms to slam and slide across the surface to avoid hitting the ground. That dive required precision and extreme tightness of muscles at impact, but I was utterly exhausted and half asleep and I really should not have done that. However, with continued urging, I got up and hopped around the pier for a few seconds and felt deceptively energized. I kicked off the pier, but really did not have enough energy or strength in me to maintain my form.

I hit the water at too steep of an angle and went straight for the floor. My hands protected my head, but I flipped over with such force that it felt like my back broke in half. I did enough damage to my lower back muscles that that it still kinks on me every now and then after all these years. Yet, then, as usual, I would endure the pain for few weeks and never considered going to a doctor.

Hiking across a Ravine

Every camping trip included some of us making a challenging hike. We would find some steep or hard terrain to push ourselves to see if we can make it. We were constantly competing on who can do more and go further.

On one camp, just up the mountains from our village, we were on the edge of an extremely steep ravine that was at least three hundred meters deep. We could not see our side of the Ravine due to the steepness, but we could see the opposite side that consisted mainly of sheer cliffs and what looked like lose stones on steep intermittent slopes.

Three of us around fifteen years old began to discuss climbing that face and challenging each other. The scout leaders first denied us permission to go, but upon our insistence, they agreed, with a clause that if we failed to make it all the way up the other side, we would have to do all the chores in the camp the next day. We entered our own clause that if we made it, we would be served all day, which they agreed to. We took the challenge and headed out. Those were not professional climbing expeditions, and we had no ropes or hooks or any other equipment. It was us against the mountain in the purest form. It took us more than an hour to get to the bottom. We would drop ourselves from ledge to ledge and climb down any trees we found clinging to the edge of the mountains and slide down any stretch that was not a sheer wall.

That was hard enough but climbing up the other side was a completely different story. We had studied the mountain from the opposing side and planned out what we believed was the best route up, but when we got to it, it did not look the same as it did from a distance and those stones were really loose. We slipped and slid on the stones more times that we cared to remember and had to backtrack to rework our route when the cliffs were simply unworkable. Honestly, the face we climbed was easier than climbing up the face we just descended, and the only other alternative to climbing up would have been walking along the bottom of the Ravine five kilometers to the coast.

Yet, we made it. Safe at the top we were less than half a kilometer from the camp and could shout at each other back and forth. They had been cheering us on all the way, and we could hear the gasps when we slipped and almost fell to the bottom.

They asked us to come back. Hell no. We were worn out and in no shape to go through that again at that time. We walked into the village atop the cliff and found a ride down to the coast and then another ride back up to where we started.

The next day we were served like kings.

CLUBING IN OUR EARLY TEEN YEARS

As we survived the initial storm and became accustomed to the chaos and mayhem of war, we simply proceeded to be teenagers in spite of it all. As naïve teenagers, we treated the war as a nuisance to be ignored and circumvented. The dangers and risk of death were not preventing us from enjoying life in any way.

By the summer of 1977, with many of us driving, particularly those slightly older than me, we started taking our night life everywhere, be it in Beirut, Byblos, Jounieh, the mountains or anywhere else we found a nice night club or bar. There was no drinking age in Lebanon, or none that was enforced during the war. No one checked ID cards upon entry into night clubs or before serving drinks. We had started drinking in our mid-teens, at our own parties, even before we started heading to those clubs.

We still spent most of our days at the beach, as there is no better place to spend a warm summer day, and there was not much else to do during the day anyway. We always had visitors from Beirut who joined us at the beach and stayed over for a few days or just a weekend.

Byblos was only seven kilometers away from our village and easily accessible but did not have much night life in the seventies. Things have sure changed since then, with old town Byblos becoming the hottest night spot in the country. However, in the seventies, our choices were initially limited to three locations on the road to the old port. Two were restaurants that sometimes doubled as a dance clubs late at night, and the third was a make shift spot that opened only in the summer as the proprietor used an open space between a hotel and the old city wall to set up a temporary eatery / dance club.

Also, as soon as we began to hit the clubs, a fourth location opened next to them, and we quickly took over that one. Two twenty-something guys had returned from France with the French fiancé of one of them and opened a pub on the port road. It was on the side and secluded, and it was perfect. It consisted of a long bar and a few tables on the main floor, with a mezzanine level overlooking the lower level, with a few tables also. It served food but was more of a drinking pub than restaurant, with the food mostly coming from the adjacent restaurant with whom they had an agreement.

We quickly became friends with the young owners and dominated the place. We were the crowd that made the pub atmosphere for others, we spent money and made the joint a fun place, and, in return, we had free reign. We came in large numbers and filled the place – sometimes our group exceeded 50 people and did not find a place for all of us to sit, but who cared about sitting. We brought our own music and took over the DJ task, and would even go behind the bar and mix our own drinks.

The place faced the sea with an open space in front that served as parking lot. One of the perks of these places was their proximity to the old port, which, at that time, had no night life – unlike today. This was an old port that goes back to Phoenician times and still functional as a fishing and tourist port after thousands of years. It has a large stone wall and tower on the sea side, which was a perfect place to retreat with girls, where no one would see you. The tower had an easily accessible ledge facing the see at about the same level as the top of the stone wall, which was more than a meter wide and perfect for a couple to mess around obscured from view. The tower cast a shadow from the city lights that made it impossible for even people on boats to really see us. The sound of the waves with the moon light shimmering on the water was just as romantic as one could imagine. We could still hear the music in the distant, but we would be alone facing the open waters of the Mediterranean.

Of course, cars served a similar purpose, but were not as romantic. Even the large American cars were still cramped and uncomfortable.

INDOMITABLE SPIRIT

The pub owners had come to count on us for their business on weekends and would do anything for us. On one Saturday evening a few of us drop by on our way from Beirut and the place was somewhat dead. The owners ask us about the others and we tell them that they did not have cars, as their parents needed the cars. That did not sit well, and they offered to go pick them up. We figured it would be too much of a hassle to pick up and deliver everyone, but they insisted, called on a friend next door and drove three cars to our village. They brought back 20 people for the night and then took everyone home at four in the morning. That is what customer service is all about.

Another 20 kilometers further south was Jounieh, which was growing in leaps and bounds during the war, as Christians left Moslem dominated areas and abandoned frontline neighborhoods in Beirut in search of safer ground. There was much more to be had in Jounieh, night clubs, restaurants, movie theaters, etc. Also, Jounieh was also closer to Beirut, which allowed us to meet our friends from the city half way and spend the night together.

Several kilometers up the mountain from Beirut lay Broumana, which had several nice hole-in-the-wall establishments in old stone basements, where we would gather occasionally as well.

Amazingly, without mobile phones and with regular phones malfunctioning constantly due to war, we still managed to connect and plan events from across the country and all get together. It is hard to imagine that today.

On the way back from a long night out, we would sometimes get hungry at about four in the morning, and would stop in Byblos at Abou-Ali, a small bakery, which would have just opened to start preparing bread for morning distribution. We would order fresh Manoushe (Oregano mix on flat bread) to quench our hunger before we get home to sleep.

Abou-Ali was a Moslem who, like all Moslems of Byblos, never left the city. They remained in the heart of what was considered the Christian heartland, were part of the fabric of the city, and no one would have wanted it any other way. He worked the bakery with his sons and it remains in the same place in the old city today, behind all the new bars and restaurants.

Most of summer in Lebanon was extremely temperate with high temperatures on the coast rarely higher than 30 Degrees Celsius and overnight lows dipping into the low 20s and often requiring a light jacket if one was to spend a long time outside. Night temperatures felt much colder with a stiff breeze blowing off the water. The mountains, which includes anything more than two kilometers from the Mediterranean, were always much cooler.

Because of the generally nice weather, much of the night life was open air, particularly outside Beirut, where the gentle breeze kept everyone cool and comfortable. There were, however, those hot spells that made even the night temperatures high and humidity made any slight rise in temperature feel miserable. Yet, we were not about to allow heat to get in the way of a good party.

Late Night Swimming

On the way back from a long night–usually after three in the morning, and on those extremely hot nights, we stopped at the beach before making it home. There is nothing like a night swim in the cool waters of our little lagoon to wipe away all the sweat and stickiness of the hot humid night. The beach was unlit, originally, and was not directly exposed to any homes. Furthermore, the rocky nature of the shore meant descending four meters of stairs from our concrete pad to get to the water, which gave us the perfect set up to swim even though we never had our bathing suits. Some skinny dipped, while others kept their underwear on, which meant that we needed some drying time before getting dressed and in the cars again.

We would linger and enjoy ourselves until mostly dry, then head home to sleep as the sun came up. It did not matter how late we stayed up, as we had nothing planned the next day except more beach and parties. We would get up late, head to the beach and start the cycle all over.

The town people within ear shot knew very well what was going on and simply ignored us, even if they heard us, and they surely heard us. A bunch of teenagers hanging out on the beach made a lot of noise, and noise travels far in the still of the night. We had that kind of relationships, where nudity did not necessarily translate to sex – not that sex was not on everyone's mind. Those who were not dating each other were simply friends and swimming naked in mixed company was not an issue. Even sharing a bed with members of the opposite sex was not an issue, and it happened more often than not.

SURVIVING A TSUNAMI

The waters of the Eastern Mediterranean are rarely calm, particularly in July and August, and even calm seas still include a lot of small wave action. However, exceptionally, there are those days when the Mediterranean turns into a lake for a day with almost no water movement.

That Sunday in late August of 1977 was one of those exceptionally calm days, and as on every Sunday with great weather almost everyone from the elderly to the infants who could not walk yet was at the beach enjoying their first summer beach days. As usual in calm seas, all Haskes, boats and anything that floats, including inner tubes, were deployed in the water. Some had acquired huge inner tubes from airplane tires that could easily sit four or five teenagers around them.

The fishermen were out in their boats as well, and the chaos of war and lack of law enforcements allowed some fishermen to take the easy fishing method of dynamite, which is officially illegal. We watched the fishing boat about a quarter kilometer from the coast getting ready. They spot a large school of fish and pulled out a large wad of dynamite that must have been at least thirty kilos as the man struggled to lift up. They lit the fuse, dropped it in the water and went full throttle to get away. The explosion resulted in a water swell about one hundred meters in diameter and at least five meters high. Then the dead fish floated all over the place and the boat returned to scoop them of the surface.

The fishermen were only interested in specific fish and only those large enough to be sellable, while the rest was left behind. We would always paddle our Haskes out and collect what they left behind as soon as they pulled off. There would still be enough fish to feed a small village, and it was easy catch and a shame to let the fish go to waste. This day was no different as three of us headed out towards the fish on a Haske. One took his diving gear to go for what does not floated as dynamite that size kills everything including lobsters and other creatures on the bottom that do not float, and two of us stayed on the Haske and collected the fish we deemed good for our use.

As we paddled around picking up fish I looked towards the horizon and was surprised to see that the water out there looked higher than us. I asked my friend, "Is it just me, or does the water on the horizon look higher than here?"

He took a good look and said "It looks like it, but it cannot be. It must be an optical illusion."

Logically the water could not be higher in one place than another, but the illusion was getting more acute. The horizon water was rising ever higher as we stared at it and wondered what was happening. It was not getting higher, but closer, and thus looked higher. It was a Tsunami from an earthquake far away, and then we began to rise with it and all the other waves that followed, as Tsunamis are not a single wave, but a series of waves like ripples in the sea.

The first few waves were at least ten meters high, and when we were in the trough between the waves we could not see any of the mountains just a kilometer away, while when we rose atop the waves we got so high that we could see villages behind the first ridge in the mountains. Naturally, we lost all the fish we had collected, but that was not even on our mind. The other guy jumped off and swam to shore to try to help anyone who may be caught in the waves near the rocks and I headed off to try to find our diving friend.

Far away from rocks there was little danger for me but battling the waves and maintaining the direction I needed was not an easy task. I eventually found my friend and get him on board. We were both expert swimmers and experts at handling the Haske so we proceeded to where we needed to get it out of the water. I paddled as he secured his gear on the flat surface of the Haske to not lose it.

As we began to enter the small bay towards the pebble shore, we heard faint screams coming from the other edge of the bay. The worst of the waves had passed but there were still massive waves coming. Between the rise and fall of the waves we could see an inner tube too close to the rocks with to kids on it. We were not that old – I was fifteen and my friend was seventeen – but these kids were eleven and twelve. A big difference at that age.

We turned around and headed out to help them, paddling against the incoming waves. They were caught between the main rock formation and a small independent rock. They held tight to the inner tube as it bounced on the rocks with every wave, protecting them from striking the rocks themselves.

We had plenty of experience playing with waves on these rocks and understood intricately the dynamics of the sea. We also knew the rocks intimately and knew exactly where they were and how the water swirled around them. We approached from the shore side to avoid being crushed into the rocks, maneuvered between two underwater rocks and held our position near them. I kept paddling to counter the push and pull of the waves, bobbing up and down as we instructed them to break away from the rock and let the waves bring them to us.

They were no strangers to the sea either, but they were just too young and not strong enough to deal with this situation on their own. They swung themselves around the independent rock and came crashing towards us as my friend grabbed the inner tube with them hanging on. He dropped in the water and let them onto the Haske as he was better at swimming that tide than they were. He implored them to secure his gear while he swam alongside of us.

We headed towards shore, but with such waves we could not just paddle all the way in. The bay was shallow with rocks in it, and the receding waves were exposing the floor of the bay at least thirty meters out before the next wave crashed past the pebble beach and over the concrete walkway, smashing into the patio walls of the houses beyond.

I got to the edge of the floor exposure from retreating waves and begin paddling backwards to hold my position. That was where they needed to get off and ride the waves towards shore. Again, they were no strangers to the sea and a little instruction would do. We told them to ride the top of the wave while remaining horizontal and swimming as fast as they can. When the wave passed them, and it always did, they needed to drop their feet and stand on the bottom, maintaining their position or even walking forward as the wave retreats and then catch the next wave the same way.

If you work with the waves, use their power to your advantage and always respect the power of the sea you will survive. They did, and as instructed, when the last wave deposited them on shore they ran like hell from the next one.

My friend and I had the more difficult task of doing the same with a Haske and gear on top of it that weighed a good hundred kilos after being in the water this long. We had to swim the waves while controlling the drift of the Haske between us, and when we stood during retreating waves we had to lift it off the floor to keep it from being ripped to shreds by the rocks.

Four waves later we made it to shore, and a friend had come out to meet us and help us out. He yelled to us to let the Haske swing towards him on the last wave as my friend grabbed his gear off of it. He really regretted that call. As my friend let go of his end the Haske swung with a vengeance and struck him in the legs before he could catch it, laying him on his back with it on top of him.

I was still holding one end and lifted that high enough for him to slide out from under it with the retreating water, almost standing it on end in the pebbles as the wave receded. He got up, grabbed the other end and we ran up the beach, as another wave caught us before we climbed up to the concrete walk way. We hold our ground as well as we could, sinking knee deep into the pebbles.

Every next wave was smaller than the one that proceeded it as the Tsunami ripples died down and, by then, the waves were still making it over the concrete but with little or no force. We lifted it up to the concrete and climbed after it. Then we hauled it away.

We looked out, and there were others still flouting out at sea. By now the waves were getting a little more manageable, and by the time they came ashore, it was normal rough seas and we helped them out. In retrospect, we could have simply lingered out at sea for a few minutes as the waves died down, but we had no idea what was happening. We were not familiar with Tsunamis and their relative short durations. Our experience was with storms that generally get worse with time, not better, and lasted for days. We did not even consider lingering. We were in survival mode based on what we knew.

Within half an hour the sea was back to the exceptional calmness of a lake. It was later that night when we heard on the news about the underwater earthquake and the resulting waves.

There were several deaths and many injuries along the coast that day, but luckily none in our village. None of the elderly or the very young got crushed into the rocks by those first waves. With the help of the able, including my friend who swam ashore, everyone was spared, including the two youngsters we pulled from between the rocks.

Haske Flip

Paddling the Haske standing up was not an easy task, as it was not that stable. It took a lot of balance and agility to remain standing as we paddled from side to side, but we enjoyed the challenge and would push our luck in battling the rough seas, which made it even harder to stand up straight. With practice we managed to be able to stand and paddle even in one to two-meter waves, bopping up and down and balancing the sideway slants from the waves.

Entering our little lagoon standing up in rough seas was another matter altogether. The waves would bounce between the two rocky sides creating a lot of turbulence. Often as the wave divided and slammed into both rocks it would converge again in the middle with an upward splash. despite that, we tried against all odds, and sometimes succeeded.

On one particularly rough day, I decided to brave the entry standing up. I could barely manage to stay standing in the open sea, but at fourteen, I believed myself invincible and went for the entry. As I got to the most treacherous segment, I encountered one of those splitting waves. It was a particularly violent one, and lifted the Haske off the water surface, tossing me up above it. I should have just jumped off, but I was too stubborn and tried to stay with it hoping to land standing. The Haske turned on its side and I landed straddling the narrow edge with a bang. That hard edge mashed my groin like nothing I had ever experienced, and I just about passed out as I slid off into the water. With excruciating pain and nausea, I tried my best to hold on to the haske, not just to remain afloat, but also to keep it from drifting into the rocks. Others quickly stepped in to help, they held it and helped me up on it to drag me ashore.

I did not walk straight for a couple of weeks before the pain finally subsided. Luckily the edge hit the side of the groin. Had it been dead center, I would have needed hospitalization.

One would think that would be a lesson not to try that again. NO. It became a challenge to succeed, and I would try it over and over again, as did others, until we got it right. However, we learned to jump off when we were tossed in the air and not try to land on a tilted slippery surface.

REFUGEES IN THE VILLAGE

The war eventually displaced some Christians from the North of Lebanon into our village and the surrounding areas. Their arrival infused a new element into our village life that was almost alien to us, as these were real village people, mostly farmers and herders, with no urban experience, while ours was a village in name only where all residents were highly educated and extremely urbane. We were people who used the village as a country retreat only.

The refugees eventually adapted to our life style, but not without some initial tension and some extremely comical mishaps. Every one of them was armed to the teeth as members of the militia, but only a few actually participated in the fighting, while the others mostly acted as reserve forces and enjoyed playing with their guns.

The refugees also viewed the locals with suspicion. Knowing that most of the locals actually resided in West Beirut, and were Orthodox Christians, not Maronites, the refugees made the immediate assumption that the locals were all leftists, thus they acted upon that belief. Consequently, they were initially not that friendly but with time things changed.

The conflict that displaced those people from the north also shifted the dividing line along the coast from the edge of Tripoli, 40 kilometers north of us to within 7 kilometers from our village. The front line was manned by the Lebanese Army, which had barracks at that point, while the Christian militia stationed their check point at the northern edge of our village.

Shortly after their arrival, the check point that was set up in our town came under a surprise attack. A car with four men disguised as nuns drove through the check point in broad daylight around noon and opened fire on those manning it, killing three and wounding four.

One of those wounded was not actually part of the check point contingent but was changing his tire on the side of the road next to the check point. He was, however, armed. As bullets began to fly, he grabbed his hand gun and started to load it when a bullet struck him just below the left shoulder immobilizing his left arm. As the left hand dropped dead, the gun in mid load snapped on the skin of the right hand between the thumb and index finger. He could not shoot, nor could he let go of the gun, as it just dangled from his hand. He tried to shake the gun off as he hid behind his car but could not.

The attacking car just sped off within seconds, leaving the dead and wounded behind. That guy stopped the first car he saw and asked to be driven to the hospital. His wound was minor, but the bullet had cut a tendon that had temporarily immobilized his arm.

Word got to back those in our beach house and those included the young man's brother-in-law who heard that the young man was shot, but did not know how badly. Within minutes of receiving the news, the brother in law ran home, slipped on his military boots without even tying the straps, slung his ammunition vest on, grabbed his M-16, and started running north, wearing nothing but his bathing suit. Others tried to stop him while calling out: "Where are you going?"

"To Zghourta." He screamed. "They killed Georges." Zghourta is where the attackers hailed from.

Laughing, the others implored him to at least get dressed before he single-handedly invaded Zghourta. He was livid and in partial loss of his mind as the others were joking about him scaring the people of Zghourta with his ugly big belly if he did not get dressed before attacking.

He could not be stopped much to the chagrin of the others who were trying to stop him, However, he did not go more than twenty meters before he managed to calm himself down and realize that no one else was heading in his direction just yet. He returned home, got dressed and then rationally went to find out what happened to his brother-in-law who was at the hospital in Byblos – 180 degrees in the other direction.

That night a small contingent of commandos snuck across the dividing line and killed several Syrian soldiers, who were actually the masters of all who fought with them. That sneak attack brought the first and only direct mortar attack on our village the next day - Four small mortar shells in total. The mortars landed in empty fields away from the houses, but one missed my head by a very small margin. We were walking up a set of stairs that connected two roads on a steep section of a hill when we heard the whistle of the mortar. We quickly dropped to the side of the stairs as it landed about fifty meters away down the hill. Judging from where it finally struck the ground and the angle it struck, the mortar shell could not have missed our head by more than two meters. We were on the back side of the hill relative to where the mortar came from and as the mortar descended so did the hill at about the same angle where we were. When the hill and the mortar have the same angle, the mortar keeps dropping at the same distance from the ground, until the ground flattens out to intercept it, which is what happened fifty meters away.

Another three mortar shells fell in other open fields and, as suddenly as it began, it was all over. It was simply some muscle flexing that never resulted in a battle. People on both side of that dividing line were not partaking in a war on each other for anyone's sake. The Syrians needed the cover of a local conflict to start a war, and at the moment in time they were not getting it.

Flexing Their Muscles

As those people lived among us, we gradually got to know each other fairly well, with some close relationships developing over time. In spite of a different background, and a general discrepancy in educational level, most people are decent and friendly, and when living next door to us, could lead to friendly relations.

INDOMITABLE SPIRIT

Many of the young men who manned the check point also spent a lot of time in our midst at the beach. Thus, even those who were not our friends, still knew all of us very well, yet, when they stood their positions at the check point, some of them felt they had to pull rank and flex their muscles to show off their power. Maybe it was their inferiority complex, seeing how much more educated and socially positioned we were, or maybe it was jealousy from watching us flirt and play all day with girls at the beach.

Regardless, of the reason, some on occasion, got nasty. One particular incident was as I returned from a trip to the north and approached the check point in broad day light, I hailed a guy and said "how are you". He barked back with a mean demeanor, while pointing his gun at me "No how are you or anything. Pull over and get out of the car."

Instead of pulling over, I asked the idiot to step aside, and called out to his commanding officer, who was looking in the other direction and standing a short distance behind. The commander was an Army Sargent, who doubled as support for the Christian Militia, and who was a very nice and reasonable man. As a refugee, he did not occupy any house per se but he and his family were allowed the use of the basement of an army officer's house in the village. His kids attended the local school free, and he was grateful for all the generosity.

As the check point dude attempted to prevent me from calling out, the commanding officer heard me, turned around, and came straight at us with a warm hello, forcing the check point dude to back down. At that point I could have driven off and gone on with my business, but I wanted that type of arrogant behavior to stop once and for all. I said to the officer: "this idiot sees us every day at the beach and whenever we pass him here, he harasses us and acts like he does not know us. Can you do something about this?" The officer turned to him and said, "I know you are at the beach all the time and cannot possibly miss these guys. How could you not know who they are?" As I have stated before, we were the loud crowd, and in spite of the war zone we were in, we were always laughing, having fun and trying to live the life any young person would.

As the guy fumbled his words trying to find any excuse for his behavior he received a stern warning that he would pay the price if he ever even looked at us the wrong way. He and others were ordered to treat all the local residents with respect and dignity. Eventually all learned to be civil and polite, as it made for a much more pleasant atmosphere for all. What I did by standing my ground that day, helped in making our occupied lives less annoying and more manageable.

Fear of an Invasion: Night Swimming

We never stopped our night swimming activities in spite of the fact that so many strangers were in our midst. The cool water after a long night of sweaty dancing was just too irresistible and this was our town; we were not going to allow anyone to cramp our style. However, the newcomers from the north had no idea what was going on. Some of them had never even seen the sea before. Few knew how to swim, and none had ever considered swimming in the middle of the night.

Late one night as we laid on the rocks in the moon light drying off from a swim, we heard faint footsteps on the rocks. The sound of the steps was coming from every direction and clearly in a stealth fashion. We sat up and looked around to see half a dozen armed men approaching us, battle ready, guns loaded and aimed directly where we sat.

The moon was particularly bright that night which allowed us to clearly recognize each other from a distance. As the females in our group scurried to cover themselves in the presence of strangers, we asked them what was going on. With a straight face, they told us they came to investigate because they thought there was an invasion. "An invasion!" We replied with shock. "Do you really think invading forces would be hanging out at the beach making as much noise as we were making?" we asked. Embarrassed at their apparent stupidity and bewildered by our presence, they asked us what we were doing. They could not fathom the idea of swimming in the middle of the night. That was an alien notion with which they struggled to reconcile, but they soon left us alone apologizing particularly to the ladies for disturbing our swim.

Ironically, after a couple of years in our midst, they began to take to the beach at night and even installed large flood lights to facilitate their swimming. Needless to say, that cramped our style and ruined our night swimming experience. We had to take our action elsewhere.

FLIRTING WITH DEATH
FLYING ROAD BLOCK

The war was meant to terrorize and segregate people, and nothing was more effective than "flying" road blocks that resulted in perpetual uncertainty and fear.

Anytime and anywhere a sudden road block could emerge without warning or any significant reason. These road blocks were called "Flying" road blocks because they would swoop in without warning and then disappear just as quickly, often times taking with them several people who were selected based solely on religious affiliation. These road blocks were designed to propagate and solidify the image of a divided nation at war with itself.

Despite their randomness and unpredictability, they most often popped up at crossings between various cantons of the country, thus providing a higher probability of quickly grabbing people of the opposite religion as they crossed over. Even though it happened all over the country, I only needed to worry about those picking Christians. If they were looking for Moslems, I would safely make it through.

Yet, in spite of all these attempts at blocking the roads, we continued to cross back and forth between the two sides of the city chasing parties and other entertainment. We were not going to let armed mercenaries ruin our lives even if it killed us; and it came close on more than one occasion.

On a Sunday afternoon in 1979, as we returned from a weekend at the beach, we crossed from East to West Beirut along the port road and came upon one of those "flying" road blocks in an area known as Normandy. That once pristine seaside district sat at the edge of the demolished downtown and had literally become the garbage dump for West Beirut when garbage could not be transported to the proper destination. The stench was nauseating and required people to hold their breath while driving through it. How anyone would willingly stand in the midst of the garbage to man a road block is beyond me, but there they were, standing guard, ready to pick up unsuspecting victims on their way back home from the weekend.

The two of us, being Christians, were a perfect pick. We were removed from our car and taken into one of the partially destroyed buildings nearby. They shoved us into a crowded room containing more than twenty people who were all fretting for their lives.

From across the hall we could hear the screams of those who were currently being interrogated by the armed men. We never knew whether they were being questioned violently, or these bastards were just having fun beating up Christians. After some time passed, one of the armed men would come in and drag another poor scared victim across the hall for more screams of agony. We could not see what was going on, but the sounds were enough to scare the bravest of brave. One after one they were dragged out. It appeared random as they did not specifically seek anyone by name, even though they had our ID cards.

After a few minutes, which felt like ages, one young man came in. His approach was calmer this time, and he called out my name while scanning the room for a response. I believed this was the end. Questions were rolling through my head: What have I done now? Why am I being singled out by name? There was no way to pretend that I was not me as they had my picture ID, so I responded and surrendered to my fate.

When faced with what one believes is certain death one either freaks out uncontrollably or goes into a calm surrender. I had a strange kind of calm come upon me like I had never before felt. I walked with this guy with a confidence that did not match the situation in any way plausible. He led me to another room and closed the door behind me just as they were removing a body from the same room but through another door. The group commander closed the other door and turned around with a smile. "What are you doing here?" He asked.

It took me a few seconds to take that in and recognize the man. He was one of those who joined our school at the beginning of the war when he was displaced from another part of the country. He certainly did not fit in and did not last even half the academic year. He had come from one of the rare schools in Lebanon that still taught math and science in Arabic. I am not sure if any of those still remain today but they did at that time and he had a very hard time adapting to the mainstream education system. Everyone made fun of him and ostracized him, a form of what today is referred to as bullying. Teenagers can be cruel whether past or present. Since he left the school three years passed and I had not seen him or heard from him. There was no reason to as he had dropped out of school and joined one of the many pop-up militias full-time thus we had absolutely nothing in common.

At that moment, I stood staring at him, knowing my life was in his hands. My mind raced to recall the days when he was in school. I remembered feeling sorry for him and trying to help him. We did not become friends as we did not have much in common but I was friendly to him and stood up for him a few times when he was being bullied. I always hated bullies and detested meanness. I also tried to help him understand math in English. Or so I recall, but I could not help but wonder under the circumstances if I had ever done something wrong to him that he would want revenge? How did he remember things? A million thoughts went through my mind in a split second. It was as if time stood still.

He chuckled and came around the table between us to place his hand around my shoulder. "You should see your face." He said and broke out into a loud belly laugh. I was still not sure where that was going. "You can breathe now. You are safe." He said as he laughed uncontrollably.

"I am?" I asked, still not absolutely sure.

He gave me a big bear hug that almost crushed my ribs and said: "You were the only person in IC who ever treated me like a human being. I wish I had one of those other bastards here instead." I gave out a nervous laugh of relief and tried to joke with him about that, but, by now, the relief of knowing I was not going to die released massive doses of adrenaline into my system that caused me to shake like a leaf in a hurricane.

He pushed me onto a chair and said: "You need to relax before you can get out of here." And called on his guys to bring a Pepsi.

"Get out of here?" I asked "In one piece?" "Alive?"

He laughed and shook his head. "You are a kind soul. You do not even realize how much your actions meant to me. I would not let anyone hurt you." I did not really think I had done that much, but when someone feels isolated and alone, any small gesture can take on a significant meaning.

As I drank my Pepsi and got the necessary dose of sugar in my system to calm me down, I regained enough of my composure to remember I had a friend with me. I told the commander that I needed to take my friend with me and he sorted through the ID cards on his desk, found the card and then posed as he looked at the picture. "I know him. He played guitar." He said.

I said: "Yes, he plays guitar."

"I did not really know him, but he looked like a descent guy." He said. "If he is your friend, no one will touch him." He called on his men to get my friend.

He walked us to our car, which by now had been moved away from the main road, wished us well and told me if I ever needed anything, I should contact him. He told me where his unit was located and I left. I had just added another contact I could use to save my life if the need arose.

My friend, from experience, had not even questioned what was happening inside. He knew we were getting out alive and went along without saying a word until we were clearly out of sight. Experience taught us not to interfere with a good thing. You did not want to speak and piss anyone off. Silence was always golden.

After we drove off, he took a deep breath and said: "I am not sure what you did in there but thank you." He did not remember the commander, even after I explained who he was. He told me he was grateful I was nice to him. It never hurts to be nice to people, as you never know when or where payback might pop up.

We headed to the party awaiting us. A few shots of vodka and some great music was what the doctor ordered to undo the stress we had just been through. I really needed a warm embrace that evening and slow dancing never felt so good.

This was our lives. Constantly flirting with death as we attempted to lead a normal teenage life in the shadow of war. Dancing on the edge of the abyss.

INDOMITABLE SPIRIT

ADAPTATION: REFUGEES AND LOCALS

Slowly, the presence of the northern refugees all over our area became a reality we got accustomed to. Within a year, we got to know each other, and in spite of the vast cultural and educational difference, we got along as well as could be expected, as they adapted to life in our village.

They eventually got used to our endless partying and flirting and even began to do the same. The younger among them even joined in the fun and became friends with some of the locals. However, that did not come without incidents, most of which were extremely comical in retrospect.

George. the same brilliant man who had planned to invade a distant town in his bathing suit, settled into the job of simply acting all important on the beach. He took over one of the two shaded areas we had built on the shore and made it his own. Those areas were wood canopies covered with bay leaf branches that allowed us to get out of the sun when playing cards or just relaxing so as not to bake in the direct sun all day. He confiscated one of them whenever he was at the beach. However, we still used it whenever he was not around.

He had found a derelict wooden telephone pole and sliced it into short stumps that he used as seats under the canopy. These also came in handy for us in more ways than just sitting as some of the girls would use them to float on when they wanted to spend a lot of time in the water. Irrespective of the use, they always brought them back to the canopy.

Floating Seat

One day a girl decided to head out in a different direction and simply abandoned the wood stump to float away at sea. Not a brilliant or considerate act, but she was a young teenager and was not thinking clearly.

George saw his seat floating away from his window and flipped out, grabbed his .45 hand gun and charged towards the beach to find out which bastard threw his seat in the water. Two years after having arrived in our village, George knew everyone of us by name. He was not really a bad man – just a little unhinged. He mostly stumped around cursing everyone and threatening the end of the world if the seat was not returned. He even fired a couple shots in the air for good measure and demanded we tell him who threw it in the water.

We did not reveal who the culprit was, but we did offer to go retrieve it. In fact, we told him that a couple of the guys were already on their way to get it knowing that such information would bring the whole ordeal to an end.

Just as we almost succeeded in calming him down, he spotted a stranger who was parking a little moped up the hill and coming towards the beach. The stranger, Sammy, was actually one of my sister's classmates who had dropped in to spend the day at the beach.

George lit up as he saw the stranger because it gave him someone to take his frustration out on. Thus, George intercepted Sammy and grabbed his back pack which was still on his back and dragged him away. Poor Sammy did not even know what had transpired. All he knew was that he was being dragged away by an angry armed man threatening to make him "pay for it."

"Pay for what?" Sammy kept asking. "What did I do? I just got here."

George did not get too far before one our close friends (who was a member of the militia military police) showed up to spend the day at the beach. We pointed out poor Sammy being dragged away and went with him to free the poor soul. It did not take much for the military police to get George in check, particularly that Sammy had not done anything.

Free from George, Sammy headed back to his moped to return to Beirut. We implored him to stay and enjoy the day, but he was adamant that he did not want to get killed that day. With assurance from the military police that no harm would befall him and having driven more than an hour to get there, he finally decided to stay, but he asked the MP to let him know when he decided to leave, because Sammy would not feel safe from George without the MP around.

Sammy ended up having a good time at the beach and we treated him to dinner and drinks at the pub in Byblos that night.

Shooting at Boats

George had never seen combat or been at the front lines, but he loved his guns and loved to play the military man.

One afternoon he spotted a tour boat in the water. Those were small flat top boats with seats and a canopy for shade. Several such boats operate out of Byblos Port for people wishing to get a nice view of the country from the sea and would sail slowly about half a kilometer from shore past our village regularly.

This particular day however, was going to be different. George came down from his occupied chalet with an M-16 in one hand and his eighteen-month-old son in the other. He held the M-16 by its handle and grabbed one arm and one leg of his son with other hand and dangled him like a suit case. As soon as he reached the beach, he dropped his son on the floor and told him to "watch Papa shoot". He then squatted next to the infant and fired the M-16 right over his head towards the boat. He missed the boat – intentionally – but scared everyone on the boat so much that they jumped off.

George cracked up laughing at the poor terrorized people and his son began to cry from the shock of loud gun noise. He did not appreciate his son's fear, and thus began to yell at the infant to toughen up and be a man.

As he was chastising his child, people began to get back on the boat and he fired at them again causing them all to jump back into the water.

Again, he let out a loud laugh calling them cowards. The infant began to cry more and got slapped this time for being weak.

We tried to stop this, but George was enjoying it too much, and kept pointing out how funny it was to see them jump off in terror. Well, he was shooting at them, what did he expect? And, the poor little boy was crapping his pants.

Eventually, George's wife arrived at the same time that he ran out of bullets. The look on her face and her physical demeanor portrayed her as a woman with a vengeance. She could not believe he was shooting at the poor people and at such proximity to her son's head. George was the one slapped at that point and she looked like she wanted to kill him.

It was now our turn to laugh as this tough man was apologizing to his wife who was letting him have it and he deserved it.

Dynamite Fishing

Before civilization caught up with George, he decided to try his hand at dynamite fishing, but he could barely swim and knew absolutely nothing about fishing. He just saw others throw dynamite in the sea and pick up fish and thought he could do the same.

He showed up at the beach with a stick of dynamite and began to ask which one of us would throw it for him. He was actually afraid to light the dynamite and wanted someone else to do it. He had seen a friend blow his hand right off and did not want the same to happen to him but to him, our hands were dispensable.

None of us were interested in playing with dynamite, and we told him there is nothing to blow up in our little lagoon anyway. He needed to take it somewhere else but he was not backing down. He cursed us for being cowards and said "Fine, I will do it."

He walked up to the edge of the concrete and called out to a young man on the rocks across the lagoon to point out where the fish were. That young man also told him that there were no serious fish in the small lagoon we swim in – at least none worth dynamiting.

By then everyone had come out of the water in anticipation of this idiot throwing a stick of dynamite in the swimming lagoon. Wanting to bring the ordeal to an end, the young man reluctantly pointed to the middle of the lagoon and said "There are some here. Throw it."

George lit the fuse, and as scared as he was from the dynamite lobbed it hard enough to clear the lagoon, and it landed on the rocks between the legs of the poor young man he had been talking to. I have never seen a barefoot man run this fast on jagged rocks. Adrenaline and survival instinct make one do amazing things. He was taking five and six-meter strides as he bolted away from the dynamite. The dynamite slowly rolled off the rock and exploded just as it hit the surface of the water. It shredded the surface of the rock where it exploded but had absolutely no effect on anything beneath.

The moron did not even give the fact that he almost killed a man any thought, but actually thought he would have gotten some fish, and asked us to go get them. By then the young man had made it to the other side and bared down on him. The young man exhausted every curse word he ever knew and possibly added a few new ones too.

That was the last of George's fishing career. It was too dangerous for everyone else.

STEVE AND OUR MOSLEM FRIEND

One of our close Moslem friends, Hani, from Beirut just did not feel secure enough to ever join us at the beach. As much as he felt like it, he just never managed to muster the courage to cross over, and always feared he would be picked up due to a mistaken identity episode.

One Friday afternoon, Hani's father heard us urging him to join us for the weekend, after he had told us we were lucky to be spending time at the beach. Hani's father joined us in urging him to go, telling him that he – the father – crossed into East Beirut all the time for business, with no problems. After all, he assured Hani that he would be with us and would not have a problem.

With the insistence from his father, Hani decided to go for it, but requested we ride with him for his peace of mind. That was fine with us, and the next morning we headed to Monsef. We spent a fun pleasant day at the beach and then, in the evening, headed out to introduce Hani to our pub in Byblos. We were a large crowd as usual, many of whom already knew X from school.

Late in the evening as we sat for some food on the patio outside the pub, along came Steve, straight from the front line somewhere, still fully armed, unbathed and looking like a killer from hell.

Steve was not his real name, but a nickname he earned in the war. In the early days of the war, the dividing lines in down town Beirut were still fluid and shifting as various forces vied for control of different buildings. In one battle, Steve found himself trapped on the fifth floor, as the Palestinians came up the building towards him. With no other way out, he jumped from the window of the fifth floor. He landed on a dirt pile, rolled down, and just took off running with absolutely no injuries. From there on, his friends, who witnessed that feat, nicknamed him Steve, on account of "Steve Austin: The Six Million Dollar Man.".

INDOMITABLE SPIRIT

Steve was one of the fiercest fighters in the Christian Militia, but also an extremely kind-hearted man with an exceptional sense of humor. He was one the northerners who hung around with us at the beach and sometimes joined us in the evenings, but usually not dressed as he was on that night. He was usually bathed and dressed for the occasion. I am not sure why he had passed by that evening, in full battle attire but when he saw us, he felt he had to stop to say hello.

He sat on the empty seat facing me, which happened to be next to Hani, and the barrel of his gun literally fell in Hani's slap. As Steve said his hellos, with the usual chatter, I noticed Hani turning blue due to sudden lack of breath. I instantly knew what his problem was, and said jokingly "You can breathe, Steve is a good guy."

Steve turned to him and asked if he was ok, given his seriously flustered look. I explained to Steve that Hani was a Moslem, and this was the first time he had crossed over after the war and was worried what people like Steve might do to him. That explanation almost gave Hani a heart attack, as he did not know Steve, and thought he would welcome the opportunity to kill any Moslem he found, especially given the way he was dressed that night.

Steve gave me a quizzical look and then asked my friend: "Have you killed or hurt anyone I care about?" Hani quickly retorted with arms raised "I have never killed or hurt anyone. I am a peaceful man. I carry guitars, not guns."

With that response, my laughter, plus Steve's knowledge that this guy is with us and thus not the enemy; Steve handed Hani his M-16 and told him "If anyone so much as looks at you the wrong way, shoot him." Hani really did not want the gun, and as Steve insisted, I could not stop laughing at the sight.

Finally, I asked Steve to drop it, as he was freaking Hani out because he had never handled a rifle in his life, not even a shotgun. Steve backed down and kept his gun but persisted in explaining to Hani that he and his faction do not hate Moslems, but just the ones trying to kill them and take their country. All others who want to live in peace are his brothers. Steve then told Hani that if he ever found himself in a jam in the Christian area, to just use the name Steve as a reference. With that settled, Steve left to go bathe and get some sleep after three sleepless nights on the fronts. We had a few more drinks, danced a little, and had a grand time for the rest of the night.

By around four in the morning as we cleared out of the place a friend from our village asked me who I was riding with and I pointed at Hani's small Honda Civic that we rode in. He looked at it and said "No problem. Just toss it in the trunk and hop in. We will ride together." Those Civics were tiny in those days compared to the huge Chrysler New Yorker the other guy was driving, and may very well have fit in the trunk, but we did not try. We drove two cars home.

A couple of weeks later, as we sat on the beach, we noticed Hani in his Honda Civic pulling in, unannounced and unaccompanied. Glad and amused by his new found courage, we asked, what made him come alone. He replied with a wide grin "I have Steve watching my back. What do I have to fear?"

Laughing, we pointed out Steve on the beach, whom X would have never recognized in Steve's clean and shaven state. Steve bought him a beer, and thus X began to frequent our beach often, and definitely whenever he felt like it.

That was the world we lived in. Fearsome fighters who doubled as the most gentle people when away from the fronts. Christian militiamen who welcome Moslems into their homes, and vice versa, as long as the others were not trying to kill them.

STRIP DARE

In spite of our ability to head into town whenever we wanted, we still held many parties in our homes in the village. It was summer and every night was a party. Going out every night was too expensive, so we would gather at our usual spots and party all night.

Several of my friends from the village had August birthdays, as did I. In particular, one close male friend two houses down from our summer house had the same exact birthday as me as well as a close female friend of mine whose birthday was four days later. Because of this coincidence, we (the birthday trio) would often hold one big birthday party for all of us sometime in late August.

In 1979, having grown into our late teens, the party included many people from other places, and some friends from Beirut. It was a sizeable party of more than a hundred people held at the home of the female amongst us. Due to the amount of people at the party and the size of the living room (which doubled as the dance floor), anyone not dancing would step outside on the sea facing balcony for the cool breeze coming off the Mediterranean, and the crowd also spilled out onto the west balcony off the family room facing the beach, and even occupied the stairs which led to the clearing below the house.

As we (the outside seated people) chatted outside, I began having a serious urge to take a swim. Many others agreed but said they did not have any bathing suits with them.

"Who needs bathing suits!" I said. "Let's just strip and go."

They laughed, joked and teased, but no one seemed up to it, especially given that this crowd was a mix from all over the country and not our small close knit group that swam together regularly.

As I persisted in effort to convince them that no bathing suits were necessary, one girl from Beirut challenged me by saying, "You would never dare strip and go swimming here.". She knew not what she was daring me to do. She gave me just the opportunity I needed to go cool off in the sea, and I reciprocated by daring her to join me. Believing I would never do it, she agreed but told me I had to strip right there on the balcony and walk naked all the way down to the beach that was about fifty meters away thus passing in front of three houses which lined the pathway to the beach.

I took the challenge on condition that she would do the same, and, again, she not believing that I would actually go through with it, agreed. I knew she was not willing to do it, as she was a stranger to most people there but I had my chance for a swim, and I took it. I began to take off my clothes slowly, giving her every chance to back out but she did not until I was completely naked. When she realized I had actually stripped, she panicked and called out to her few friends for help. I was not about to embarrass the poor girl who just gave me the gift of a dip in the sea. It would have been too cruel to force her out of her clothed and cruelty is not in my nature.

Thus, with a shrug, I turned around and strolled off the balcony and down the stairs butt naked in the direction of the sea. One of the witnesses to the strip scene ran in and told the host "HE DID IT! HE TOOK HIS CLOTHES OFF AND WENT SWIMMING!" She came out to see my "extremely untanned white butt shining in the moon light", as she put it.

By the time I had finished my swim, her six-year old little brother was standing ashore with a big towel and said "Mom says wrap this around you before you come back." Apparently, someone also told the Mother who was in her bedroom while we were partying. The mother was a nice lady from Texas who married a Lebanese. We spent so much time in her house and she treated all of us as her own children. There was a lot of love there, but she really did not appreciate my strip show in her house.

I obliged and returned with towel wrapped around my waste to find the poor girl who challenged me still cowering in the corner praying that I would not force her to strip and dip. I knew I would never do that, but I took pleasure teasing her and pretending I was going to make her do it. She was rescued by another girl who pulled me to the dance floor inside, still naked in a towel. It was a slow dance as she defended the girl who reneged on her dare on the premise that she was a stranger and would be too embarrassed to strip.

I told my dance partner that the girl should not have made the dare if she was not willing to go through with it. I certainly gave her ample opportunity to back off.

My dance partner agreed and said "If I had made the dare, I would have joined you."

Hmmm. This was an outsider with whom I have not skinny dipped before, but would not mind it at all, especially alone, so I dared her "You do not have the courage to do that. You would have cowered out also."

A few sentences later and she was eager to prove me wrong and decided to strip down and go for a swim. She yanked the towel off me in the middle of the dance floor and said "Let's go," and began to unbutton her shirt.

The host quickly intervened, wrapping the towel around me from behind saying "As much as Mom loves you, she will kill you if you keep doing this shit so take it to the beach."

We asked her for another towel and headed to the beach. The idea that we could see all the houses from where we were just added to the excitement. Many occupants still had their lights on and were out on their patios but they were in the light and we were in the dark, so even if they could hear us, they could not see us, particularly in the water.

An hour or so later we rejoined the party, cool, refreshed and with big smiles on our faces.

The host pulled me into her bedroom where she had gathered my clothes. "Get dressed already. No more dancing in towels."

She still until today tells people about my white butt shining in the moonlight. I guess some images just never go away.

NOT YOUR STANDARD SCOUTS
LATE TEENS

By our late teens, scouting took on a whole new meaning. We were graduating into leadership positions, but most importantly, scouting became another venue to gather and enjoy ourselves. All the discipline and rigor associated with scouting was discarded in return for our own version of things.

Once we turned sixteen, we decided we were too cool to sleep in tents. The mixed camping trips still segregated the group by gender and age, with each of the six groups (three age groups per gender) having their own area with their own leaders, but some of us had other plans. We – boys and girls - would drag our sleeping bags closer the fire and sleep next to each other, even sometimes using each other's stomachs as pillows. The leaders finally gave up trying to stop us, and some even joined us since, as they were not that much older than we were and they were also our close friends.

We would spread some of the sleeping bags open on the ground, and then share the other open sleeping bags as quilts covering more than one. On one particularly cold night high in the mountains, the wind started making really cold late at night, so we decided we needed closed sleeping bags. However, lacking enough bags, we shared. One girl and I got in the same sleeping bags, zipped it up, and slept comfortably sharing body heat and protection from the wind.

We heard some choice words in the morning when the leaders woke up to find us cuddled in the same sleeping bag. They worried about the little kids learning the wrong lessons. The kids turned out just fine, and the sight of us did not disturb them that much. It was the two of us who got talked about for a while, but it did not really bother us, as it was all in good humor. She still tells people that we even shared a sleeping bag when telling people how closely we have known each other all our lives.

Our troupe should have won an award for being the least disciplined in Lebanese scout history. Yet, we excelled in every competition, and won almost every federation competition we entered. The fact is that while others were stuck on tradition and the way things were always done, we were free thinkers, moving forward as we believed best. We went way outside the box, and bent, sometimes even broke, the rules.

We did so well that the federation commissioned us to help in the formation of four new troupes during the last three years I was in the scouts. Lucky for them, they did not have to camp with us and get completely spoiled. We just taught them the basic principles and helped organize the newly formed troupes.

Boy in the Nunnery

One of the Camp sites that we frequented in our later teens was at the grounds of a nunnery. As was customary when campers used the site, the nunnery provided a source of water and the use of their land.

it was during one of the longer camp period, a five days and four nights to be exact, the ladies feeling they could not go that long without a decent shower, worked out a deal with the nuns to use the indoor showers. The alternative would have been to bathe with jugs of water as we males did. The nuns made it very clear that permission was given to females only, after all this was a nunnery but still the guys felt left out.

On the second day one of the guys decided he was going to sneak in and take a shower regardless of the deal made and the warnings issued. To camouflage himself, he placed a towel over his head as he approached the showers with one of the female campers. As the showers had access from the outside and he and the female did not need to go through the main facility thus, he managed to get in unnoticed.

However, as he began to take his shower, one of the nuns showed up to offer assistance to the supposed girls she had just seen walk in. The nun instead of offering help to the females, comes face to face with a naked man in the showers.

Not only was she shocked about the actual agreement violation but also the ethical code of females and males showering together. It was actually the later which had her freaking out and calling on the mother superior all the while praying to God for forgiveness regarding what she had just seen.

As for the male camper, he did not even take the time to rinse himself and just took off running towards the woods soapsuds and all. He entire focus was on getting out of there before Mother Superior showed up. For all he knew, she could be bringing with her the nunnery whipping team with their mean switches to whip him for his evil deed.

The females also took off running to avoid being identified because no one wanted to be blamed for allowing a man to shower in the nunnery. They rationalized that If they ran, the nuns would not know who exactly was complicit in the crime.

I was oblivious to all of this when I encounter my friend running half naked with the soapsuds dripping from his hair and his clothes bundled up in his hands. He yelled out at me to meet him with a jug of water and continued running towards an area below the level of the camp. He clearly needed water to rinse off regardless of the reason he found himself in that condition, so I obliged. I ran into the camp storage area and grabbed a twenty-liter jug of water and followed him.

I knew exactly where he was headed, as we had, the day before, found a nice setup to double as a bathing site. The site was a two-meter long slab of rock that was surrounded by rocky terrain which allowed the person bathing to avoid standing in muddy ground during the water pouring process. This location also helped the person pouring the water as he would not have to lift the heavy jug over his head because all that was needed was for the jug to be leaned over the top of the cliff and the water would pour over the bather below.

As I helped my soap covered friend to rinse off, he filled me in on what had happened prior to be bumping into him. I could not stop myself from telling him that the nuns were going to castrate him and turn him into a nun as punishment.

In the middle of this scene, the girls show up to rinse off as they could not possibly go back to nunnery without being held as culprits to the crime. With so many soapy bodies to rinse off, I headed back for more water.

By the time we got back to camp, the nuns were there in heated discussion with the camp leaders about the egregious transgression of a man bathing in their bathrooms. Had they caught him just walking in, it might not have been so bad. But they caught him in mid shower and in mixed company. No, No. No. Not in a nunnery.

We hung back until it was over as we did not wish to confront an irate mother superior and her disciplinary team. The nuns could not identify the female culprits, so they imposed punishment on all by terminating showering rights for everyone. they would have thrown us all off their land had it not been for the pleading of the camp leaders and their promise to punish those responsible.

The nuns left in a huff and then we entered the camp. It was not hard for our camp leaders to identify the suspects since we were walking back with empty water jugs, wet hair and wet clothes.

Instead of punishment, the leadership seemed amused by the whole ordeal. They did not care about showering rights and had thought the showering agreement cut against the idea of roughing it out in the camp. Denial of showering rights was punishment enough.

Scout Raid in Kour El Hawa

At eighteen I was part of a raid on a camp by the younger scouts on the edge of the cliff we had hiked a few years earlier. The camp ground was actually situated among almond trees and surrounded by a massive rock retaining wall along the edge of the cliff thus creating a terrace of soil for planting. The kids who were camping, had assumed that the cliffs and boulders already provided perfect protection against any incursion from that side so directed their attention to guarding the other side.

The campers had clearly not anticipated a commando raid coming up the cliffs, but they got one. We snuck around the almond groves and along the top of the cliffs to climb up the rock wall which was a rubble wall with boulders the size of small cars forming the outer shell.

As I made my way across the boulders, I spooked a large bird that had been sleeping between them and it attempted to fly away into safety. Instead, it flew straight into my open jacket and got tangled there for a few seconds before it managed to find a way out and disappeared. The night without moonlight was extremely dark and I was perched on the edge of a steep cliff trying to remain stealthy and maintain my footing in a precarious position. Needless to say, my encounter with the screeching bird inside my jacket was nerve wrecking. I did not even know what hit me at first, all I knew was that something extremely noisy was suddenly bouncing off my chest.

I managed to remain silent and maintain my footing on the ledge, but the noise the bird made brought the guards to the top of the wall to check it out. I had to hold myself in a frozen position in order to evade detection as my heart raced at two hundred beats per minute. With all the adrenaline racing through my veins it was hard to maintain the calm and silence but I succeeded.

As the guards hovered over me trying to figure out what was happening below, they left the field open for the other three of my comrades to sneak in from other points along the rocky wall and steal the flag which belonged to the campers along with a few other things as well. As was customary in a camping raid, a few of the campers were taken along with the booty.

My comrades would later thank me for causing the distraction which allowed them free reign in the camp. When I explained what happened, they laughed and told me they were glad I did not lose my grip and fall. Actually, so was I as that would have been a very painful fall.

PARTY MAHEM

We continuously tried to ignore and overlook the ugly war around us and proceed with our lives. However, there were those times when our fun would be directly disrupted by idiotic armed men, yet we managed to overcome the disappointment.

One of such disruptions occurred in late September of 1979 during a party one of our friends had thrown at his house in the village. Many of the invited people were from Beirut and consequently would have to spend the weekend at his house.

The house was located at the top of the village but, as usual, at times when there is no beach, we gathered in the center of town in the afternoon prior to the party. That was the intersection of the main road and the road to the church, where the only small store in the village was located. We would linger on the low walls surrounding houses and had access to the store for drinks and treats.

There was quite a crowd of people in their late teens on both sides of the road. About forty of fifty teens joking and yelling across the narrow road was standard behavior in our village but not to the two men driving through that particular evening. As they drove down the road which was now located between us due to our large crowd, someone yelled out something the men in the car did not understand. They immediately hit the brakes and came to a screeching halt and then backed up with ferocity. The man occupying the passenger side was halfway out the window before the car actually reached us. He was screaming at the top of his lungs "WHO IS YELLING AT US?!?"

A bit of back story: the men were brothers from the North of Lebanon. They were two of the displaced occupants in one the houses in the village and were known to be half-wits with extremely short tempers and drunk more often than not. Because we were aware of who they were, we quickly apologized and explained that we were yelling out at each other and not them. Unfortunately, the truth did not sell. The men were just too drunk and stupid to comprehend that friends would yell across the street at each other.

As some of the crowd tried to reason with them, I and some of the others tried to shepherd the out-of-town people away from the scene. The drunk men had been around the village for a couple of years and knew us well. But in several other altercations it was the people the men did not know that were on the receiving end of their anger. In addition to being out-of-towners, some of them were Moslems and thus would really get the brunt of this if it got out of hand, so we shuffled to get them in their cars and headed towards the party house. Unfortunately, the men saw the cars leave and became furious. They wanted to know who left and why. They began to drive recklessly up and down the road screaming at people, threatening them, and waving their guns out the windows. They even blocked the road for a while forcing people to drive five kilometers out of their way to get to their homes.

When one of the ladies from the village tried to convince them to let her pass by innocently telling them that she is a decent person just trying to get home, she set them off even more. They yelled out at her; "WHAT? ARE YOU SAYING WE ARE NOT DECENT PEOPLE?" That led to prolonging the road blockade.

Finally, everyone managed to get to the party. In order to help keep things at bay one of the invitees brought along a friend from the next town who was an officer in the militia Military Police. He brought his gun with him and camped out on the front porch in case either of the idiots figured out where we were and decided to seek revenge.

The older brother of the party host heard the story of what transpired in the village square and decided he could help in calming the situation as he had served his compulsory military service alongside one of the two men and thus knew him better than anyone. He told us to enjoy the party and headed to the village house the men and their family were occupying.

The party went on with the usual music, alcohol and fun, as if nothing had happened. But, two hours later the older brother had not yet returned and we began to worry about him. True he knew them but was not friends with them and definitely not prone to hang out all night with them. It was doubtful they had much to talk about being that the brother was an intelligent college student and they were morons. We began to wonder if he had been killed yet there was not much we could do but wait. We felt secure in the fact that we had our armed guard at the door so we went back to partying.

Finally, the older brother showed up almost three hours later and way past midnight. He was annoyed, but laughing. "What happened?" we asked. "We thought they might have killed you."

He crackled and said: "The mother fucking morons had no idea what I was talking about."

We all looked at each other with puzzlement.

He explained that when he got there to the house they occupied, they were watching TV and drinking; they received him with a warm welcome and invited him in to sit.

The brother explained that shortly after he sat he said, "I heard there was a problem."

"What problem?" they responded. And then continued with, "Who is giving you problems? Tell us, and we will take care of it. You know how much we love you". He tried to explain that he did not have a problem but had heard that they had a problem with some people in the square earlier that evening. He told us that by the looks on their faces, his words were not registering and the few brain cells they had were already fully numbed by alcohol. They had no recollection of what they had done earlier and clearly had no intention of following through on an incident they could not remember.

The brother, clearly satisfied with what he saw, got up to leave but they insisted he stay and have a drink. That type of people took offense if you refused their generosity and considered it a form of disrespect that you deemed yourself above having a drink at their house. Given their state of mind, he would likely get shot if he refused, so he stayed for a drink, and then another and another while all the time they were numbing his brain with idiotic chatter. But what did he expect? After all, those were the two brothers that once shot each other while arguing over JR and Bobby from the TV show *Dallas*. One of them intentionally shot the other in the foot because of a disagreement about who they liked more. The shooter then put his victim in the car and took him to the hospital all the while telling him that the gun shot should teach him not to disagree with his older brother.

DRUNK MORONS with guns.

Thankfully none of us got shot by the Morons that night.

HIGH SCHOOL SENIOR YEAR

1979-1980 was my last year in high school, and like all high school seniors, we had anxious anticipations of a life changing transformation. Even though most of us were not venturing too far, with the largest number heading to AUB across a narrow street, it was not going to be the same. We would not be in the same classes or have the same schedules. Life would be different, and we knew it. We had spent a decade together and came to age together and everything we had come to know was coming to an end. Consequently, we wanted to milk it to the last drop.

Our generation was different than all others. Those slightly older than us were mature enough when the war started that their character was not defined by the chaos of the first few years of war. Those younger than us did not really remember the pre-war Lebanon and had grown up knowing the established division of the country once we got past the initial chaos. We were the people who were old enough to remember what was and to realize the massive transformation in our lives that resulted from the war but we were young enough that our personalities had not yet fully developed before the war came.

Thus we were the war generation in all its facets.

The teenage years are defining years in the development of anyone's personality. These are the years where our experiences define who we become as adults. For us, our experiences in our teens were ones of extreme uncertainty and undefined situations where everything was fluid and changing by the second. The only certainty were our traditional and moral codes that were handed down from our forefathers, and guided our behavior and actions. Yet, even those were being challenged by the war and the hedonistic nature of the times.

We became immune to uncertainty. With every close encounter with disaster, and every brush with death we became more brazen in our attitude toward the war and life in general. Every time we were confronted by danger and survived; every time we managed to cheat death and win we became more desensitized. We stopped depending on the promise of a tomorrow and began living only for today. Still, till now I can recall the constant nagging feeling that I was missing out on something at that time; the feeling that we needed to get as much in as we could while we still could. With that feeling came a callous disregard for any rules that limited our enjoyment of life. According to our teachers, we were the most disruptive and chaotic class they had ever taught. We were not mean or destructive in any way, but we never tired of pranks or practical jokes. We would cut classes and sneak out of school at will and would regularly challenge the established norms. In some cases, we even took to setting our own rules as they suited us.

In order to counter this, the school administration took to continually shuffling us around into various sections every year to break up the cliques that appeared to be most unified, but that did not really work. We maintained the same behavior and anyway, most of our pranks happened outside the confines of the classroom.

The school buildings with thick stone walls and large windows dated back to the late nineteenth century. Our classroom was located directly above the teachers' lounge that had a balcony over the building entrance. One day, between classes, one of our classmates decided to climb out the window and monkey around on the ledge over the balcony. As the teacher walked into class, I immediately closed the window, lowered the shutter and sat right next to the incriminating window.

The ledge hanging classmate tried to get back in. He managed to open the window and then tried to move the shutter but since I was leaning up against it and he did not have much leverage standing on a narrow ledge, he could not get it opened. The teacher, not knowing anyone was outside, told me to stop messing with the shutter, so I nudged my classmate and he jumped to the balcony three meters below. A couple of minutes later another teacher who had been sitting in the lounge, came to our class dragging our classmate behind him. The lounge teacher looked at ours and said, "You seem to have lost one."

It did not take a genius to figure out what had happened. Our teacher told the ledge hanging classmate to take his seat and then turned to me and yelled, "GET OUT." That actually suited me just fine as I was not a fan of his classes where he just made us read from the text book. I could do that myself and at my own time. So being kicked out of class actually gave me time to head to Mehyo's for a cigarette and relaxation.

Mehyo was a fixture in the area outside of our school and AUB. He operated a small cart that he permanently parked on the street every day. It was a narrow and tall glass enclosed cart with two wheels at one end and handles on the other. It was crammed with candy and cigarettes and these were the sought-after items of our youth. He also had an old-style cooler, the type you put ice in to cool drinks, chained to the fence of AUB. He would have ice delivered every morning to cool the drinks he kept in it. In addition to those two things, he strung a rope across the fence and hung newspapers and magazines on it for sale. His little makeshift business and its location allowed him access to everyone who came to both campuses. Consequently, he knew everyone in both the school and university. He appeared poor but we found out that his meager business had made him a fortune. He managed to put all his kids through college (one became a doctor and another a lawyer) and owned two buildings in Beirut that were worth millions. Nevertheless, he could not imagine life without being there as the permanent fixture among all the students.

His family continually argued with him to stop the business as he no longer needed the income. They told him he was embarrassing them since people in the community were accusing his children of not taking care of their father and making him work like this for a living. I was present one time when he told his son "You bastards. This business is what gave you everything you have and you look down on it." He continued "What do you want me to do, sit at home and wait to die? This is my joy in life. I love seeing all these kids and doing this work."

He truly loved what he did and it showed. Thus, in return, everyone loved this kind and generous man. He had a memory like an elephant and really knew everyone by name and even remembered all their preferences. He would give people items on credit and kept a record of these on a tiny notebook in his apron with a pencil stub behind his ear – a stub that never seemed to shrink or grow into a new pencil – maybe he just took the pencil remnants of his children.

His entries into the notebook were gibberish to all of us. One time as I watched him make an entry after a staff member from AUB picked up two magazines a drink and two chocolate bars, it appeared to me as if he just scribbled something that was no longer than one word and was completely incomprehensible to me. I asked him: "What language is that?" He said "Mehyo language" and laughed.

He truly remembered everything. Once, I bought something and he did not have enough change and owed me a quarter. I left for summer the next day and did not see him until October. Yet, when I bought something, he gave me back what appeared to be the wrong change. I had completely forgotten about the quarter so I told him that he had given me the wrong change. He then reminded me that he owed me a quarter from June. Just amazing – not just the memory, but the honesty. It was not the value of the quarter, but the principle behind the act.

In any event, his cart became a hangout location during breaks. He also sold single cigarettes to students who could not afford a pack, or did not want to carry a pack and be caught by their parents.

When I got to Mehyo's that day I had been kicked out of the classroom, I found him needing to go to the bathroom thus he asked me to keep an eye on his stuff for a few minutes. While he was gone, a lady passed by and picked up some magazines and candy then told me to have Mehyo put it on her tab. I did, but my teenage scatterbrain could not remember her name. I told him what she took and he asked "Pregnant?" gesturing a hump over his stomach. I said "Yes." He confidently entered a brief scribble into his notebook. He recognized who it was from the items she took.

On another occasion as we were hanging out during break in front of classroom building near faculty cars, I leaned up against the front of a car without knowing that it had accidently been parked in neutral without the handbrake pulled. Due to the weight of my body leaning on it, it rolled out of place. Our immediate reaction was to push it back into place but then mischief struck. We looked at each other and instinctively understood that we were given a golden opportunity for a prank. So, we casually pushed the car out into the driveway, blocking traffic to the school and innocently headed to class.

A few minutes later we heard horns beeping. We could see the car from our classroom window and watched as an irate teacher was stuck. The owner of the car did not know that she was the subject of the irate beeping until someone called her to tell her that her car was blocking traffic. She came out confused as to how the car got there. We could not stop laughing as she ran back to get her keys and moved the car when all they needed to do was push it as we did but what did they know?

Eventually, one week before graduation, we got a class visit from the assistant principle. He spent fifteen minutes chastising us for all our known shenanigans and all the complaints he was getting from teachers and finally said: "If I hear one more complaint. Just one. None of you will graduate this year."

I raised my hand. Annoyed, he barked out: "What!"

I calmly asked: "Are you willing to endure us one more year?" Of course, I was highlighting the consequence of us not graduating.

He glared at me as if I had killed the golden goose. As others in the classroom snickered, he must have changed colors a dozen times before he finally managed to breathe and that saved him from suffocating. The image of him waving his finger at me with his mouth open and nothing was coming out is still vivid in my mind. He was at a loss for words and his anger was not helping. Finally, he just huffed loudly, shook his finger at everyone and stomped out of the classroom. I turned around to see our teacher shaking his head. "You are just unbelievable. I never thought anyone could ever stupefy him, but you just did." That was the kind of power we felt we had, being that we had no certainty of tomorrow coming.

Despite all that happened, we graduated and our teachers and school administration were glad to see us move on to become someone else's nuisance.

Senior English-French Battle - 1980

Lebanon is a trilingual country. Most schools are either predominately English or French but our school had both an English section and a French section so there was always a type of rivalry between the two. Students in the opposing sections were constantly competing in just about everything. A tradition that grew out of this rivalry was the end of year water balloon fights which included seniors of each section. It was not a planned duel, but rather a series of sneak attacks against each other, and sometimes balloons were dropped from windows on unsuspecting targets below.

Our senior year took on a whole new dimension, as did almost everything in our lives. Our attacks started early and lasted much longer. We also took the fights to a level beyond just water balloons. In those days we still used old-style ink pens that required cartridges and what better a weapon than a cartridge of ink emptied into a water balloon and tossed on someone thus turning them blue, red or black. True it made a big mess, but it created more of a challenge for everyone as well. Being soaking wet in warm weather was not a big deal, but the ink was a different story so we started coming to school in old clothes that we did not mind being ruined.

The attacks continued to escalate until a challenge was offered by the opposing team to meet on Saturday for a full battle. Everyone had similar ideas of enhancing the weaponry beyond balloons so we went to all the juice stores we could find to collect orange peels and any discarded parts of fruits. We even hit grocery stores and asked for their fruit and vegetable discards and brought eggs. It was going to be nasty and we came prepared.

We met in the narrow street between IC and AUB; the French section on the lower end, and the English section on the upper end. A note of caution: an egg may break when it is hit, but when it hits a human head from fifty meters away it feels like a rock, and it really hurts. I had one hit the back of my head and in spite of me having a very strong head, it almost knocked me out.

The fight was scheduled to take place on the last week of school and AUB students had finals coming up. The AUB dorms were situated right along that narrow street where the fight was to occur and our loud ruckus was preventing the AUB students from concentrating on their studies. Their response to our disturbance was idiotic at best as they threw eggs at us from their windows and did not care what mess they made while we did not care if they hit us because we were already messy. But, they were in their rooms thus when we began throwing eggs back at them in retaliation, those eggs landed into their windows and even if we did not hit them directly, the eggs would cause a mess in their rooms. That really ticked them off enough to throw glass bottles at us. With glass raining down on us, a small group decided to charge the building to grab the instigators. As we ran up the steps to the dorm another glass bottle headed our way and right at my legs. I jump for the bottle to miss me and it hit the stairs and shattered sending the hard-bottom part into the ankle of the guy behind me. He ended up needing quite a few stiches in his ankle as a result of that.

Others who were not a direct part of the fight had called the police and by that time two jeeps were speeding down the narrow street. We were not ready to explain any of this to them thus we scatter into the school and AUB campuses. They did not follow, as their objective was to stop the messy behavior and by scattering us, they had succeeded.

A bunch of us from both sections, English and French, headed to the beach to attempt to wash of some of the remnants of the fight. This was just a game and school rivalry, not a war, and we were all friends after all. We headed down through the AUB campus, through the tunnel under the coastal boulevard that connects the main campus to the AUB beach and proceeded to jump into the water with our clothes on. They were stinky and messy, and the sea was the most efficient way to clean them and avoid a major scolding from our mothers. We jumped into the water fully clothed then got out and stripped down to our bathing suits while we let our clothes dry in the sun and we spent the rest of that day on the beach.

Senior Dance - 1980

One week later, school was over, and it was time for the graduation party we had been waiting for. The party was planned to take place at a seaside resort – Summerland – which was located south of the city. It was a beach/hotel with sprawling grounds, pools, and waterfront beach. The party was in a hall that opened up to the main pool, and from there the space opens up to a vast area where sunbathers spread out during the day.

It was a very nice place that eventually got surrounded by some nasty neighborhoods during the war as hordes of homeless war refugees occupied what was once the empty land surrounding the resort.

The school administration insisted we all ride buses there to avoid any potential problems with individuals driving through the neighborhoods surrounding the resort. We gathered at the school and eventually filled up quite a few buses as our graduation class had more than a hundred students in the English section and a little less in the French section.

The celebration was a formal party to mark our achievement in managing to finish high school despite all the hardships we faced and we were dressed to the hilt in suits and night gowns, but kids will be kids. Some of us were horsing around near the pool and ended up in it, as one fell in and dragged another and another until there were seven floating around the pool in their suits and gowns. Some of us took advantage of the sprawl to head towards the beach with. Away from the party and the teachers, with lounge chairs and a nice breeze, it was a perfect setting for one final rump while technically still high schoolers.

We had our last hurrah with pictures and all. A bitter sweet night, as our pride in graduation mixed with a nostalgic realization that an era of our lives had ended, and things would never be the same again. Some of those kids, I have never seen again since. They are but a distant memory. A beautiful memory, but only a memory nonetheless. We knew that we would most probably never see each other again and tried to make the evening last as long as we could but we had come in buses and had to return in buses that had to leave at the scheduled time.

We lingered a bit at the school saying our goodbyes, not wanting to let go of high school but we had to. Off we went, each to their own home and onto the next chapter in their lives.

We had supposedly grown up.

INDOMITABLE SPIRIT

SAND BAGS ON CLASS ROOM WINDOWS

We spent the next three weeks after high school classes ended studying for our Government Baccalaureate Exams. The GBE is a standardized test in Lebanon, without which one does not graduate regardless of school grades. To minimize the possibility of cheating and standardize the exams, the sessions were not taken in our own school but rather we were assigned to a different school and seated mixed in with students from other schools.

Our class assignment was posted in early July 1980 and was at a school right on the front-line dividing East and West Beirut. And, I mean right on the line. The school campus literally straddled the line, with the east gate opening up into East Beirut, and the west gate opening up into West Beirut.

There was no active fighting at the time of the exams, but in a quintessentially Beirut style that could change at any moment and without notice.

When we arrived at the school on Monday, all was calm. It was a nice sunny summer day, not too hot, but just warm enough to make one want to relax and enjoy the weather, but it was time for some of the most rigorous examinations we had ever taken. The first day we were scheduled for a four-hour Math Test from 8 to 12, followed by a three-hour Logic Test from 1 to 4, with a one-hour lunch break in between. Once the tests were handed out, no one was allowed out of the room, not even to use the bathroom. We were in for the duration, and anyone who left the room remained out and did not get to finish the exam.

Furthermore, every student was thoroughly searched on the way in by police and soldiers to prevent anyone from bringing in cheat sheets. Everything was searched, and they even took cigarettes out of the boxes to see if papers where rolled into them. Despite all the diligence, students still got their notes through. One of our classmates was too lazy to study, but extremely innovative. Photography was his hobby, so he wrote out his notes on regular paper, then took pictures of them and developed the pictures the same size as the negatives. He had a full page the size of a negative that was actually legible. No one could write that small legibly. He snuck the photos in his big kinky hair.

After exams were over, we showed one of the photos to an officer at the gate, who could not believe it and could not stop laughing. He said that this guy should pass on account of ingenuity, if nothing else.

Given the location of the school, the class rooms all had sandbags in the windows, to ensure that students sitting in their seats were not in the direct line of fire, when fighting erupted. Even though we had already been through five years of war and had gotten hardened and relatively desensitized to the notion of war, the sight of sand bags in the windows was a little distracting.

We already knew that we were sitting smack in the line of fire, should anything happen, but the sand bags became a glaring reminder of that fact as we tried to focus on the sea of calculus problems in the exams. They, however, provided a strange kind of re-assurance of protection.

After a few snide remarks about the sand bags and jokingly wondering if they were set up properly to protect us, we settled in to receive the tests. Silence filled the room, except for the hushed sound of pencils and pens against paper.

About two hours into the exam, the silence was broken by a loud explosion that could not have been more than a couple of hundred meters away. Before anyone could remark on the explosion, it was immediately followed by a rattle of gun fire, and then others of all calibers, which quickly grew like a crescendo into a full- fledged battle right at the door steps of the school. The building we were in was not receiving any direct hits but that could change at any time. The battles were close enough that a mere change in the direction of fire would cause a direct hit to the building even if the fighters did not move a single meter.

The sound of gunfire grew closer and farther away in a futile deadly dance, interspersed with rockets and artillery. The truce had been broken and everywhere people were joining the fight, each from their own bunkers.

Sure, we were protected from normal gun fire while we were behind the sandbags however, a mortar hit would tear the whole room apart, sand bags and all. Furthermore, we knew that we would soon have to leave the room and head out into the unknown. Our heads were filled with questions. Was this a minor skirmish that would subside soon? Or, would it grow into a major conflict that engulfed the city? What was happening to our cars out there? Would we be able to get home? Would we be able to get lunch between exams? Then, of course, those mental questions became spoken ones, and gave way to analysis of what everyone thought was going on.

The room was filled with students from both sides of the divide. At eighteen and nineteen years old, some of the people in the room were also active in the militias on either side and could have been out there shooting at each other but instead they were inside the same room debating what was happening. The debate quickly heated up, while the exam monitors desperately tried to end it.

Finally, the head monitor issued an unequivocal warning "anyone uttering another word will forfeit the exam and will have to leave the room." He loudly yelled at all to go back to their work, saying "ignore the fighting and focus on finishing the test."

For those who complain about being distracted by footsteps in the hallway, try this one on for size. IGNORE THE ARTILLERY BATTLE OUTSIDE AND FOCUS ON CALCULUS.

INDOMITABLE SPIRIT

It was not a simple task, but we had done it before. By then, we had gotten used to going to school and taking exams in the shadow of war. We just were never positioned between the two warring factions. That was a new experience. Had this been our first experience with war, I am sure we would have all failed miserably, but our war experience had taught us to endure what most teenagers cannot even imagine. We completed two more hours of the exam to the sound of guns and explosions close enough to make the building shake violently, and managed to get good grades.

Then came lunch hour. The fighting had not yet subsided, and, in fact, appeared to be intensifying and spreading. We were by then hearing the sounds of war at varying distances and in multiple directions. Those who finished early got to leave the room, and I was one of those early students – a few minutes early – and we headed down to the ground floor to check out the situation. There were police and security people at the school gates all day and they had been witnessing the fighting and communicating with their counterparts elsewhere, so we figured they were in position to fill us in.

They told us that it was a minor skirmish three blocks north of us and spreading into the old downtown a kilometer away. Minor, in the Beirut lexicon, meant that it was limited to the local forces, and no major mobilization of re-enforcements was in play, and Large Artillery and Rocket Launchers have not been deployed in a massive bombardment of large sections of the city. However, minor still involved mortar fire, RPGs and vehicle mounted B-7 and B-10 artillery, not to mention every caliber of bullets you can imagine, including ant-aircraft guns aimed horizontally which is not something anyone would wish to traverse.

They also said that sporadic skirmishes had broken out to the south of us but had not lasted and were on and off low-level activity – the kind of shooting that tells the other side "We are here." Those bullets can still kill us if we got in their way.

Listening to all this, we asked "So, where can we get lunch?"

One officer jokingly said "I guess four hours of tests make you hungry, huh?"

We explained that we still had another three hours of exams and seriously needed the food. He pointed out a decent sandwich shop a couple of blocks away, but told us we cannot head straight to it because we would be exposed to sniper fire at the intermittent intersection. We had to walk around three more blocks to the south where we would be protected by an earthen mound and approach the shop from the other direction.

"How about the fighting on the other side?" we asked." Is there any sniper fire from that direction?". "Not yet." Another officer chimes in, "but be careful, you never know."

"Be careful" was a standard warning everyone gave. I never knew exactly what that meant in situations like this. How could we possibly know if a sniper had taken up position on top of a building and was just waiting for us to come around the corner? How could we possibly know when any of the armed men decided to pull the trigger?

Nonetheless, we accepted that warning as usual and said "We will be careful."

We waited for a couple more of our friends to emerge from the test and headed out for sandwiches. The fighting was literally behind the restaurant, where the back of the building was being showered by bullets and the occasional RPG. However, those were concrete and stone buildings that prevented bullets from going all the way across.

When we arrived, the servants were handing a large order to some fighters picking up lunch for their crew. Everyone had to eat. We thought we would ask them what was happening, but they appeared as clueless as the rest of us.

"Someone started shooting" they said, "and, someone responded, and then all hell broke loose."

"Who started, and why?" we asked.

They could not even tell which side of the line the first shooter was on. Like so many of the battles, they started and ended without much reason. It could simply be a misfire that triggered responses that took hours to subside. Too many young armed men in close proximity.

We finished our food and drinks and headed back around the building to class. The fighters wished us luck on our exams and headed back into the battle. We wished them safety and told them to "be careful." They shout the same back at us.

Just before 4 pm, we finished our second test and headed out of the building. By then, the battle had settled into earie sporadic rattles of gunfire. A bullet here and bullet there, then a long machinegun run. There would be no rhyme or reason to it, as if these guys had bullets to spend.

We again checked with the soldiers at the gate about the safest route back to our neighborhood. They obliged with detailed explanation of which roads were closed and which were open.

We thanked them and head out to our cars.

"Be careful." they told us, again.

We dropped each other home, as we had shared rides, and settled in for last minute refreshers for the next day's exams – Physics and Chemistry.

Our parents asked us how we did in the exams and discussed the tests like nothing else happened. We did not even give the events of the day another thought. It was just another day in Beirut.

Two more days of the same grueling exams in the midst of a war zone. The fighting would ebb and flow as the days went along, but never died out.

Our last exam was "History of Arab Science," a fairly interesting subject, in retrospect, about early scientific developments in the Middle East, but our teacher was an obsessive man who forced us to memorize the book instead of understanding the material and we learned to hate the subject. Furthermore, we were Math and Science majors heading into Engineering and Medical school and did not feel the subject had any importance at the time.

Several of us calculated the minimum we expected to get on each of our previous exams and determined we had already passed. The exact grade on those tests is irrelevant to proceeding with our studies and it was only important to pass, which was determined by the cumulative grade from all subjects. We could fail one subject and make up for it with high grades in another as long as we did not get a zero in any of the six exams.

We had the grades so all we needed to do then was answer a few questions to avoid a zero and head out to the beach. We asked the monitor when we could leave as he was passing out the exams and he looked at us with a puzzlement that said "You have not started yet." We repeated the question "How long do we have to stay here to be counted as taking the exam?" He told us we could leave after forty minutes.

We start answering the questions we found to be the easiest while regularly checking our watches. At exactly forty minutes we stopped in mid-sentence and got up, handed the exams in, wished the monitors good luck and walked out. They watched us with bemusement. Maybe they thought we would fail, but we did not.

We had all this planned from the previous night and drove to the tests ready to go. Those heading to the beach up north rode together and had their stuff in the cars. We had come into the school from the West side, but now drove around it and headed into East Beirut and then north to the beach – through the battle lines and gun fire.

The stress of the examination was over and we needed to relax on the beach. Summer vacation was upon us.

We were all still alive, and tomorrow was another day.

Time to Party, just "be careful."

SCOUT CAMPING IN CYPRUS-1980

In the summer of 1980 the older crew in the scouts decided to organize a camping trip to Cyprus. None of us knew much about Cyprus or where we would go, but we wanted to take a trip outside the country and Cyprus is less than two hundred kilometers across the water. The alternative close country would have been Syria and no one would even contemplate that. Cyprus is not much different from Lebanon, except they spoke Greek, but, otherwise, the people culture, etc. was very similar.

A couple of twenty-year-old guys made a preliminary trip to look for a camp ground, and found a nice stand of pine trees next to the water owned by a seaside restaurant near Larnakes and made a deal with the owner for food and use of bathrooms and showers. We planned to be there in September after the wave of European tourists subsided, otherwise the owner would have no time for us.

We spent ten days on the Island. Twenty guys between sixteen and twenty and one girl – she was the girlfriend – later became the wife – of one of the leaders of the trip who wanted to come along. Luckily, we had one guy who had no interest in doing anything other than lounge in the sun and sleep, which allowed the rest of us to tour the island without having to worry about guarding our stuff at camp.

One day we decide to rent cars and drive to Limassol and Nicosia, but Cypriots drive English style on the left side of the road with the driver seat on the right side of the car. It was hard enough to adapt on city and coastal roads to Limassol, but when we headed over the mountains to Nicosia, it got really dangerous.

Mountain roads in Cyprus like those in Lebanon are narrow and winding with a lot of hairpin curves with asphalt that is barely five meters wide and no dividing lines. We were used to this kind of roads and did not think much about it, except for the wrong side of the road.

On narrow roads like that, with sparse traffic we always drove in the middle of the road until we met someone, we moved to the side, made way and proceeded.

On straightaways all was fine, but then we came across someone as we took a tight turn we instinctively went right as he instinctively went left. We were both heading to the same side of the road and we end up running him off the road cursing and making all sorts of vulgar gestures in the process. We tried to apologize but our hysterical laughter got in the way. No matter how much we told ourselves we need to remember to go left, whenever surprised by another car instinct kicked in and we drove them off the road.

We kept insulting each other and taking over from each other, each claiming they could do it better, but we all fell victim to the same instinct. Thus, two days later we returned the cars and abandoned driving as it was getting too dangerous. If a car did not kill us, we feared some angry Cypriot might shoot us, so we decided to stick to Larnakes,

The beach was sandy, unlike the rocky beach we were used to, and we took to playing games only possible in wide shallow waters. As all twenty of us were in one-meter deep water horsing around, a stranger came rushing between us and suddenly keeled over with a blood-curdling scream of pain, as the water turned instantly red all around him. We hurriedly helped his friend carry him back to shore to find a massive gash across the bottom of his foot that almost sliced his foot in half.

Once the ambulance had taken him to the hospital, we returned to the water to find out what could have done this and found a large sharp piece of metal sticking out from the sand. We had been stepping and falling all around it for days, and yet managed to miss it all that time. We entered the water with shows the last two days we were there. That incident has given me a phobia of sand beaches to this day. You can see what is on the rocks, but you cannot see what is just below the sand.

It was not all games in the water, and sticking to Larnakes was not that bad. There were plenty of girls on the beach and a lot of tourists around. We, or some of us, had our share of trysts on the moonlit beach.

On the night before last, four of us and the girl decided we need to find a night club. We asked the restaurant owner who told us "five hundred meters." while pointing down the road., so we figured we could walk that distance and did not need to waste money on a taxi. We started walking and walking, with nothing in site. After walking more than a kilometer, we came across a small snack shack and asked about the night club, and, again, he said "five hundred meters" and pointed down the road. Well, we had come this far and we could walk another five hundred meters but the girl complained about her shoes hurting and her boyfriend carried her on his back.

Another kilometer or so and still no sign of a nightclub, someone again pointed down the road and said "five hundred meters." By then the boyfriend was getting worn out from carrying her. She is lightweight, but a kilometer is a long distance, so I take over as mule.

Another kilometer, another "five hundred meters" instruction, and another mule. It was getting ridiculous. After walking more than four kilometers and carrying a girl on our backs and then being told another five hundred meters, we relented and ask them to call a taxi for us. The man was insistent that there is no need for a taxi, but by then we were convinced Cypriots had no sense of distance. We were not trusting him and insisted on a taxi.

He clearly had no sense of distance, but that time it was the reverse. The nightclub was around the bend less than one hundred meters away by then, and we looked like fools getting onto a cab for such short ride.

I only wish the nightclub was worth it. It was a little place with a scratchy music box and a tiny dance floor, and there was barely anyone there except for a few local drunks. However, we had made a great effort to get there and decided to make the best of it. We had a few drinks, and the loving couple had a few dances, while the rest of us watched as there was no one to dance with.

We certainly took a taxi back. We were half drunk on ouzo and certainly not in any mood to walk four kilometers back.

A couple of days later we packed up and headed home. All-in-all, it was a great trip, as we bonded and enjoyed new experiences and had a great time.

COLLEGE YEARS
Those Were the Days

By the time I turned eighteen and entered college, the war had been around for five years, and in spite of the eternal hope of people predicting the end of conflict almost every day, the worst was yet to come. However, I can honestly say that the next two years were the best years of my life in spite of the fact that we witnessed some of the most vicious battles. As young adults with complete mobility, we took advantage of every opportunity to live it up.

Some of my classmates and childhood friends left to attend college abroad, but most remained in Beirut, primarily attending the American University of Beirut (AUB) and the Beirut University College (BUC). The two were less than one kilometer apart in Ras Beirut. AUB was almost connected to the International College, where I spent my high school years, and BUC was up the hill where I lived on campus. That meant we all remained very close, but college brought new friends who joined the university from other schools and places, expanding our circle of friends even further.

One would think that with age and experience we should have gotten a little more responsible and cautious, but it was the opposite. The more dangerous and chaotic things got, the more defiant we became. We were determined to resist in every way possible all attempts at subjugating us. We were in a way daring the world to try to hurt us. If we were to die, we were going to die while daring greatly, with a smile on our face, enjoying life, and throwing a party, not cowering underground and miserable.

As I lived on campus and hung out with students, I was already familiar and even friends, with many of the upper-class students. However, then

I was on campus full time, not just after school, and I was part of the crowd rather than the younger outsider.

Deep down, we all knew those days were numbered, although no one wanted to admit it or articulated it, we knew that soon we would be scattering around the world and away from each other. The war in Lebanon had limited work opportunities for fresh graduates, and those slightly older than us were leaving in droves for jobs in the oil rich Arab world, Europe or the US. Others were pursuing post-graduate degrees all over the world, and that would be the lot of many of us.

Before the age of internet and social media, that would be the end of any close relationship, and we would literally lose touch with a few exceptions. We would always be friends. but we would not be spending our time together as we were in college.

We spent more time partying than studying the next two years. From college campuses to ski resorts, to beaches, to night clubs, we were constantly in search of a good time, and made friendships that would transcend time and space. Decades later, when communications allowed us to reconnect from across the globe, it was like we never left each other. We searched for each other and found ways to get together after all those years.

As the son of the Dean I could study tuition free at BUC so I join the Engineering Dual Degree program. The college had not yet grown enough to field a full engineering school and had dual degree agreements with several US Universities. Students would spend their first two years at BUC and then complete their studies through two years in the US. The Engineering school was small, had no specific building, and we took classed with the science students.

Although an Engineering Student, for me the fine arts school was the place to be. It was where all the pretty ladies studying theater and communications hung out. Engineering students were mostly nerdish and studying all the time. That was not my scene.

The main entrance of the Fine Arts Building opened to the theater with a large gathering space in front of a full glass wall. Outside the wall was a two-meter-wide ledge that stretched the width of the building with open stairs down to the ground. The upper floors of the building overhung the ledge, creating shade in the summer and shelter from the rain, unless we had a down pour.

That ledge became my "office" for two years. I would call it my office, because I was always there, except when I needed to be in class, and I tended to skip a lot of classes. This was where I hung out with friends and made lasting memories.

Not a Morning Person

Nonetheless, this was engineering school, and some amount of work was necessary. That meant working into the early hours of the morning, and very rarely going to bed before midnight. I was never a morning person anyway and early classes where not my favorite. I would often arrive late, even though I was only a two-minute walk away from the classroom.

In one particular 8am linear algebra class, I had a young professor who was new to the college and did not know who I was at first. As I arrived late the first time, he questioned me, attempting to establish authority, as he was barely out of college and expected he would not receive the same respect as the older professors. Without much thought, I told him I was stuck in traffic and proceed to find a seat. Traffic is horrendous in Beirut, and that is always a valid excuse. He explained that I should leave earlier to insure timely arrival. I nodded, trying to ignore the snickers from around the room and hoping he did not notice them either.

The next class, I had a flat tire. The time after that, I had a hard time finding parking. I was starting to enjoy that and waiting to see how long it would take him to figure it out. It did not take him long at all. He noticed the snickers and by the second time he asked and found out who I was, but he seemed to enjoy the game also, and was waiting for me to run out of fake excuses.

I did not run out of excuses, but eventually, he tired of the game, and simply told me to shut up and take my seat. "Walk faster next time" he said with a smirk that said I am not fooled.

I always had a tendency to skip classes as they were mostly boring for me. The professors spent a lot of time explaining material to insure everyone got it. However, I already got it, and felt like I was wasting my time, and became disruptive. Often professors were glad to see me absent. Many times, I was specifically requested to leave the classroom so others could concentrate and learn something.

However, the 8 am math class was one class I had to attend regularly as it was advanced math with no text book. Yet, I still missed a few classes anyway. As the ski season set in, those Monday morning classes became a real chore after a weekend of almost no sleep, skiing and partying. Often, we drove down from the mountain on Monday morning, barely making it on time.

My Chalet mate and I would begin falling asleep in the back of the class, and the professor found it amusing and would ask us about the weekend. "How was the weather in Faraya? Was the party worth it?". One time he cynically offered to bring in some mattresses for our comfort since we clearly were not getting enough sleep in Faraya.

The raging war all around never prevented us from enjoying life to the fullest. In fact, looking back at it, the war and the ever-present threat of death, led us to push life to its extremes. We wanted to get the most of it while it lasted, because tomorrow may never come. The chaos of a sporadic and unpredictable conflict created an extremely high level of uncertainty, where no one could say what was going to happen the next day or a week down the line. No matter how connected and informed you where, there was just too many actors on the scene, anyone of whom could turn the tables at any time.

So, we lived day by day, hoping for the best and expecting the worse. Ironically, having extremely low expectations produced very satisfying results, since outcomes were mostly better than expected. This perpetual exceeding of expectations created a strange positive sensation in an otherwise negative environment that allowed us to enjoy every moment.

A common response to the quintessential question: "How are you?" became "Alive." A strange answer to anyone not living in a war zone. That habit persisted with me long after I left Lebanon, and people got that quizzical look on their face, and often chuckled as they found it a funny response. However, for people in a war zone, "*alive*." represented a valid response. It said, I made it through another day of this mayhem, and I was still there. In a twisted psychological way, it was an act of defiance that said they could not kill me yet. The term also implied hope. Alive, meant you got to live another day, in spite of the omnipresence of death all around. It implied that this is a new day, and a new lease on life. It produced an eagerness to capture the day and make the best of that gift – the ultimate carpe diem

The closer we came to death, the more meaning life had for us.

SNEAKING INTO THE GIRL'S DORMS

As was the norm in many colleges in those day, the girl's dorms had an eleven o'clock lock down rule. The main entrance to the building got locked and any student not inside would need to wake up the dorm monitor and deal with the consequences.

The monitors were not older student, but two staff members who lived in the dorms. Those were older unmarried ladies and did not have much appreciation for late nights by the girls. More importantly, they did not appreciate having to wake up and go down to open the door for every student who wondered back at every hour of the night. That would be tiresome and annoying, and the girls would pay for the nuisance.

However, by eleven the party was just starting. There was no way these girls could be back by then. So many would end up sleeping in cars if they had nowhere to go until the doors opened in the morning. They could not even get into the campus as the gates would be closed.

My friends were in luck, as I could sneak them in whenever they needed to, as long as they remained quiet and not wake up the monitors. Certainly, the monitors knew about many of those cases. If a girl was not present at lock down, but was in her room the next morning, there would be only one explanation.

It did not need to point at me as many girls helped each other. The ones inside would leave their window open and then walk down to let others in. But, why wake up anyone, when a key is available. There was also the question of how they got on campus but that still did not mean I was in the dorms.

One Friday night we arrived at the dorm at about three in the morning and she was drunk out of her mind. It took all I could do to keep her from waking everyone up even before we entered the building as she laughed hysterically. She was certainly in no shape to climb up three flights of stairs to her room.

I normally tried to stay out of the dorm at night. Everyone in college knew me and I did not want to embarrass my father when he hears from the monitors that his son was traipsing around the dorm at night. He never thought I was a saint, but asked I minimize embarrassing him whenever possible. It was easy to oblige on this issue as anything that could happen in the dorm could happen somewhere else before she got back to her room, and I had access to comfortable accommodations on campus.

However, this time, she was not getting to her room without help, as she was too drunk to climb the stairs. Either I got her there or took her somewhere else. We were staying in Beirut that evening and I did not have another place to take her. I finally carried her and climbed up the stairs. I almost suffocated her with my hand on her mouth to keep her quiet.

As we got to her room, I saw two beds. One was completely bare, with no sheets or anything, just a mattress. The other was messy but made up. I asked her which one was hers and she giggled and laughed and told me everything was hers. I knew she had a roommate, but I could not see anyone there. I thought, maybe her roommate was out of town, which would explain the bare bed, so I dropped her on the messy bed.

Boy, was I wrong. Her roommate was actually under the messy quilt but was so tiny that it was not that apparent in the dark. As my friend hit the bed and her roommate, she jumped up screaming in terror, as she had no idea what was happening. That only aggravated the uncontrollable laughter and I was trying to shut both of them up before they woke up everyone in the dorm.

Her roommate was staring at me with quizzical eyes, wondering what on earth I was doing, as I placed my hand on her mouth. She knew me and did not make a sound after the initial scare, and we were both trying to shut the other one up. I told her I had to go quickly and she needed to handle her roommate from there. She agreed and told me to hurry before the monitors came down from the upper floor. There was certainly a lot of noise.

As I exited the room several girls had popped out of their rooms to check out the commotion. I asked them to help her and play interference with the monitors as I made my exit. One pushed me into her room and closed the door as she saw the monitor heading down the hallway. Another two went into my friend's room to keep her quite while others intercepted the monitor. They made all sorts of excuses about nightmares until the monitor left. They made sure the monitor cleared the stairs and back to her room, and then gave me the all clear to get out.

The next day, I ran into the monitor on campus and she had this big grin when she saw me. She put her arm around my shoulders and said: "Do not do that again."

I tried to play dumb and asked "Do not do what again?"

She said "I am not blind and the hallway is not that long. Plus, I can tell the difference between drunk laughter and nightmares."

I was not sure how to respond to that. I was busted, and no amount of BS would suffice. As I stared at her with mouth open trying to find the words, she leaned over and kissed me on the cheek. 'I am not dumb either. I know what is going on. I just do not want you to set a precedence. Take it somewhere else."

She had known me since I was a little kid and did not want to embarrass my dad with that, but she had a point. If I got away with that, soon other guys would be in the dorms too and would point to me asking why I got away with it and not them. Relieved, I explained that I did not bring it there, but just needed to get her to her room because she was too drunk to get there on her own.

She said "Do what everyone else does. Get other girls to help her, but please stay out of the dorms at three in the morning. I do not want to hear from the parents of the more conservative girls."

She had a point there also. Not all the girl's families were open minded and modern. Some held very conservative believes and if they heard about men in the dorms late at night, they would raise hell. I would be getting everyone in trouble and that did not serve anyone well.

From there on, drunk girls got to wait in the lobby as I woke up their friends to come get them. I still had to sneak into rooms to wake girls up, but it was quiet and no one saw.

My parents were glad I left before they moved into the penthouse atop the dorms. My father became president the summer I left the country and they moved into the President's penthouse. That would have been interesting.

Well, you cannot have it all.

INDOMITABLE SPIRIT

SKIING: CONQUERING THE MOUNTAIN

I had always been interested in skiing, but never got the chance to do it. None of my family skied. And, they never even came close to a resort, except to take us to play in the snow a few times when we were little kids.

Then the war came, and all the ski resorts where either in the Christian area or required driving through them. Thus, none of my classmates in West Beirut skied, and neither did I, until I got to college. There I met a group of die-hard skiers that included national champions and international competitors., and we rapidly became friends in early fall.

That was my chance to learn from the best and enjoy the mountain. I loved the sport from the very first day and could not get enough, and, from there, I was on the slopes any day possible. We had season passes and would hit the slopes in mid-week even if for only a couple of hours.

I was always very athletic, playing multiple team sports, advanced Tae Kwan Do, and expert swimmer, which made skiing a little easier to learn. However, the first few days were extremely painful. There are muscles used extensively in skiing that I never knew I had. But, with strong athletic abilities and determination I pushed through and got to the upper slopes within a couple of days.

After a few runs on the learner's slopes trying to master turning and stopping, one of those champions asked me to join him up the bigger slope. It was at the bottom of the mountain and not a very long run, but it qualified as an intermediate to advanced run due to steepness. That was a tug lift that we braced between our legs and sat on it as it dragged us with skis on the snow to the top. At the top you were supposed to let go and use your upward momentum to turn quickly before you begin to slide backwards.

INDOMITABLE SPIRIT

Of course, he did not explain any of that as it was second nature to him. He rode the tug behind me after helping me onto mine, which was not easy the first time. The lift is always moving and you must grab the swinging pole as it passes by, place it between your legs as it tugs you hard uphill. If not properly aligned, you would be dragged on the ground.

As I got to the top, he was yelling at me to let go of the tug and I could see what the ones in front of me where doing so I let go. But, the skill necessary to properly turn was not there yet, so I slipped and slid and ended up on my ass. I got up as he dismounted next to me laughing. I did not appreciate his smugness one bit. He had been skiing all his life, and I had just started.

He pointed downhill and said "This way." Like I really needed that instruction! Did he think I was going to try skiing uphill? It would have been better if he provided more useful instructions before kicking off and leaving me standing there. For a beginner who could barely stand on his skis that slope looked like a wall with a parking lot at the end of it that I was certain I would land in.

I was really not ready for that but I was not about to be humiliated by walking down the slope. I considered my options and realized that if I descend to the right, the slope is steeper but I would intersect the beginner slope instead of the parking lol. There would be a lot of people in the way, but it was better than cars in the parking lot.

Wedges do not work too well for turning and slowing down on steep hills and I became a rocket heading down the slope until I got to a shallow enough ground to use my wedges, which were not that effective at that speed either. I plowed through the poor beginners like a knife through butter tossing quite a few on the way before I came to a stop.

It was my first kamikaze run, and my friends seemed to take pleasure in watching me crash through everyone. I was their comic relief that day, but they were still disappointed that I did not actually fall. I was tougher than they thought, and I managed to ram into everyone else and remain standing.

When they finally stopped laughing, they began giving me lessons in real skiing. At the rate we were skiing and the crash course in professional skiing, I improved quickly and developed the necessary skills to keep up with the experts. However, I still lacked the years of practice they had and remained the kamikaze skier that everyone enjoyed poking fun at.

Mountain Gypsy

The first year, I had no place to stay on the mountain, and initially would drive up in the morning and back down late at night. However, soon I started taking a small bag with me and find a place to stay with friends where ever there was a space.

A few weeks into the season, I came across another college student on the slopes, whom I knew, but we were not that close yet. After skiing together for a while and her giving me more pointers on proper skiing, she asked where my chalet was. I told her that I had none and would stay were ever I find space.

She had a nice small chalet near the slopes and invited me to stay with her. Not a bad idea, I thought to myself, but did not want to seem too eager to go. "Are you sure?" I asked, "I do not want to burden you. I can find a place with the guys."

"I would love to have you over." She said. "Please."

I did not need too much convincing and spent the weekend with her. That night, there were no nightclubs or big parties for me, but just a cozy evening in front of a warm fire. We did not get too much sleep, but we got more rest than the other nights out.

INDOMITABLE SPIRIT

We would repeat that a few times, but I must have stayed at ten different chalets that season. That was just the nature of the ski crowd, somewhat communal and everyone shared their chalets.

Skiing became a passion. The freedom I felt on those slopes was just exhilarating. The challenge of catching up with skiers that were so much more advanced than me always gave me a rush that kept me coming for more.

Furthermore, the night life on the mountain was fantastic and just made the experience so much livelier. Great friends, beautiful ladies, and kamikaze skiing was my cup of tea, and I could stay there all winter if possible.

Instead of allowing the war to interfere with our joy, we turned it around. We would use any interruption from the war to head out to the ski resort and leave the ugly world behind. As soon as classes were disrupted by political rallies or fighting, we would head for our cars and off to the mountain.

No matter how fierce the fighting got, there would always be some crossing available between West and East Beirut. We would find it and regardless of the danger posed by crossing we went through. We defied the war and turned the disruptions into enjoyable play time.

No one was going to stop the party.

Dislocated Shoulder - 1981

I started running the expert slopes long before I was really ready for them. I just had to push myself to make up for years of experience the others had. I could take a fall as good as anyone, and I was tough enough to make it through the worst falls,

However, there are limits to all of us. On one of those exceptionally steep slopes, as I gained uncontrollable speed, one of my skis caught something and I went flying into an endless tumble. It was one of those comic images, where skis, gloves, goggles and everything else was flying in every direction. Strangers were converging in my directions as they thought I would not walk away from that.

I was mostly fine, except my right arm had at some point dug into the snow hard enough to push my sleeves, Jacket and everything all the way to my arm pit. The shoulder hurt as I stood up, but I did not give it much thought. I continued to ski for the next three hours.

The pain did not really kick in until I finally stopped and the muscles cooled down. By the time I got to Beirut, I could not lift the arm at the shoulder. For the next week, I could not even lift my arm to place it on the desk to write. I could do everything else, but not lift it. I would use my left arm to place my right on the desk.

I was never big on hospitals, but I asked a relative I saw during the week who is a doctor what he thought. He checked it out, asked and few questions and then told me I probably dislocated the shoulder, but it went back into place. He could not tell if anything was torn inside but given that there was no swelling he thought there was probably no serious damage. He told me to rest it and hang it in a sling and see how it develops, and if it does not improve quickly, I should see a doctor.

I did not use a sling and the next weekend I was on the slopes. It was improving, but still hurt for the next month. I did not want any doctors to impede on my skiing by telling me I should not do that, so I just endured the pain.

At least it was just a dislocation. A friend actually fractured his foot on the slopes and finished the day in pain. He rode with me to Beirut that day and half way down as the foot cooled down he was screaming at every curve that put pressure on the foot. I had to help him up the stairs to his apartment. The next day he showed up to college in a foot cast. He skied more than four hours on that broken foot.

INDOMITABLE SPIRIT

INDOMITABLE SPIRIT

DEFYING A 1981 SNOW STORM

On a winter weekend in 1981, we arrived early at the ski resort as we had no late-night activities scheduled in Beirut. I was staying with a friend at his chalet in Faraya village at the base of the mountain that weekend, and we were in a hurry to join other friends for the night. We quickly moved the luggage to the trunk of my car and sped off in his, without entering the chalet. From there we decided to drive back down to Jounieh on the coast for the evening.

It was well after midnight when we came back up the mountain. By the time we got to Ajaltoun, we found a solid thick coating of snow on the ground even at half way up the mountain and a winter blizzard was well on its way. There was no doubt that there was much more snow at higher elevations and getting thicker.

Yet, a blizzard that limited visibility to barely the hood of the car, with blowing heavy snow did not phase any of us. All we could think off is thick fresh snow on the mountain the next day, and we were determined to head up to be ready to ski the fresh snow in the morning.

If we lingered the roads would close as no snow plow would be operating in the pre-dawn early morning hours. So, up we went, the only two cars on the road.

By the time we arrived at Faraya village - 1200m -there was more than half a meter of snow on the ground and driving was getting seriously treacherous. We debated staying collectively at our place and head up in the morning. However, with electricity failing under the heavy snow, our chalet had no heat. It also had no fire place.

The chalet was effectively a third-floor apartment in a concrete building. It was sparsely furnished with a table and four chairs and mattresses on the tile floor. It did not even have curtains to provide the slightest bit of insulation. Humidity inside the apartment was already forming ice sheets on the glass panes.

Our friends were driving a 70s Chevy Blazer with four-wheel drive and oversized snow tires, and they believed they could make it to their chalet at the foot of the ski slopes – 1900 meters -where we could enjoy the warmth of a fire place.

The thought of having the slopes all to ourselves in the morning before the snow ploughs cleared the seven-kilometer winding road between the village and the ski resort to allow the crowds up, was too enticing.

So, the seven brilliant nineteen-year-olds made the decision to go where no man should ever go – up a steep winding mountain road with almost a meter of fresh snow and rising, and blinding blizzard conditions in regular cars in the pre-dawn hours. The blazer with oversized tires is still just a car, but do not tell that to the superhero driving it. He believed it could do miracles. He would later flip it trying to drive it up the side of a mountain.

My 74 Plymouth Valiant was already buried in snow and was not the most effective snowmobile. We decide to use my friends front wheel drive Fiat 127 on the way up. But, with snow already half way up the doors, the only way up was to follow the Blazer as it ploughed a swath through the snow.

The plan worked for a while, but the snow was getting thicker with every passing moments and every additional meter in altitude. Wind was creating snowdrifts in some places higher than the cars.

About half way up, even the Blazer was having a hard time overcoming the thick snow. By then we were facing more than a meter of snow on the road and the only way for the Blazer to move forward was to back up and charge the snow, plowing a few meters forward before getting bogged down. Then backing up and repeating the process.

INDOMITABLE SPIRIT

Looking back, I cannot help but wonder WHAT THE FUCK WERE WE THINKING? We clearly were not.

In spite of the tracks made by the Blazer, the Fiat was much lower to the ground and was still getting stuck in the remaining snow, and we had to emulate the Blazer's charge to clear the remainder.

The blizzard was intensifying, creating blinding conditions with high winds blowing snow in every direction. It was insane to proceed, but we pushed along regardless of the irrationality of our efforts. Once again, the indomitable spirit of youth overcame all reason and rational thought.

Charge up a mountain in a complete White-Out with a can-do attitude fit for the looney house.

To make things worse, the Fiat began to stall every time we charged the snow and fail to restart. We had to get out and push it downhill then put it into gear to jump started it, and we charged again only to stall again and repeat the process.

Up to our waste in snow and blizzard conditions brought snow into every article of clothing we had on. Body heat and the warmth inside the car melted the snow which then froze into ice as we stepped out into sub-zero howling wind.

Two hours into this exercise in futility, by about 3:30 am we were exhausted and developing partial hypothermia. We could not feel our toes or fingers. The only thing keeping us from freezing to death was our constant heavy lifting and pushing of the car. And that effort was getting harder as the snow got thicker and utter exhaustion set in.

There comes a point when even utter fools come to their senses – or maybe it was the primordial instinct of self-preservation. We finally decided it was time to abandon the insane notion of making it to the resort and head back down to our cold apartment in the village. However cold it might be, it could not be worse than the conditions we were enduring. At least we could get out of our freezing wet clothes and lay down and rest wrapped in worm blankets.

The guys in the Blazer refused to give in and decided to proceed on their own. They were even crazier than us. They hurled insults at us for being wusses and losers and charged on.

We later discovered that they never made it to the top. They were forced to abandon the car soon after we turned back and hike the last two kilometers on foot. The fireplace was certainly a welcome site by the time they made it at dawn. It took them more than an hour to stop shivering.

Heading down the mountain was not as easy as we thought it would be. Even though gravity worked to our advantage, the snow on the road had grown even thicker, burying all the tracks we created on the way up. Snow drifts in some places rose higher than the top of the car. We had to dig through it by hand and push the car through the remainder.

At some point you start getting the uncontrollable urge to just lay down – a standard result of hypothermia and exhaustion. They say that when you freeze to death you actually fall asleep and never wake up. We were almost there.

We finally made it to the apartment just before dawn only to find my car buried under a mountain of snow. We were simply too exhausted to dig through the hardened snow to access our luggage and decided to make do without our clothes. It was well past 4:00 am and we desperately needed sleep. We could barely stand.

Since all our clothes were soaking wet and frozen, our only option was to sleep naked and wrap ourselves in all the blankets available. Yet, that was not enough as the temperature inside the apartment was substantially below freezing by then.

The apartment was not designed for this. The windows were leaking and the place was extremely humid. The wool blankets felt cold and humid they were hardening as they froze in that temperature.

We did not get any meaningful sleep that night. Every time I dozed off, I was awakened by the cold which was numbing every extremity. I had to get up and move around to maintain blood circulation and keep from freezing. That cycle repeated several times until the sun came up around 7:00 am.

We painfully put on our frozen cloths and headed down for our luggage, in search for dry cloths. The site was horrific. The snow plows had an early start and managed to pile even more snow on my car. The thought of gaining access to dry cloths was enough to overcome our exhaustion and dig through more than three meters of crusty plowed snow piled over the trunk.

Finally, in dry cloths, we headed out into the village to find something to eat and seek a mechanic to look at my friend's car which was refusing to start at this point. We could not even jump start it.

The only auto shop in the village was closed, but, luckily, we found food as the local baker lived above his bakery. He had not opened, but being regular customers and in dire straits, he obliged us with a couple of sandwiches.

We had no access to the ski slopes as the roads had not been cleared yet and more snow was on the way, so we waited around in front of the local store for the mechanic who never showed up, or cleared roads, which also did not happen by mid-day. We were soon informed that the roads were a mess and would not clear that day. The electricity was still out as the power crews could not get to the downed lines – no heat in the apartment. And, the temperature was well below freezing as we stood in the frigid wind.

Snow was still falling gently, and we were freezing. Our situation was getting more ludicrous by the minute. Exhaustion and freezing temperatures gave me a headache like no other. That was not fun anymore. We prided ourselves on being tough, but that was insane. We all have limits.

We finally surrendered to our fate. We were not getting to the slopes that day and had nowhere warm to stay on the mountain. We decided to leave my friend's car and head down to Beirut in mine, returning for his car later.

It took some more hard labor to get the car out of its spot. The snow ploughs had stopped a couple of meters short of my car, which meant we needed to remove the mountain of snow it created before we could move, and we had no shovels. It had to be done by hand.

Then came the need to enter the car, where the doors were also completely buried. Luckily this was an old car with manual window levers. We cleared enough snow to crack the door open and reach in to roll the window down. Then went through the window, started the car and backed out. We cleared the hood so we can see, but did not bother clearing the roof, as we figured it will slip off as we drive.

It was a long trip down as the snow had covered roads almost to the coast, where there was no available equipment to clear them. And most of the road was under a thick layer that remained unmolested, as all sane people had remained indoors.

When my friend got out of the car at his house in Beirut, he finally realized why we were getting all these strange looks from people all along the road. The ploughed snow had solidified around the ski rack on top of the car allowing it to stay in place all the way home. I had a block of frozen snow on top of the car more than a meter high.

But, by that time we were not going to worry about it. The temperature in Beirut was above freezing, and it could take its time melting away while we slept.

By the time I made it home after depositing my friend, I was ready to collapse. It had been 36 hours since I slept and I had spent almost 24 of those in hard labor under freezing conditions. I crashed into bed at 6:00 pm and did not wake up until noon the next day.

I never appreciated a warm bed in a heated room more than that night.

Oh, and our friends finally got off the mountain on Monday, without ever getting to ski the fresh snow. It took two days to clear the three meters of snow that fell overnight. Three meters in 24 hours is a lot of snow even for a ski resort. Roads must be cleared and equipment must be freed from the snow. And, even the lifts themselves required some work, as the snow piled up higher than the level at which people got on and off.

That did not happen before they needed to head down and back to school.

At least the roads had cleared for them on the way down.

PLAYS AND ACTING

In addition to hanging out with the girls at the Fine Arts building during the day, I participated in student play productions in various capacities. I was mostly support crew, helping build the sets and assisting backstage but I also acted in some as well.

Most of that activity occurred in the evenings and often stretched late into the night as we got everything ready for the play. The fine arts students received grades for their work but we (the volunteers) simply had a great time helping. During my two years at BUC, I was involved in more than 20 plays, and got to know and befriend a lot of exceptional people and made lifelong friends, with relationships spanning far beyond the confines of the play production. We spent a lot of time together at the ski resorts, beaches and other forms of entertainment.

As is customary in the theater, every production ended with a "cast party" which was held for the cast, crew and friends. I attended almost all of them. Sometimes I was not even part of the current play, but always got invited to the party. Those parties were full-fledged celebrations where the enrolled students finally got relief from the stress of putting on a play production and we all danced the nights away as if there was no tomorrow.

It made no difference what was happening around us, and even if there was a flare up in fighting, the party had to go on. We found a way to make it happen. If the venue had to be changed at the last minute, it did, but party we must.

College campuses were a kind of a haven for students in a war-torn city. The students included family members of all the militiamen and as such the campuses were spared from the bombing – with a few exceptions. They were a place to hang out in relative safety and enjoy life, forgetting what went on outside - Most of the time.

As I lived on campus, I had the pleasure of enjoying the company of all who lingered on campus. One could say I always had a lot of guests.

With all this social activity, I would not get to my studies until late at night, certainly no earlier than 10pm, after all the fun stuff is done. I never needed to study much, as I always had a somewhat nonchalant attitude towards studying and was also blessed with a strange mind that could absorb and decipher information very quickly with minimal exposure to input. Furthermore, my field of study (engineering) made it easier for me as comprehension of the main principles with a keen analytical ability would suffice; there was no need to memorize a lot of information.

There were always classmates who gladly shared classroom information and notes from classes I skipped in return for my help deciphering the main principles and helping them understand and pass the course. This type of educational exchange simply allowed me more play time as they attended classes.

Palestinian Camp Late at Night

Around 11 pm one evening, as we worked on stage set up for an upcoming play, one of the girls who was helping started to pack up to leave because the person with whom she was riding home needed to go. Another girl quickly volunteered my services in lieu of the ride she had already secured because this would allow her more time to work. Offering my services was standard practice as any ladies stranded on campus at night could always count on me to come to the rescue.

By about 1 am it was time to call it a night so we headed to my car to drive home both the girl who volunteered my driving services and the newly stranded one. It was at that moment when Lama said "Remember. You need to take Lamia home also but drop me off first since I have an early class tomorrow and cannot afford to spend the night in the car."

"What? Wait! All night in the car!" I said. Turning to the Lamia, I asked "Where do you live?" Most people lived within a five to ten minute-drive from the college when there was no traffic. Since it was already 1 am I knew there would not be any traffic so what could Lama possibly mean by saying that we would be spending all night in the car

Lamia replied: "I thought you knew I lived in Fakhani."

"FAKHANI, THE CAMP?!?" I exclaimed.

She said "Yes."

Fuck me was the only thing I could think. Fakhani was a Palestinian camp south of the city where all the high-ranking PLO officials lived. It was a military fortress and not a place for a Christian from Byblos to drive into at that time of night.

At 1 am, if I did not take the poor soul home, she would have had no other way to get home. But If I was going to be forced into danger, the person who volunteered me was going to go along for the ride. I looked at Lama and said: "If I am to die tonight, you are going with me, since it is your fault that I am having to take this trip anyway."

Lamia tried to ease our angst by explaining that her father is a very high ranking PLO member. She assured us that we would be Okay. In my mind I was thinking, yes, maybe we would be safe near her home but what about the way back when we would have to get past all the other Palestinian strongholds?

Lama complained about being forced to go with me but relented after truly realizing what she had gotten me into. To be fair to her, she had not known where her friend lived either. We both knew she was Palestinian and knew she was connected to the upper echelon but that did not necessarily mean she resided deep in the Palestinian camps.

Thus, our adventure into to the unknown began. Heading there I was not too concerned because I had the daughter of a high-ranking PLO official in the car with me. As we approached the entrance of the Fakhani headquarters we could see that the guards were on full alert. The camp did not usually have visitors that late at night. I drove up to the guard on duty and lowered my widow. He was mid-sentence when Lamia leaned over me and interrupted him. She introduced herself and immediately received a full attention salute. She continued her explanation that I was simply dropping her off and leaving. She instructed him to remain at the guard post until I left in order to ensure no issues which might occur with any potential replacement. My presence at the camp at that time of night was enough to cause alarm and she knew it. I appreciated her attention to detail but still had to say: "Not good enough." We would still need to drive by the Sabra and Shatila camps on our way to get home. Thus, I added: "Ask for a car to escort us all the way past the camps. PLEASE."

We had to wait for an officer to come and authorize this request as it was beyond the authority of the night guard. The officer told us a car would be waiting for us when we returned from her house which was a couple of blocks away.

After dropping her off we saw that a car was indeed waiting and drove in front of us all the way back to Ras Beirut. When we reached our neighborhood and no longer needed the escort, we stopped and thanked them and then went on our way. All the way back Lama was chastising me and saying "You were never in danger. You could have been escorted like this and been safe without keeping me up this late."

I argued back with: "No way was I going to go without YOU. You got me in this situation, and you endured it with me. Next time ask where people live before you offer my services."

"Why did you not ask?" She said implying that I was as much to blame as she was.

I did not agree with her point of view and told her "Well, I did not know I was taking her home until we reached the car. You volunteered my services without asking."

She tried to sweet talk me by telling me how much she appreciated my constant kindness, generosity and willingness to help. While all that may very well be true, there are still limits and that adventure was a little bit over the top.

INDOMITABLE SPIRIT

GREEN LINE CROSSINGS

In spite of the war, crossing back and forth between different zones was constant as we were venturing out all over the country but most of the crossings were simply passing through demarcation lines with little to no fighting taking place. However, despite how simple the crossings often were, we almost certainly had to worry about coming across someone in a bad mood, or someone who may have lost a dear one and were hell bent on seeking revenge. Whatever the lines were, none compared to crossing the green line which separated East and West Beirut. Even when there was no actual fighting, you never knew when a sniper would take position and start shooting people just to disrupt movement. If you were lucky you would not be the first in their sights.

On one of those rare occasions, I found myself driving alone across the green line. It was relatively calm with no major fighting anywhere that day. According to the news, all crossings were supposedly open so there should have been nothing to worry me from taking my car and going my way. I had my own music on which meant I was not monitoring the radio for sudden developments, a big mistake that we seemed to have repeated too often. However, I had the latest Eric Clapton on tape and was just enjoying myself while stuck in traffic.

The straightest route is down the middle of Beirut from the college to Ashrafieh through the Sodeco crossing, and then on to the mountains. After half an hour of heavy slow as molasses traffic through Basta, everyone in front of me veered either right or left, with no one going across. That should have raised a flag in my mind, but with Clapton milking his guitar at full blast on my stereo, I did not stop to think. It only later dawned on me that there was no check point on the West side of the green line, as even the militiamen had taken cover. However, then with the road cleared, I floored the pedal across the green line without a moment's hesitation.

I calmly came to a stop at the permanent Lebanese Army checkpoint on the other side to find that I was the only one on the road. As I looked around, I noticed a hand sticking out the door of the building in front of me waving me to proceed. I slowly pulled forward and leaned over to roll down the right-side window as the hand was attached to a man who was obviously inside the building. He yelled at me saying: "GO. GO. GO." and did not even attempt to exit the building.

I kept driving for another fifty meters or so and pulled into a gas station to fill up. I noticed the man at the station looking at me like he was seeing a ghost. He kept peeking around the wall towards the green line and then back at me. Finally, he asked "Where did you come from?"

I said "Ras Beirut. Why? What is happening?"

Again, he took a couple of careful peeks around the wall and added, "Now? You just crossed over? Now?" There was a small road between the gas station and the green-line but no one drove around there when there was sniper fire. Anyone needing gas usually came to the station from the other side.

I began to hear the questions in my head: Did I miss something? There was nothing happening, yet everyone acted like they were about to die. I said "Yes. Now. Why? What is wrong with everyone?"

He told me there had been sniper fire and several people had been shot while attempting to cross over the Green line, and, he continued, "even the Army is hiding" I realized that. I had just encountered the hand that was waving me on from the building about 50 meters back. But the gas station owner was not done yet and he said, "And, you casually cross over! You need to get out of here. I need to shut down now."

Since my miraculous crossing was already done and I was not shot, I asked him "Can I get some gas before you shut down? You are safe here behind the wall while I fill up my tank." He laughed, shook his head and started pumping gas into my car. I paid and drove off to pick up a friend from Ashrafieh. She asked me which way I came as she was concerned I would not make it due to the fact that snipers had closed the crossings.

I ceased the opportunity to explain that I was invincible and snipers would never prevent me from getting to her. I got a big slap for being a fool and then a bigger hug and kiss to wipe the slap away. She was glad I did not get shot and so was I. So now it was party time.

I guess it was just not my day to die. That day never came as much as we dared the grim reaper. Maybe the snipers took pity on this fool. Or maybe they heard Clapton and just enjoyed the music. Who knows? All that I knew was that I was still alive.

Putting the drama behind us, I got my girl and drove up to the ski resort where we met up with our friends for another weekend on the mountain. We enjoyed Clapton all the way.

INDOMITABLE SPIRIT

STREET THUGS ON CAMPUS

Everyone knew where I stood on the issues and how I felt about the Leftists/Arabists and their Syrian and Palestinian enforcers. We had our share of heated debates and arguments. That being said, educated civilized people can disagree vehemently and still respect each other. We remained friends in spite of our diametrically opposed views.

Yet, we had our share of close calls and confrontations with bad elements from outside the student body.

For, example, we had been planning a concert grouping several local bands for some time, and as it was winter time, the concert was to be held indoors to insure rain did not disrupt the concert, and we picked the main auditorium in BUC as the venue.

We had spent a lot of time and energy organizing and promoting the event and more than two days preparing the space for the concert that was supposed to take place all Saturday afternoon and evening. Friday evening. we had just finished setting up the stage, and decorating the auditorium and the bands had already brought in all the musical equipment, when a group of militia-connected student showed up.

They informed us that there had been fighting in South Lebanon and Israel had bombed several villages along the border. They demanded we cancel the concert in solidarity with the people of the South.

"What do we have to do with any of this?" yelled one of the organizers. "We have been working on this event for months. Look around you."

After a brief argument where the organizers refused to back down and insisted that we had nothing to do with the war in the south, the antagonists left, but not for long. They returned with armed militiamen who warned everyone that they would ensure the concert would not proceed.

All our work was wasted. Everyone had to concede to "solidarity" with the poor dispossessed people of the south, as they called them. When people with guns declared their intent to stop a concert, it would stop. They would make sure no one got in. They would make sure to scare everyone away. They did not like us having fun while others suffered. We all had to suffer in solidarity.

The armed group was led by none other than Ali who would later become the most wanted terrorist on the planet. However, back then he was just a street thug enforcing militia dictates on schools and universities.

I would come across Ali again under different circumstances that year, but, that time, I was the one not backing down. That encounter took place when the students had declared a strike in March of 1981 to contest rising tuitions and decided to have a sit-in in the administration building to press their case. There was nothing unusual about that, as students often complained whenever tuitions were raised and they would shut down the school as their political leaders negotiated with the administration. I had watched my share of those leaders meeting my father at home, as the offices were occupied by the students.

Ironically some students would show up in brand new luxury cars to complain about not being unable to afford tuition. Each car would pay the tuition of several students through graduation, and I would tell them that and point at the fact that my father – the administration – could not even afford to buy me my own car. They would insist that they were supporting the less fortunate and not asking for anything themselves, but the fact was they were obeying their political leaders' orders.

As my father was the administration, I certainly was not party to the student movements, nor were any of my friends. As soon as the college shut down, it was time for us to head out to ski or the beach, depending on the season.

We lived on campus, and my car was parked inside the gates, next to our building and the administration building. The striking students knew that and understood why I was leaving, and would let me out, even when the gates were technically shut for all. These were my classmates and would sometimes joke about me being a spy among them for the administration.

That day was different.

I said hello to the students at the gate, got in my car and started moving, expecting the gate to open. As I turned the car around to get out the gate I saw the striking students arguing with one of the outsiders assisting in the closing the campus – the same thug - Ali.

I pulled up close to the gate and could hear him swearing at everyone and denying exit to anyone. I got out to discuss this, assuming that as usual the students, whom I knew, would eventually let me out.

He was not backing down and would not let me leave, so I told him his issue was with the college administration, not me, and he had no right to infringe on my freedom of movement. I told him he could shut down the offices all he wanted, but how dare he interfere with my skiing time.

He did not appreciate that one bit, charged at me and shoved me against the car, telling me to go back or else. I had always tried to control my temper, particularly when dealing with this type of people for survival. However, there were times when arrogance made my blood boil and fogged my judgement, and that was one of those times. My martial arts training kicked in instinctively, and without much thought, I sprung back from the car with a swift punch that literally knocked him out and broke one of his front teeth.

As he laid motionless on the ground, the students freaked out. The outsiders were seething but were outnumbered by students who did not want the issue to go any further. The students managed to open the gate and get the others out of my way so I could speed out of there.

As I exited, one friend among them told me to stay away until he sent word. I greatly appreciated that but was already well ahead of him. As they were opening the gate, I had told one of the college gatemen, who witnessed the whole event, to get word to my father. I knew this required intervention.

The gatemen had known me for years, since I was a boy, and we had a nice respectful relationship. We had been raised to show caring and respect to everyone, particularly the menial laborers, without whose work none of us could live. They performed honest work for which they deserved to be respected, and, in return, we always had their gratitude and care.

The militia leadership was contacted, Ali was restrained, and I was safe to venture as I wished without fear of retribution. The students who knew him could not believe I physically struck him, yet, in a way, they seemed to enjoy seeing him go down. They may have been politically and ideologically on his side but did not appreciate his mean demeanor.

Nonetheless, that was not a smart move on my part. I could have gotten myself killed by any of the armed men present. Yet, I would live to be foolish again.

The next time, some Leftist/Arabist students decided to have a political rally on campus. In preparation they erected a large flagpole with three divisions to support three flags: The Lebanese, the Syrian and the Palestinian. The stand was in front of the Fine Arts building and could be seen by everyone across the whole central campus and I could see it from my bedroom.

There was nothing unusual about these types of political events, and I usually ignored them, but, as I got dressed, I saw them raising the flags with the Syrian flag center and higher than the others. Palestinian Flag on the right and the Lebanese flag on the left and lower than both.

That was too much for me to swallow. If they wanted to wave their own flags, fine, but this was Lebanon and the Lebanese flag should always fly center and above all. I picked up the phone and called the guidance office, whose director was a good friend of the family and also closely connected to the Socialist Party and the Syrian Nationals Party among others. She knew these students well and had their ear.

I told her what I was witnessing and demanded they switch the flags immediately. She tried to calm me down, telling me to let it go. "They will be finished and out of there in an hour or two."

I just could not do that. Not for a single minute. I told her I would be up there in ten minutes and if the flags were not switched, I was bringing the whole stand down. I did not care about all her warnings that I would get killed, as I was just seething and ready for a fight.

Finally, she pleaded with me to let her handle it, and asked me to stay home until she had a chance to talk to them. I agreed and stood on my bedroom balcony watching across the tennis courts. She got there within the minute and began talking to them, and after a few minutes of stern retribution from her, they switched the flags. The Lebanese Flag flew center and high.

She turned towards me and gestured in a way to ask if I was satisfied. I nodded and proceeded to campus. Most students had seethed at the original flag placement but did not dare say anything, and were glad I did and noticed her gesture in my direction, as did the people who raised the flags.

The demonstrators had a few choice words for me when I got there, but I was not the coy type. I had a few choice words of my own and it almost got physical before some of my friends from the other political persuasion intervened. They kept telling me I would get myself killed some day.

Well I did not get killed. I stood my ground and had the support of most people there.

WAR COMES TO THE MOUNTAIN

By late winter of 1981 a fierce battle for the control of a strategic city in the central Bekaa valley was in full swing. The Christian Lebanese Forces were fighting to take full control of Zahle, a large Christian city just over the Lebanon Mountain range and incorporate it into the territory they control. The city, however, strategically controlled the Beirut-Damascus road and all access between the northern and Southern parts of the Bekaa valley. This made retaining control of the city of paramount importance to the Syrians.

The peaks of Mount Lebanon immediately overlooking the city became an integral part of the battle field as they represented two critical factors in the war. First, the mountain passes were the main supply lines between the Christian controlled areas and Zahle. Second, they strategically overlooked Zahle to the east and Beirut to the west.

The mountain battles had forced the closure of all the upper slopes of the Faraya ski resort which we frequented. Those higher elevations were in the direct line of fire of the Syrians and manned by the Christian Lebanese Forces and the Lebanese Army. The remaining slopes were within meters of the fighting but protected by a mountain ridge from direct fire. They were definitely within range of mortar and artillery shells. However, in a quintessentially Lebanese fashion, life went on in the shadow of a raging war, and we continued to ski the lower slopes.

As was customary in the Lebanon wars, battles had a tendency to expand into other parts of the country without warning in an effort to increase military pressure or divert the forces of the other side from the main battle field. Occasionally additional battles erupted simply because someone refused to be left out of the fight and did not have a presence in the area of the initial battlefield.

In spite of the dangerous proximity to the fighting and the risk of a spreading war cutting us off from our homes, we could not resist heading to the ski resort on that early April weekend. Conditions were ideal, as there was still a lot of snow on the mountain, while the temperatures had risen enough for skiing in short sleeves on that sunny weekend.

As usual, we headed out into the mountains at the end of a late Friday night party in Beirut to avoid the Saturday morning traffic towards the ski resort. This time it was seriously unnecessary, as most people were not about to leave their homes in anticipation of worsening security conditions.

However, not the indestructible youth, who were intent on living life to the fullest under any conditions. As usual, we barely slept a few hours before hitting the slopes at 8:00 am, then skied all day and partied all night, enjoying the fact that we had the mountain almost all to ourselves.

The surreal proximity of the fighting did not faze us. The main chair lift to the upper levels was in constant use by fighters ferrying to and from the mountain battles. Military helicopters constantly hovered overhead, snow ploughs and other snow-worthy equipment were in constant movement. Furthermore, the deafening din of gun fire and explosions were omnipresent.

We were behind the lines of a full-fledged battle, but we skied on. We even used a lift that was designated for mid-range dismount because the top part put us in direct sight of the Syrian soldiers. It was a nice steep slope that we just had to ski, and the trick was to let go just before the top to avoid sniper fire. We would dare each other to get as close as possible to the top, often getting so close we had to duck to keep our heads from being exposed. Flirting with death had become a popular game.

We had no radio or TV in our chalets. We had no need for them since the chalets were only for showering and changing clothes and storing our gear, and we barely even slept during the weekend. So, we were oblivious to developments elsewhere in the country.

Early Sunday afternoon we ran into a local who was shocked to see us still hanging around. He exclaimed "what are you still doing here?" To which we casually and cynically responded "Skiing!" He proceeded to explain that the fighting had engulfed all of Beirut and there were no open roads to the western part of the city. Soon after, the ski resort shut down as the fighting seriously intensified - meaning bullets and shells were now coming over the mountain ridge that had shielded us up till then.

Military equipment was piling up near the slopes and even a field hospital was erected to treat the wounded before they were driven to hospitals farther down the mountain. We were now inside the battle zone, not only across the line from it, and thus we were forced off the mountain.

Crossing Over

Some of us lived within the Christian controlled areas and had direct access to their homes. All of us had either village homes or relatives within the area to be able to wait out the fighting. However, I and two others of us decided that we were better off heading home. Why we made that decision completely eludes me today, and I cannot think of any rational reason that would necessitate doing so, but, then again, I have grown older and wiser since those days. Thus, back to that time, we decided to follow each other in three cars as we had come in, brought the three young ladies who were with us individually to their homes in east Beirut and then headed towards the southern edge of the dividing line, which included an army-controlled crossing that was always the last to close during fighting. This planned course would lead us through some of the roughest Palestinian and Moslem shantytowns but would help us avoid crossing under fire in the completely devastated downtown.

However, a more direct crossing to get home – the National Museum Road - was another option in the vicinity, thus we decided to check if it was passable. The fighting had died down and conditions were fairly calm when we approached the army check point on the east side. Ahead of us and totally in sight was a three-hundred-meter straight boulevard that cut through the abject destruction known as the 'Green Line' and allowed passage into West Beirut.

We asked the soldier manning the checkpoint if there were any snipers – a common occurrence during the war- on the road. He told us that on that day eight people have died attempting to cross but said there had not been any sniper fire for past 20 minutes. We asked if anyone has come or gone through during those 20 minutes as we knew that snipers need targets to shoot at and would surely have been silent if no one was crossing. Unfortunately, he confirmed our suspicion by telling us that no one had attempted to cross within the past 20 minutes.

This newly highlighted situation required a serious meeting of the minds. To the amazement of the soldiers who found it necessary to call their captain to witness what they must have deemed utter lunacy, we got out of our cars and began analyzing and strategizing about how we could cross without dying.

The captain arrived in time to hear us reasoning that the absence of targets for almost half an hour – some time had passed by then – meant that the snipers would have relaxed their postures and put down their guns, and no longer posed in the ready position with eye on their sight and finger on the trigger. Snipers generally have a limited view of the road with a short kill zone. As such, we concluded that if we gain enough speed before we enter into view, we would pass through the relatively short kill zone and out of view so fast that the best the sniper could do was take an ineffective wild shot at us.

INDOMITABLE SPIRIT

Before the captain could pull his jaw off the floor we turned and asked him to point out precisely where the sniper kill zone was on the boulevard. Still in shock from our wild plan he proceeded to point out the stretch of road before he snapped out of it and yelled "ARE YOU CRAZY!?" We replied with the utmost calm and composure by asking him if he was denying us permission to cross. He shrugged and said something to the effect that if we were so eager to die, who was he to stop us. We asked the soldiers to step out of the way as we backed our vehicles far enough away from the check point to gain the most speed before we entered the kill zone.

We made it through with only one wild shot scraping one of the three cars, but to our dismay, we realized as we reached the end of the passage that our plan was not fully thought out. Had it not been for our exceptionally good luck, we would have died on the other side by paranoid militiamen fearing for their lives. As we exited the kill zone we found ourselves approaching the check point on the other side at about one hundred and fifty kilometers per hour with only a few meters to stop. We hit the brakes, down shifted and turned the cars managing to barely avoid running over the check point as we screeched past it sending the young men manning it into every which direction.

We were surrounded by armed men looking on with amazement and concern at all three of us and asking what we thought we were doing. We told them we were headed home from the ski resort, which only added to their amazement that we were skiing in a war zone and now zipping through sniper fire. They let us through without even checking IDs, tapping the top of the cars and wishing us luck. One yelled "God save the brave souls".

I am still not sure if they really admired our bravery or simply thought we were so far over the edge and thus not worthy of their time. Craziness and stupidity often draw sympathy from others.

When I got home that evening I was the last thing my mother expected to see. With telephone lines disrupted earlier that day, she had naturally assumed I would stay on the other side and wait until the roads opened. Even if the mountain resorts became unsafe, I could head to Monsef (my village) and stay as long as necessary. I did not need to take this risk – neither did the others for that matter.

As she saw me open the door, she walked down the hallway and slapped me across the face yelling "ARE YOU CRAZY! WHAT WERE YOU THINKING?! CROSSING IN THESE CONDITIONS!?" Then she hugged me and did not let go, telling me with tears in her eyes that one of those days my guardian angel may not be there to save me.

I can only say she was right, but this was our life in a war zone. And, the guardian angels never let us down.

MISSILE WATCHING FROM A ROOFTOP

The city was engulfed in war and there were no classes the next day under such conditions. We gathered at a friend's house who lived in the tallest building of his neighborhood on top of the hill that was surrounded by old mansions. The roof top had a clear view across the city and perfect for watching the fighting. We could see many of the frontlines and all the mountains east of Beirut, and had a perfect vantage point for watching all the action

The Syrian army had taken over a half-finished skyscraper that we could clearly see on the edge of downtown from which they could dominate the city. They had hoisted rocket launchers onto the upper floors of the unfinished concrete structure and were firing at East Beirut.

On the opposing side, the Lebanese Forces had positions atop another skyscraper on the east edge of downtown and the Army was responding from the hills east of Beirut. We were less than a kilometer from the Syrian positions and almost directly behind them, but we could see the other positions.

We could not see the rockets leaving the Syrian positions, but we could see the white smoke coming out the back side when they fired. The army was using guided Milan missiles that we could actually see headed towards the Syrians. We would watch the trail of the missile until it hit the building, and while some would hit the outside of the building, others managed to enter the open structure and destroy the launchers.

A direct hit on a launcher and ammunition sent a large ball of fire through all sides of the building, as all the ammunition exploded. We would jump up and down cheering the army as it took out the Syrian launchers one by one. The fact that some missiles and bombs were coming into our neighborhood did not deter us from maintaining our position on top of the building.

Suddenly, the metal door to the roof opened with such force that it sounded like one of those missiles had hit the building. The father of the other visiting friend had found out we were on the roof and came calling, and he was an officer in the fire department and not someone to mess with. He walked right up to his twenty-year-old son and slapped him hard enough to lay him down on the roof, then he turned towards us and said "YOU. GO HOME. YOU GET DOWN TO YOUR APPARTMENT."

"Yes sir." We both said as we watched him drag his son off the roof rattling off every insult he could think off. He could not believe we were actually standing on the roof watching missiles fly while everyone else was in bomb shelters.

We got off the roof, but we got the satisfaction of watching the much-despised Syrian army blown to bits for a short while.

SUMMER OF 1981

That summer between the two college years I spent in Lebanon was as hectic and chaotic as can be. I attended summer sessions to insure I completed all my credit requirements within two years for the dual degree, yet, we still had part of the summer free, and of course, we were everywhere during the school session as well.

By that time, my father had acquired the use of college car, and had his car all to myself. Having grown into adulthood, with the complete freedom to wander all over the country, and new friends from college, life took on a whole new dimension.

Furthermore, the people renting the adjacent house from us all these years, had left and the two were opened onto each other. That provided additional rooms, that were not furnished, and ideal for those large groups of friends who came over for weekends. As it was originally a separate apartment, it had its own entrance that allowed us to get in and out without much disturbance to everyone else in the house.

All friends were welcome, they brought sleeping bags, and packed into those large rooms at will. We had a fantastic beach available free and it came with free lodging as well. What more could they hope for. Others, who were not that close often brought tents and camped at the beach for a few days.

My classes in the summer were in the morning, leaving the whole day free, with the flexibility of doing anything I felt like. While on weekends the beach was packed with people, including my friends, weekdays were generally quite with few people, except for the young kids who did not have school. That was the time for any intimate trip to the beach, whenever I wanted to spend time alone with a beautiful lady, and I took advantage of that often.

My grandparents, in their old-fashioned ways, did not appreciated my bringing ladies alone, particularly different ones every time, but it never stopped me. They would chastise me and ask what type of women would come spend the day alone with a man. Try as I did to explain to them that times had changed from when they were young, they never bought into it and were never happy with it.

On one occasion one of my lady friends tried to take a shower and found no hot water in the bathroom she was using. There were two separate hot water tanks for the bathrooms, and she needed to use the other one. She wrapped herself in a towel and walked through the living room to get there, right in front of my grandmother. That freaked my grandma out, and she would not stop rattling on about it, until the girl came out of the shower, at which time she tried to maintain civility. However, her demeanor said it all, and my lady friend knew she had made my grandma uncomfortable.

We were all over the place, even when gasoline supplies were in serious shortage. The Syrians had been trying to squeeze the Christians into submission and had interfered with deliveries into the area. Gasoline never ran out, but we were limited to twenty liters per filling at any time. Furthermore, sometimes gas stations would not even give us any, if they did not know us, thus saving their gas for their regular customers.

My 1974 Plymouth Valiant did not go too far on twenty liters, but luckily, we were not that far from an abundance of gas just to the north of us. We would cross over the dividing line, and barely ten kilometers away, we could fill up the tank at an even cheaper price. I told my friends that, and they would fill up there every time they came to visit and not worry about limiting their trips.

One of those days, three large American cars headed to fill up, and found the power disrupted at the gas station. The owner told us we could pump the gas manually if we wanted, and pretended it was not that hard. The old pumps had a crank lever that we could turn and pump gas out, and we spent the next hour taking turns turning that lever, as it was exhausting and very slow compared to electric pumping. We never did that again, and whenever the power was out, we would leave and return when it came back.

With gas available to everyone, people where coming and going at will, and I never knew who would show up and when. They would show up and tell me they were staying for a couple of days, taking the accommodations for granted. I loved the company, and never bothered me for one second. The communal mentality of the ski resort had transferred to the beach, and we just continued the party uninterrupted.

Disrespecting the Sea

Having played the waves all our lives, by the time we reached adulthood we had gained enough experience to make it look easy for anyone not familiar with it. My out of town friends knew enough to stay away in really rough seas, even though many were expert swimmers and divers. They knew enough to respect the power of the sea and realize they did not have the skill we mustered over the years. Yet, there was always an arrogant idiot, who refused to listen to reason.

One late morning my friends arrived from Beirut to find me playing in four-meter-high waves. They called me from the concrete pad and I dove in and headed into the lagoon to meet them. As I climbed up the steps I found them arguing with a friend of theirs who wanted to try his luck. I barely knew this guy, but he was a large man, built like a refrigerator and believed that his strength made him able to do it better than me. He was not listening to them telling him that I grew up on these rocks and had the necessary experience that they lacked.

With him insisting and heading there regardless of my assistance, I told him to come with me on condition he listened and obeyed any instructions I gave him for his own good. I gave him the standard physics explanation about water weight and force and told him "You will stand where I tell you. If I tell you to move or jump, you act immediately. You do not have the luxury of asking why or debating. The waves will crush you and drag you on the rocks."

He agreed, but apparently just to shut me up. We swam out to the Blata, as we got there, he headed straight to rocks with extreme lack of knowledge and ended up rolling up the slope and dragged partially back along the flat surface. He was lucky the wave he caught was a relatively small one. I followed him up on the next wave and turned to see a monstrous wave cresting just off the rocks – the highest yet that day. I told him to run down the slope and dive head on into it as hard as he could and swim out as I descended the slope to meet the wave.

Instead of listening to me, he stood at the top of the slope – the most dangerous place to be with that type of wave – and assumed a sumo wrestling position to confront it, giving it the maximum surface to strike. He ignored all my yelling and held his position. I knew what he was about to endure, and lucky for him I had enough experience to save him part of the agony that was coming. I did not dive into the wave nor tried to resist its pull back, but instead I allowed the wave to carry me up following him as he tumbled and scraped against the rocks.

Experience that included a whole lot of cuts and bruises over the years gave me the ability to run and walk up the rocks with the waves without falling over. I also knew the rock in detail, and knew were the holes and sharp jagged edges were to manage to run and walk with the way without injury. I kept my head above water and could see him intermittently as he flailed in the curling water, and finally, caught up with him as the wave was reaching the end of its range twenty meters up the rocks. I grabbed him and nail him in a depression in the rocks to keep him in place, and prevent him from being dragged bag to sea by the retreating water, which could do even more harm.

As the wave pulled back, I told him to get up and move inwards, but he was livid, and he kept yelling at me "How could little you do this? I am twice your size and I could not handle the wave". I told him "If you wish to live to learn why, you better get your ass up and move before the next, even bigger wave, hits you."

He moved as he saw what was coming our way – survival instinct - but did not stop cursing me and yelling about how I could do this. Everyone else was laughing hysterically at him and telling him "We told you." That only made him madder and added to the curses coming my way, as if I was the cause of his pain.

He had cuts and scrapes all over as he tumbled and dragged across the rocks, but luckily no real harm. I collected a lot of Tayyoun for him, which is a small shrub that grows along the coast with moist sticky leaves, and when mashed and placed on a wound, it stops the bleeding and disinfects the wound. We had used those plants extensively over the years.

As we placed the mashed Tayyoun against his wounds his attentions turned from cursing me about the waves to screaming about the burning sensation from the application. He finally calmed down enough to listen to reason, and I tried to explain this in physics terms, again, explaining that the bigger he was the more surface the wave had to push on and the harder it would push him. As an engineering student he understood the principle. Then I explain how we prevent the wave from having a flat surface, which he also understood and finally conceded that he acted stupidly and was arrogant by not listening to me. He had to endure a lot of pain for his arrogance, and I hope that was a meaningful lesson regarding listening to the advice of people who have more experience than him.

LABNEH IN SHTAURA

One Friday night in in the summer 1981, or more accurately Saturday morning as it was past three after midnight. Our party in West Beirut was dying out and we were getting ready to cross over to head to the beach. This was preplanned, and all had their stuff in their cars, including tents for those who needed them.

Everyone was hungry and would not be able to sleep without eating, so I suggested we stop at our friend Abou-Ali in Byblos on the way to our village for some manoushes. The bakery would be open by the time we got there, and everyone agrees, except one. He wanted a Labne sandwich, so we promise to find an early grocery store to get him some labne on his manoushe.

"Shtaura" he said.

"What! Are you nuts!" another retorted. Shtaura was over the mountains in the Bekaa valley across quite a few check points and through multiple not so hospitable terrain. They went on about it being three in the morning and dangerous and out of our way, but he held his ground and insists that by the time we made it out through all the check points they would be open for breakfast. Plus, he insisted, we had nothing pressing waiting for us, so we could sleep all day when we finally arrived at Monsef - big deal. We would be up for the evening party.

Somehow that all made sense to some of us. Shtaura is renowned for its labne, and people swore by the great sandwiches, especially on fresh bread. However, driving two hours in each direction, crossing multiple military zones in the predawn hours for that would be considered flat out crazy to most, but not to us. "Why not" was the response.

Not everyone agreed, so one car headed over the mountains to Shtaura while the others headed straight up the coast to sleep and wait for us.

We crossed into East Beirut and started up the mountains through the Lebanese Forces check point and then the Lebanese Army check point before we would need to cross into Druze territory and then Syrians and Palestinians.

The soldier at the Lebanese army point checked our ID cards and asked where we were headed, curious as to what would bring us there. None of us was from anywhere near the area and it was past four in the morning by then.

"We are going for labne sandwiches in Shtaura." We told him. He cracked up laughing in disbelief. We reassured him that we were just going for sandwiches and then headed back to the Byblos area.

"Yeah. Sure." He says. "Bring me some." he continued as he let us through. We promised to bring him back a sandwich and drove off.

It was past five in the morning when we arrived in Shtaura. The sun was not out yet, but darkness was lifting. We turned to the man who started all this and asked "Where do we go from here?"

"Hell if I know." He said.

"You idiot brought us here and you do not know where to get the sandwiches?"

"We can ask." He said. "They would know."

They who? It was still mostly dark and all sane people were asleep. We were the only lunatics lost in a part of the country none of us was familiar with at that hour, so we drive around looking for a bakery as we figured they would be open and making bread by then.

We stopped and asked the first baker we saw where we could get labne sandwiches, and he asked if we were going hunting given the hour we were driving through and the fact we did not know where to find a sandwich. It would have been better to claim we were hunters, at least we would look sane. No. The idiot took pride in his insanity and boasted about driving up from Beirut just for the sandwiches.

The baker seemed amused by the story, but I am not sure he really bought it. He told us we were in luck, as he made labne sandwiches - The best labne sandwiches according to him. Well, how would we know if that was true or not?

We ordered sandwiches and sat down on the one small table he had in the corner and enjoyed them. By then, we were really starving, and when one gets really hungry all food tastes really good, so we will never know if he had the best sandwiches or it was our hunger. Not that it really nattered anyway, as none of us could find the place again if our lives depended it.

We got up to leave, and suddenly remembered the soldier whom we promised to bring back a sandwich. We ordered four sandwiches, enough for everyone manning the road. Army soldiers always deserve our kindness. The baker actually began to believe our story and was looking at us with a mixture of amusement and petty. He must have thought we were really crazy and he would not be wrong. Looking back at it, I think we were crazy also.

We drove off as daylight was taking hold and reach the army check point a little before seven in the morning. We asked about the soldier that was manning the upwards traffic three hours earlier., as we did not have a name but only a description.

"Why do you ask? He said. We told him that we promised him a labne sandwich on our way back.

He broke out into a big laugh. "No way!" he says "You were telling the truth!"

He told us the soldier had told all of them about that as an example of all the bullshit he hears from people. He thought our story topped all in being unbelievable. He was saying "Can you believe people expect me to buy this crap." Well it was not crap, we had sandwiches for him. He had just not met nuts like us before, or, maybe, the other nuts hid their lunacy and gave a reasonable fake excuse.

He asked us to pull up off the road to allow traffic to pass through and called on another soldier to go wake up George – I still remember his name. George was up all night manning the check point and had only gone to sleep at six, but he got up anyway to see us. That was too much for him let it pass. An officer also showed up to see the crazy people as he put it jokingly.

We gave George the sandwiches and told him we got enough to share with the crew. We asked the officer to allow them to enjoy them, as the army is strict on these things. He agreed with big grin and said given what we had just done, it was the least he could do, but he insisted he got his share. Who were we to deny him.

We drove off oddly content with another act of daring stupidity. By the time we reached our beds it was past eight in the morning, the sun was up, and so were my grandparents. They were wondering why all my friends were camped out at our house when I was not there. I was too tired to discuss it and certainly was not about to tell them that story. They already thought I was crazy enough, so I said I just needed to sleep and will explain later.

FEDERATION SCOUT CAMP

Past high school, my scout activity had seriously tapered down. All The parties, girls, skiing, and other fun activities just did not leave any time for the scouts. However, I remained part of the troop and partook in any event I found interesting.

In the fall of 1981, the federation held a leadership training camp, which was held in the hills above Beirut, near the defense ministry. Troupes from all over the country showed up trying to impress everyone with their discipline and abilities, but we were there to have fun, as usual, and by then the open-air sleepers were all in the leadership.

Friday night, after setting up camp, the federation leadership made a tour to inspect the various sites and found us laying in open air. They objected and began to tell us how we should be in our tents. Boys here, girls there. This is the scouts, blah blah blah, but we were not listening. Eventually, the troupe leader told them not to waste their breathe, we simply do not know how to sleep in tents.

Right next to us was a troupe that came from Zahle, over the mountains and were somewhat intimidated by the whole ordeal. They were new and did not know what to expect and to their luck, we get a hold of them. By the end of the weekend, they were as undisciplined as we were, and enjoying it.

Saturday morning, they marched everyone to a spring a kilometer away to wash up and brush their teeth. One of the girls had an uncle who lived nearby and suggested we head there to wash up and have some nice coffee. Sounded like a good idea, but how do we get out of the crowd, so the other girl and her told the leaders that they need to go to her uncle because of woman reasons. They eventually had to spell it out and tell them they had their periods and needed a real bathroom and the leaders relented and allowed them to drive there.

INDOMITABLE SPIRIT

A friend and I straggled in the back of the long line marching towards the spring and as the car came by we hopped in the back and laid low as we passed the whole line. We used the bathroom at her uncle's, shower, had coffee and then returned. The group was at the end of their march back to camp when we caught up with them so we hopped out of the car and pretend like nothing happened.

Saturday night was campfire night, and the federation had specific rules on how to sit and how to wrap your blanket or sleeping bag over one shoulder, etc., all of which we did not care about. This was an instructional camp to teach us how to teach the younger scouts, but we were already beyond repair. Plus, it was a warm night and wrapping ourselves in sleeping bags was torture, so some of us got tossed out of the gathering for failing to follow protocol and were told we would not be served dinner, which consisted of bread, cheese, spam, and a baked potato.

There were better treats in the camp storage up the hill that we preferred. We had seen the leaders bring in some delicious cheese pastry, and other goodies and put them in the portable fridge earlier, and already had our eyes on that. With everyone busy at the camp fire gathering, we could sneak in and indulge ourselves and so we did. Two guys from the Zahle group had decided to skip the fire for some reason and saw us, so we invited them to join in the feast, and they never said a word.

We saved some for our leaders as we knew we would be accused of this when the would be found empty. We preempted that by offering our leaders the treats before the federation guys came knocking and made them complicit in the crime. Then we relaxed and watched them defend us, or themselves to the federation. Our illustrious leader actually turned the tables on them telling them that the rules said we should all be eating the same stuff. Why would they be treated to something better? And, of course he denies we did anything. There was no evidence of a crime so they could not pin it on us.

In any event we did not care. It was our last year in scouts, and we just wanted to enjoy ourselves.

INDOMITABLE SPIRIT

CHALET 70

In our second year of college, four of us decided to get our own chalet in Faraya, the main ski resort we frequented. Most of our friends' families owned or rented a chalet in the ski resort, and we had gotten tired of sleeping on people's floors, or driving back and forth every day.

The owners of Chalets near the slopes did not like renting to young people, and almost all had a standing rule of only renting to families. They feared young people will not take care of the facility and end up causing a lot of damage.

We had to lie and cheat to get our own, and we rented under the name of only one person, who pretended his family was renting it. It was dishonest, but necessary, if we were to have a place on the mountain. Thus, Chalet 70 in the Avalanche complex became our home for the winter of 1981-82, and, in essence, became the communal chalet of everyone we knew.

The Avalanche was built on a cliff high above the road below it with a magnificent view of the valley leading to the sea. It was a series of buildings along the road above it with one single building in the middle situated farther back placing it literally on the edge of the cliff, and that is where our chalet was.

Our balcony stood more than 50 meters above the road, and the mountain just dropped further down from there. We would joke about our secondary exit off the cliff for those we do not like. We had to walk down a series of steps to get to it, which during the winter were constantly buried in snow. In fact, the owners cut steps in the snow and then we had to walk around to our front door, which would be completely below the top of the snow.

The snow would often reach the level of the bedroom balconies on the second level of the chalet. On one occasion, a friend was visiting and slipped down the snow all the way to the chalet and ended up hanging off the balcony rails. I was in the bedroom when I heard him scream and then a loud thud. I looked out and there he was hanging from the rail, so I opened the sliding door and let him into the bedroom.

The chalet quickly became party central. I do not recall a weekend that did not have at least 10 people sleeping there, and sometimes twenty. Often even our friends whose families had their own chalets would spend the night there to avoid driving drunk on slippery narrow mountain roads or just because.

More importantly, all our friends who did not have a place of their own now had a home in what had come to be simply known as "70". Not only did we not mind having them over, we actually enjoyed it. The ski resort was party time, and the more the merrier. They left their ski gear there, and always had a place to sleep when needed - Not that we slept that much. We would arrive on Friday, ski all day and party all night and rarely leave before Monday morning.

Saturday morning traffic was simply horrendous heading up to the slopes. So, no matter how late a night we had in Beirut, and we often had, we headed straight up the mountain. That way we would be on the slopes at 8:00 am and ready to start our ski day.

We stopped trying to be honest to people at check points in Beirut about where we were headed, as they would simply argue with us and think we are lying about going to a ski resort at two or three or four in the morning. We started telling them we were headed home in east Beirut, just around the corner. It was much less headache.

We skied nonstop for eight hours until the lifts closed with no lunch break, and always the last down the slopes. We spent so much time on the slopes we knew all the people who ran the lifts and always managed to get one more run after everyone else was done. We were young, athletic, and tireless.

The weather was never a deterrent. Sunny snowy, or even a blizzard we were on the slopes. There were times when we were the only ones, as all sane people headed for shelter from blizzard conditions, but not us. We took pride in being the tough ones who could ski through anything, even zero visibility and driving sleet at 50 km/hr – that was painful.

One day, conditions were so horrendous, that we had to beg the operators to let us up the mountain, but that was a very short day. Wind was blowing so hard up the mountain, that it literally prevented us from heading down the mountain. I stood there with skis pointed downhill and was actually being pushed up hill by gale force gusts. The wind brought with it sleet that hit our faces like pellets from a shot gun.

We finally had to traverse the hill and descend the back side away from the wind and then shuffle back around. The operators had been watching us and welcomed us with derision. One said "I told you, you did not want to go up there." Well, that day he was correct, but most other times he was not.

After the lifts closed we headed back to the chalet where removing our ski boots felt like heaven after eight hours of hard skiing. Boots in the early eighties were not as cushy or insulated as they are today, and by the end of the day, our feet would be frozen, which actually helped numb the pain from the hard edges digging through our flesh.

We started a fire and stuck our feet in front of it until we could feel our toes again. Then came the pain of the partial frostbite, yet, it we were happy and exhilarated. We had something to eat, and then off for a brief nap to ready us for the night. Sometimes we simply fell asleep in front of the fire.

A couple of hours later after we hit the showers we tried to do some studying and homework before the party began. We were college students after all, and we brought our books to party town - No computers back then, just books, pens and paper. The party never started early anyway.

INDOMITABLE SPIRIT

By ten or eleven we headed out for the evening on the mountain or along the coast down more than 30 kilometers of winding roads. We had a late dinner, and then whatever the night brought.

On some occasion we actually managed to get 3-4 hours of sleep before heading back to the slopes on Sunday, but most nights we did not. There were times when we simply came in, changed cloths and headed out to the slopes. Those were the days when we were young and relentless. We were out all night Friday and Saturday and skied two consecutive days, and still had the stamina to go out on Sunday night.

On a few occasions we drove down to Beirut on Sunday night, if we had a test or some other pressing issue early Monday morning, but it was always late because those days the traffic pattern was quite different from today. Morning commutes to work were rare, as people mostly lived in the city they worked in and the kids went to school there. However, many people exited the city for the weekend, which meant too many people were headed back into the city on Sunday evening creating traffic jams that lasted hours. We always tried to avoid that and would rather enjoy the time on the mountain and drive late than spend four hours in traffic.

We always had a full house at the chalet. Normally we always had friends and girlfriends with us, and always expected someone to stop by with no place to go. We did not lock the door during the day to allow them to access the place, and all our friends knew this. We were like one big family.

Several times we walked in on friends making use of our bedrooms with their significant others. They did not even feel the need to ask permission, but just took the place for granted.

That was "70". It was everyone's place.

At night we shared beds and some slept on the couches and the floor. We were a close group, who shared a lot of our lives together. Aside from the specific romantic relationships, we had many female friends who were regulars at the chalet and sometimes even brought their boyfriends. When alone, there was no qualms about sharing beds. It was the kind of close friendships that transcended the normal gender relations.

I have slept many times with a woman on a single bed with a single cover. That meant bodies pressed against each other and half naked, yet, no sexual relations. We sometimes even discussed each other's relationships with other people while in such positions.

There were cases of relationships developing and then ending, and yet the friendship remained. Even occasional one-night stands between friends that never ruined the relationship.

It was truly a season to remember by all measures. We bonded in ways that few people ever have a chance to do. We shared each other's joys and sorrows, counseled each other, provided advice and guidance when needed and assisted each other in our studies. We teased and harassed each other whenever possible, pestered and annoyed each other to extremes, fought and made up, but that seemed to have only brought us closer together.

The war played a big role in all this. We were living in a world where death was around every corner and any second could be our last. We raced through sniper allies and slalomed between artillery shells to get to the ski resort. We braved road-blocks of armed gangs any of which could pick us up to never be seen again. As such, we lived for the moment and did not worry about tomorrow because it may never come. We enjoyed every second we could and overcame any negativity quickly to get back at having fun. It was our way of resisting the ugliness of a war that we did not understand nor believe in. The whole world seemed to be solving its problems at our expense and in our midst, destroying everything we held dear, but we were not going to succumb to it.

We were determined to live it up no matter what the world said, and we won. We lived, loved and laughed against a global attempt to make us weep. We played between their bombardments and thumbed our nose at the invaders. We turned war obstacles into challenges that we took pride and pleasure in overcoming.

We survived, and now look back at the war years with a nostalgia often reserved for tropical island escapes. The horrible memories of death and destruction are overwhelmed with joyful memories of deep friendships, parties and playful resilience.

We are the war generation.

A Check Point Near Us

We had the chalet from mid-November to mid-May. Even though the ski season is a little shorter than that, we had to rent for six months. We would head out to the mountain for the weekend even before the snow came to hang out and party. That is what it was all about after all.

The war on top of the mountain that shut down half the ski slopes also placed a military check point by the Christian Militia just up the road from our Chalet – No more than fifty meters from where we parked our cars. Those guys had little to do any way as a Lebanese Army check point was placed past the resort on the road over the mountains to the Bekaa, and no one was ever going to attack from below since that was their territory, but there they sat.

In those early days before the snow came, there would not be that many people on the mountain and not that many people passing through the check point, which made for a very boring post. We, however, had to drive past it to get to the slopes and even get to the grocery store, restaurant and many of our friends' chalets, so we became their entertainment.

They would see us getting out of the Chalet and getting in the car, yet as we approached they would ask where we were coming from and where we were going. On the way back, they asked the same questions.

At first, we obliged, but after a few times, it was getting old and annoying.

As I approached the check point and before the militiaman could ask his idiotic questions, I yelled out the widow: "I am coming from hell and going to hell. Anything else you want to know?" I continued "Have you not memorized us yet!"

He laughed and said "We are bored and need entertainment."

I said "Get some cards and play with your friends. You are not at risk of an attack anyway. Just leave us alone."

He apologized and stopped pestering us with stupid questions. Anyway, soon the crowds came and he had enough people go through to keep him entertained. He would waive us through and pester others.

THE OLD NAG

Of all the plays I participated in "Sir slob and the Princes" stands out. That was a story of a king who set a series of challenges for those who wish to marry his daughter. Sir slob was a bumbling fool who decided to try his luck and succeeded with the help of an old nag– ME. It was a collaborative production by two students, as the play was quite complex relative to others and had a sizeable cast.

As we practiced for the play. we were improvising and changing the script all the time. Some of the changes were intentional as we thought they were funnier, but often we forgot our lines and improvised on the fly. At first, the producers of the play were getting seriously upset with us diverging from the script and making thigs up as we go, but, slowly, they started appreciating some of our infusions.

Since writing the script from a story was part of their effort, no one would know who injected what into the script. They could even get a better grade if the play became funnier, and it - It was a comedy after all. However, our lax playful approach to the whole thing made them nervous, as we had nothing to gain or lose, but they were being graded.

It turned out to be smashing success. The professors and their colleagues liked it so much that they asked us to put on two more shows one in BUC and another in AUB so more people could enjoy it. This had never happened before.

And it was all because the old nag – ME – whom everyone mistook for a donkey. I wish I could take all the credit, but I cannot. We all did our share. The donkey part, however, is mostly my fault, as I distracted the make-up artist and caused her to do a bad job. It was not that easy to distinguish facial make up between a horse and a donkey to start with.

They had brought in a professional make-up artist due to the extensive make-up required, as there was a horse, a lion, and several other animals, young students had to be made to look old, etc. She was gorgeous, not much older than us, and I was me.

I was flirting with everyone and playing around as my turn came for makeup. I had my horse suit tied around my waste and shirtless to keep the makeup off cloths. To hold me still, she straddles me in my seat, short jeans skit and white translucent shirt with no bra. With perfect breasts staring me in the face, skirt lifting up to expose panties pushing against my crouch, what was I to do.

She was bringing out a different animal in me than a horse, and my mind was already past the performance and at the cast party. I needed to convince this gorgeous lady to come along before she finished my makeup, otherwise she may not be there when we are finished the play because we did not need her to remove makeup.

I failed in that mission, as she had something else to do, or so she said. Nonetheless, I fear my flirting with her and her clear attempt to tease me by sitting on me had a serious effect on her artistic abilities, and I ended up looking like a donkey. Come to think about it, maybe there was a lesson there. When you act like an ass you may just end up looking like one.

I was feeling like I was losing my touch, but all was not lost, she would be back again and I would not be busy performing. I had only helped set the stage and had nothing to do during that play, so after makeup we were both done with our jobs and ready for recreation.

We put on one of the best plays in the history of the school and enjoyed every minute of it. That is what I call enjoying our work.

Cast Party Car Overload

That was a grand cast party, as the play had a lot of actors, who all invite friends. The party was held in a large old apartment that had high ceilings and open space, ideal for a party, and we danced into the early hours of the night.

Eventually, the crowd began to thin. One by one, people head out, until there were only nineteen of us left. It was past three in the morning and we decided to call it a night. As I prepared to leave, a girl said: "Do not leave without me, you need to take me home."

"OK." I said. She did not come with me, but she wanted to stay past her ride's departure. I only had one girl with me and could easily accommodate her.

Then the one next to her said: "Me too."

Then, another, and they begin to rattle off "Me Too."

"Wow. Wow. Wait a minute. Does anyone else have a car here?"

None had a car. It turned out they all rode there with someone else, and as their ride wanted to leave they decided they can catch a ride with me. None of them bothered to tell me and they just assumed it would be ok. No one expected that everyone was riding with me. I had a big American car, but this is ridiculous.

Someone suggested I make several trips. "Fuck, no. I am not spending the rest of the night driving around town." I told them they had to fit themselves in the car somehow and I would make one round. I was not a very long ride, anyway, as we all lived within a kilometer of each other.

Any bags, even hand bags, one guy had a guitar, had to go in the trunk to increase the squeeze capacity. Luckily, all were relatively thin and agile, as it took some contortion to get all of them in. Six guys squeezed into the back seat and five girls sat on their laps, knees crushing against the front seat and heads pushed into the ceiling.

Another three got on the solid seat next to with three more on their laps kissing the windshield. The last one, the girl who came with me had to straddle my left thigh, with her right leg between my legs and she leaned in front of me to allow my left arm to reach around her to drive. This was a stick shift, but the stick was in the dash allowing for a full seat. However, I still needed to reach the stick from between the people crammed against me and use the clutch with the leg that was straddled by a girl.

We had planned the route before we crammed into the car, as we needed to drop off the most amount of people as early as possible to gain some breathing room before they get permanently contorted out of shape. We also need to minimize the length of the trip and not end up retracing myself as I dropped people off randomly. Furthermore, I preferred to start the route downhill if possible as I was not sure the car could climb a hill with that load.

The girl on my lap was the closest to the party and we drove in front of her building to reach all the others, but she was riding with me. She would be the last dropped off because we still had some "business" to take care of before the night was done.

The car made it, and I got everyone home, and the sun was coming up by the time I got home. That was a good night - One to commit to memory.

SPEED DEMONS AND MOUNTAIN DARE DEVILS

I was the only one with a large rear-wheel drive American car. All the others had small European cars with front-wheel drive and much better designed for winding mountain roads and snow. Furthermore, I did not just have any American car, I had a 1974 six-cylinder Plymouth Valliant, one of the least stable cars that would fish tail at the mere hint of a curve or moisture.

Everyone initially joked about the "Hajji" as my car came to be known. They could not believe it could handle the winding roads and snow, but it did. I made it do what no one thought such a car can do. The more I did that, the better I got at it. I could maneuver those curves at speeds exceeding one hundred kilometers per hour, when sport cars were slowing down. I could race any of their sporty European cars any day.

Those who later drove rear-wheel drive cars would come to me for advice. They knew if I could race that car on mountain roads, I had the expertise necessary for rear-wheel driving. I taught them how to take sharp curves at high speed, how to precisely drift into a curve, and how to compensate for the drift without overcorrecting. On those mountain roads with deep ravines and no guard rails, there was little room for error.

As much as everyone made fun of my Hajji, they all eventually grew to love it. It was roomy and could carry a lot of people, it Certainly could perform in the right hands – mine - and it was safe. Old American cars were made of steel and could take a beating that no European car could take.

One evening as I drove through Byblos, not at a slow speed, I was forced to swerve to avoid a car exiting a parking in a spot that had oil on the road. That forced me completely off the road on the left and into a high voltage power pole.

It was a large steel truss pole with its base almost one meter above street level. There was a stone wall in front of it and, luckily a big rock in front of the wall. Luckily, because that rock saved the car, as it was low enough to slip under the bumper but high enough to hit the steel beam that held the radiator. When the bottom hit the rock, the car rose above the wall and hit the pole directly, bending it and snapping the power lines. It rolled back and dismantles the stone wall into rubble.

Naturally the car stalled. We unbuckled our seat belts and started to open the doors to get out when we noticed power lines dancing around us with huge sparks everywhere and people yelling at us not to get out. The car was protected by the rubber tires but stepping on the road would be fatal.

I turned the ignition and to my surprise the car started, so I backed out and took it across the road away from the power lines to check it out. To everyone's surprise there was nothing wrong with the car. The collision with the pole had barely left a mark on the steel bumper that we could not really call a dent, the engine was running with no leaks anywhere.

We proceeded on our way and enjoyed a long night, leaving thousands of people without power due to the severed high voltage lines. There was nothing we could do about the severed lines anyway and no reason to ruin our party hanging around.

I realized the next day in daylight that the steel beam under the radiator had a major dent in it, and it had bowed the whole radiator, yet, somehow, the radiator did not break. That radiator was never changed, and nothing had to be fixed. All was good.

In fact, the collision fixed my speedometer that had been messed up for some time. The needle would rise as I accelerated to a certain point in a very noisy manner and then snapped back to zero and stayed there, until I stopped and moved again, and then it would do the same thing. I meant to fix it but had not gotten to it.

That evening after the collision, the speedometer worked fine. It did not seem to accurately indicate the speed but there were no more noises or snapping back. I never cared what the speedometer said anyway so all was fine.

I told my father that I fixed the speedometer, and when he asked where and I told him. After a few seconds of confusion, he was both entertained by the fact I saw the positive in it and upset that I caused all that damage and just drove off. Oh, well.

Beyond Reason

One of our craziest acts came in winter of 1982. Realizing we were late for a rendezvous on the coast while still at the top of the mountain, and having no means of contacting the other people, it was time for the run of our lives. I would never do that again. The alarm did not go off and we woke up late in "70". We had ten minutes to be in Junieh to drive to the Cedars for a ski race that Sunday.

We hastily got dressed and hauled our gear to the cars, strapped the skis on top and only had six minutes left. We needed to take both cars down to avoid coming back up for the one we leave behind as we were heading straight to Beirut from the Cedars at the end of the day. We floor the gas peddles downhill. The other guy was driving an Alfa Romeo GTV, six-cylinder engine, five-gear and designed for speed, while I had my Hajji with three in the dash.

We made the trip of almost thirty kilometers in less than ten minutes. That is an average of almost two hundred kilometers per hour on winding mountain roads. Speeding uphill was rash enough, even though gravity worked to our advantage when we needed to slow down or stop. Speeding downhill was just simply insane, or, at least now, I see it that way

I could see the Alfa Romeo tip on two wheels around at least half the curves and was sure I was on two wheels also. I was praying he would not tip over, because, if he did, I would plow right into him and we would both plunge into a ravine in a burning ball of fire. Yet, we pushed on in a crazy drive down the mountain.

We made it, and it took a while for the massive doze of adrenaline to ware out from our systems. We were simultaneously proud of what we did and regretful for the sheer stupidity of it all. We never repeated that feat again for it was too insane even for us. If the war did not kill us, another run like that would have definitely done it.

We did not push it to that extreme but racing up and down the mountain and anywhere else was a constant pastime. Other cars became our slalom posts, as we would whip back and forth between and around them as if they were going backwards. Our driving could have killed us just as easily as the war. Yet, we miraculously made it. As they say in the Lebanon "It was the lack of enough death that spared our lives."

Foggy Lenses

Then there was the Alfa Romeo driver and his lenses. He had really bad vision and wore lenses, which in those days were thick and hard. Bright lights could easily fog up the lenses and he would need to put drops in his eyes or at least rub them enough to get his natural tears to wet them. Not a good thing when speeding on winding roads.

My first experience with the lenses, it was only the two of us in the car. The speedometer was in the middle of the dashboard between the driver and the passenger, with the RPM gage in front of the driver. As he sped up the mountain, he suddenly yelled "Lenses. Take the wheel." I was not quite sure what he meant, but he had already let go of the steering wheel and had both hands on his eyes with his head tilted backwards.

It was not the time to ask questions, I grabbed the wheel and tried to steer from the passenger seat. I was looking straight at the speedometer that read 130 kilometers per hour with sharp curves coming up and a driver that just turned blind and not letting up off the gas.

It took only a few seconds for his vision to return and retake control of the car, but it certainly felt much longer as I had to take two sharp turns and pass a few cars in the process with incoming traffic, while having no control of the speed.

"What the fuck was that?" I screamed, which is when he explained to me the effect of the lights.

"Could you not at least take your foot off the gas while fixing your eyes!" I said.

"Sorry." He said "You are right." That was easier said than done, and he would keep doing that and never took his foot off the gas. Sometimes, as he leaned back to fix his lenses he actually stepped harder on the gas.

One time, we had two girls with us and I was in the back seat. He was slaloming through traffic at more than twice the average speed when he lets go of the steering wheel and yells "Wheel." I had to reach over from the back in a small car to drive. I was crouched over, reaching between the two front bucket seats avoiding colliding with hundreds of cars we were zipping by, while he put drops in his eyes.

The girls were freaking out and shrieking like it was Armageddon. They were not happy campers. They turned to me and asked how I knew what he meant and I explained that it happened a lot. From there on they would ask me to drive, and threatened to kill him if he ever scared them like this again and I do not doubt they would have. They almost wet their pants.

FORGOING SNOW CHAINS

Most of the time the snowy roads were clear and the snow plows created a serious crusty snow barrier preventing possibility of slipping into the ravine. In fact, at some times the barrier becomes so high it felt like driving through a tunnel.

However, driving up those mountain roads were not without our share of adventure. We were young and rash and always pushing the limits of our luck. Beyond driving like speed demons around those treacherous curves, we challenged each other into the most ridiculous dares, including driving up uncleared snowy winding roads without snow chains.

As I drove up the mountain one Friday afternoon before the ski season actually started, rain began to turn to snow at the higher elevations and by the time we passed Faraya village there was a few centimeters on the ground and more coming down. Yet, we would not stop for snow chains on such thin snow and proceeded as usual.

Few wiggles and slides here and there, but it was workable. As long as I kept the car in low gear with no jerky movements we could get there. On the last stretch below our chalet and before the last U-curve that got us in front of the chalet, the snow was starting to get deep and seriously slippery. This was an early snow and very slushy, making it more slippery than dry winter snow. Undeterred and determined, I pushed on without chains.

The last stretch was fairly straight, but uneven, sloping towards the ravine in several locations. As I proceeded at constant speed, my 1974 Plymouth Valliant began to drift slowly. We were still heading up the road but at an increasing angle as the rear drifted towards the ravine and pointed the car towards the sheer rock cliff to my left.

The guy next to me began to chant "Rocks, rocks..." as I tried to straighten the car out. That must be done with care as I could very easily over correct. I was turning the front wheels slightly and stepping lightly on the gas to force a counter rotation. Finally, the car began to straighten up and we were still moving in the right direction, but the counter rotation does not stop and we began to drift in the other direction. Now we were staring at a deep ravine that opened up all the way to the sea, and my friend's chant changed to "Back to the rocks, back to the rocks..." Hitting the rocks was definitely preferable to jumping into the ravine.

We skipped the ravine and the rocks, and after a few drifts in each direction we reach the U-curve. However, the car was not turning and heading straight off road. It was time for drastic action, so I turned the stirring wheel all the way to the left and floored the gas pedal forcing the car into a spin. The car went through two and a half turns and came to a stop pointing down the road instead of up.

I threw the car into reverse and backed it up the remaining hundred meters, I hit the brakes and turned and ended up perfectly parked where I need to be. Mission accomplished. We got out of the car to cheering crowds who were out walking and enjoying the fresh snow. They thought I was showing off and I did a wonderful job. Little did they know that I had no idea what I was doing, and was making this up as I went.

Later that season we kept daring the mountain, always trying to get as far up as we can without chains. Always trying to outdo each other.

On one late nigh heading up to the mountain the snow was heavy, and I was in my "Hajji" with another guy and two girls. Past the Faraya village fresh snow was more than thirty centimeters deep, yet I decided to plow through without chains. The girls complained, but it was two in the morning and I really did not feel like hassling with the chains in a snow storm.

Half-way up to the slopes, we began to struggle in even deeper snow, and the girls kept nagging until we decided to stop and install the chains just to shut them up. We needed to lift the car to get the chains on the tires in such deep snow, so I pulled out the jack and cleared a space for it in the snow. That was a straight stick jack that hocked to the bumper, and as the weight of the car came off the tire and tilted the car slightly, the car slid sideways tilting the jack and bending the hock in the bumper.

Now we could not jack the car up, nor remove the jack as the weight of the car laid on it. It took fifteen minutes to free the jack, with all four of us lifting the car and tugging on the jack. With the jack free, I told the girl to just zip it, we were proceeding without chains.

We got back in the car and the girl next to me laid the flashlight on the seat, so I asked her to put it back in the glove compartment but she shrugged it off. As we drove, the car began to beep in a way I had never heard before, and without reason, so I told her "Hajji" wanted the flashlight in its place. I used to always jokingly talk to the car and ask it to cooperate with me when I pushed it beyond its capacity.

She laughed and ignore me, but then the glove compartment snapped open and beeping stopped. I said "See. Hajji wants the flashlight in there." She slammed it shut and told me I am nuts, but the beeping started again and the glove compartment snapped open again. She gave me this strange look and slowly put the flashlight in and closed the compartment.

The beeping stopped, and She started to caress the dashboard and apologize to the car telling it she would never disrespect it again. We never knew what the beeping was for, but it made for a very interesting story.

We made it to the chalet, where even the four-wheel Chevy Blazer with oversized snow tire had chains on. I it was a proud moment as I was the only one on the mountain with no chains.

The next morning, we get out to find the Blazer driver staring at my car next to his. " You took your chains off to pretend you did not need them!" he said. He would not believe that I made it up without chains. "you are not getting out of here without them." He said with absolute confidence.

Hmm. A dare. We got in the car and I casually drove off to the slope itself. I was the champ.

NEW YEARS PARTY – AT CHALET 70

1982 was our last New Year's eve together. We already knew that as several of us were planning to travel the next summer to pursue studies in various places around the world, including me, and some were graduating and taking jobs abroad.

It had to be a party to remember, so although there were several parties planned on the mountain to which we were invited, we had to have our own. This was our last collective hurrah, and we did not know when we would all be together again.

"70" was the natural place for this, and there was no debate about that. After all it was everyone's chalet. Everything else was a huge argument as we gathered to plan the event in early December. It is safe to say we could not agree on anything past the fact that we wanted a big bang. There was more than ten of us, and we argued for hours coming up with twenty different opinions.

At one point I stopped participating in the debate and just watched the comic arguments. Some were climbing on the dining room table in an attempt to dominate the debate from above, and, at one point, there were two on the table shoving each other off. Luckily it was made of massive solid wood. And I got never get the image of one of the guys in a dishdahe hopping and enacting his plan for inviting everyone. He kept jumping, waving his arm and yelling "All you bastards, come down to 70."

The Party

In retrospect, all the debates were a waste of time since what happened that New Year's surpassed anything we could have imagined and threw all the plans into a tailspin. All we needed to do was bring alcohol and munchies and ask all others to bring their own. They certainly did, particularly alcohol. Boy was their alcohol at that party. Maybe the guy in the dishdashe was right.

I was commissioned to prepare sangria, where the recipe called for one shot of vodka and gin each for every bottle of red wine. I poured five bottles of wine into a large bowl and proceeded to pour the vodka and gin, but I did not have anything to measure shots with so I just poured them in, then a little more. Oh, what the hell, just pour half a bottle of each into the mix.

That much hard liquor made it simply too harsh to the taste, so, to remedy that situation, I mixed in some sugar to sweeten it, then added a lot of fruits, and placed the whole thing out on the balcony in the snow to chill. All that sugar made it taste more like fruit punch than sangria, and, as everyone knows, sugar intensified the effect of all the vodka and gin that I poured in.

The party started out fairly normal, with close friends arriving first around 10 pm, followed by all our other friends over the next two hours. The chalet was beginning to brim with people by 11 pm with the crowd spilling into the upper levels and out the balcony. The chalet had two levels with a high ceiling on one side. The stairs to the upper two bedrooms were exposed with a balcony for a hallway upstairs overlooking the living area.

By midnight, people begin to converge onto our chalet from other parties, as many people did not want to split up between parties. People we had never seen before were now cramming into what was feeling like a smaller and smaller space.

It got to the point that no one could move from one place to the other. We were crammed like sardines, but it did not seem to bother anyone, as most were too drunk to care. It seemed like everyone was walking around with a bottle of something. When they got thirsty they quenched their thirst with my sangria, which they mistook for punch. That did not help much.

INDOMITABLE SPIRIT

The first girl to try the sangria actually found the bowl on the balcony. In the chaos of so many people cramming in the chalet, we had forgotten to bring it in. She brought it in and poured a glass, asking what it was. I told her it was sangria, but, upon tasting it, she laughed and said "Who taught you how to make sangria! This is fruit punch."

She chugged down the whole glass in a single gulp, tried to pour another, stopped and began to sway, staring at me and looking confused. "What is this?" leaning on the table. "My own Sangria." I said helping her to a seat as the massive alcohol and sugar mix took almost immediate effect. She had to rest for a while.

As I danced around, friends would simply grab my hair, yank my head back and pour alcohol down my throat from whatever bottle they had. Mixing drinks that way is never a good formula, but we did and did not think much about it. It was party time.

Then came some disasters.

One of our friends could not find the wine bottle opener and decided to open a bottle by pounding it against the wall. That actually works, as the pounding drives the cork out if done properly, and the walls were concrete and could not be damaged. However, the glass sliding door was not that tough. The guy standing near the glass sliding door and thinking he was hitting the wall through the curtain actually put the bottle right through the glass pane.

Everyone nearby cleared the glass from the floor and simply tossed it over the balcony rail. No one would walk on that cliff they reasoned, or maybe they did not think at all. We were all too drunk to think. It was simply a miracle that none of the dozen people in close proximity was cut by the flying glass.

Sometime later I catch one of my co-hosts, drunk silly and weeping like a child on the stairs. I was drunk enough myself that I did not notice the cause of his distress until he pointed it out. A whole step from the stairs was gone. How? I still cannot explain. These were steel stairs with a large bean in the middle and steel steps welded to it. The step had completely sheared off, and I wonder how many people were standing or jumping on it. Yet again, no one got hurt falling through. Also, none of the hundred or people who fell going up and down the stairs after that got hurt, or maybe they were too drunk to feel the pain.

Even though the temperature outside was well below freezing and our balcony door was gone facing an open valley, it was boiling hot inside with all the body heat and alcohol. There were simply too many people crammed together, and they began to shed any heavy garment. There were sweaters and jackets everywhere, and some remained after all were gone. Some people came back for their clothes, others never did. Maybe they just could not remember where they left them.

One friend came to me at one point and with all seriousness asking me "I was wearing a blue sweater. How did it turn red?" Sure enough, he was wearing a red sweater when he earlier had a blue one. Whose sweater he was wearing, no one knows. He went home in someone else's red sweater and never found his.

This same drunken genius decided to dance on the railing of the upstairs balcony, but not for long. The rail was actually a concrete knee wall that could hold him and he could reach the ceiling while standing on the rails. He stayed there for a few seconds until he got confident and let go of the ceiling, and down he went onto the crowd below. Needless to say, that was painful for many. Others thought it was fun and started getting on the rail and diving into the crowd. I am really not sure how we managed to finish the night without anyone needing hospitalization.

Then came the screams from the kitchen and someone was clearly in serious pain. We rushed in believing some idiot had cut themselves with a knife or the like, but what we found was mind numbing even in our drunken state. One guy was gifting an earring to a friend, when the friend did not have his ear pierced, and he decided to pierce it with the hearing, which does not have a pointed end. He was effectively tearing his earlobe and kept commanding him to toughen up and be quite. The poor guy could not even get away as his friend had him pinned down on the ground and insisting to give him the hearing.

We laughed about it later, but the next day the poor gift recipient had a very large swollen ear that needed medical attention, but not that night. He danced the night away after being freed, being too drunk to really feel the pain.

The Morning After

The last I remember checking the time was around 4 pm. The crowd had thinned a bit, but we still had more than a full house, and the party was going strong. I woke up at about 10 am naked in bed and I still do not know who the naked girl laying on top of me was. I had never seen her before, and never saw her again. Even in my extreme drunken condition, I still had good taste – she was beautiful - or, maybe, she was the one with good taste. I cannot be sure, as I do not remember getting to the room and certainly do not remember who picked whom up.

It was quite outside and I really needed to use the bathroom. I find my underwear among the people on the bedroom floor, step over a few and walk out the room onto the balcony overlooking the living area to get to the bathroom. It was literally a war zone and scaring the living life out of me. All I could think of was "Who will clean this mess.?"

Then a voice from below asked "Do you have a light?" I looked down at this half-dressed girl holding a cigarette, stared for a moment wondering who on earth was she, and what was she still doing there. Then I noticed as I am coming out of my drowsy state that there were dozens of people scattered all over our war zone. Some I knew, some I did not.

Annoyed by my silence, she demanded again with a louder voice "Do you have a light?" I looked down at myself just to confirm that I was actually still undressed, and still partially under the effect of the enormous amount of liquor consumed during the past 12 hours, I dropped my shorts and showed her that what was under it was not a lighter.

She was partly offended and partly amused, giggling while telling me how rude and uncivilized I was. It was my turn for asking questions, and I said "Who are you? And, what are you still doing here?"

She said "If you pull your underwear up, I will explain." and laughed. Her explanation had to wait for a bathroom break, which at this point had become a serious emergency. My bladder was about to explode and if I did not rush into the bathroom, I may shower the poor girls seeking a lighter.

I came out of the bathroom two minutes later after emptying a bladder that felt like an oil tanker to hear that she did not know where her ride was and had no way of leaving the party since the people she came with had left and she did not have a ride or a place to go. She had come to the mountain for the parties without having a place to stay, and in the party shuffle from place to place she got separated from her group. She was stuck there for now.

I needed more sleep and asked her to stay comfortable until we wake up again. I crawled back into bed next to my beautiful bedmate and passed out again for another two hours. I woke up to find her gone, which is how I never got to know who she was. I guess she too had no idea who I was and decided to sneak out before I woke. We certainly had sex and I hope it was enjoyable.

The cigarette girl was still there when I woke up, along with several others, and I told her we will get her home, but she would need to help us clean first. We did the same to the other poor stranded bastards laying around the place, but it did not work with all of them. Some had a ride but were just too drunk to go anywhere until that moment. The prospect of cleaning up the mess they made sobered them up very quickly and they ran out the door.

Nonetheless, some had a heart and seeing the scale of the job decided to pitch in.

We must have removed two tons of garbage from the place. We had to run out and buy more garbage bags because we ran out. It was everywhere, on the beds, under the beds, the bathrooms - everywhere. The white vinyl floors in the kitchen and bathrooms were black – solid black - with centimeters of sludge on them. People dragged the wet snow in with them and then collected all sorts of dirt. That was not fun.

However, we got it cleaned, including all the remaining glass from the sliding door and all the broken bottles, etc.

The breakage was another story, and the owners were not going to be happy. We could talk ourselves out of the step, claiming that it was defective otherwise it would not break. However, there was no way we could avoid responsibility for the sliding door. We had to pay for that.

It took two weeks to replace the sliding door. I think they did it on purpose since they realized they had been cheated into renting the unit to a bunch of college students and not a family, and wanted us to suffer. Yet, we found a way around that problem.

The step remained missing for the rest of the season, and we could not get them to fix it. Another punishment. They had to replace the glass because the freezing cold would damage the unit, but the step they could ignore. We eventually got used to stepping over it, after tripping on it a few times. Going up it was easy to see and it was only the third step, so even if we stepped through the hole our foot will reach the floor before we really hurt ourselves. But coming down was the trickier part, and If one missed it he will keel over and straight into the wall across – something that we masochistically grew to enjoy watching people do.

That party lived in infamy for years. It was never duplicated. There was not another group like us who bridged the various circles of friends in a way to bring them all into the same place and there was not another chalet that would be open for the carnage we did.

We still recall that night with pleasant nostalgia as we do most of that season. A friend recently suggested we should try to rent that chalet again just to try to relive those days and I doubt we could. Too much time has passed and I believe that we would ruin our memories by trying to relive them.

A FOGGY TRIP TO THE MOUNTAINS

Sometimes, what is called fog is nothing less than a dense cloud sitting on the mountain. The mountains rise steeply from the sea that often clouds over the Mediterranean slam straight into the mountain and slowly creep up. Visibility is reduced to almost nothing.

Friday evening following our infamous New Year's party we encountered some of the densest of those clouds ever on the way back to Faraya. Half way up the mountain, which is where those clouds generally get stuck, we could not even see the front hood of the car. Usually you could still see at least a meter or two in front of the car, but not that night.

Cars had pulled over to the side of road to wait it out, and those who did not absolutely need to ascend the mountain where turning around and heading back down. However, we decided we had driven this road so many times we had it memorized and determined we could make it.

We could see the ground below when we stuck our heads out the window that we reasoned would keep us from going off the road and into a deep ravine. We knew exactly which direction each curve would turn and all we needed to see is the edge of the asphalt to stay the course. Insane, when I look back at it. What if there was another car heading the other way with the same crazy reasoning? We would collide head on before we even knew the others were there.

I watched the right edge from the passenger seat and the guy in the back looked out the left side. We guided the driver along the way "Getting too close. Back the other way." Over and over as we crawled up the mountain. We were barely moving to insure proper response to road edge warning. We were crazy and out of control, but not stupid. We had enough sense to self-preserve - sometimes.

We figured we would make it through the cloud soon enough and then continue the trip normally. Usually the clouds are not that deep – top to bottom, and at some point, we would emerge above the clouds and into clear skies. We had often looked down on clouds from the mountain while in full sunny conditions up top.

Not that night. The cloud stayed with us all the way to the chalet. We were never sure whether the cloud was simply that large or it creeped up the mountain with us, keeping us company along the way. Either way, we had to drive in below zero visibility for almost fifteen kilometers. At one point the driver asked for his books, as he jokingly said he was not seeing anything anyway and only responding to our left/right commands. Might as well get reading done. That did not happen. We needed him alert and responsive. This was not the time for microbiology studies, or we may turn into a million microorganisms at the bottom of a ravine.

We finally made it to the chalet and are relieved that we had survived the nerve-racking experience, but we had forgotten about the broken glass door in our chalet, which has now let the cloud in. We walked through the door and could not see a thing. There is no way we are sleeping in the cloud, and the chalet was freezing and extremely humid.

Back to the car and back down the road several kilometers to the nearest store that could sell us plastic and tape to seal the sliding door. Two hours later, we were back at the chalet, started a fire to try drying up the air inside and proceeded to seal the glass, placing plastic over it and taping it all around.

It held for a few minutes until the wind started to gust, blowing the plastic inwards and peeling the tape off the glass. We re-taped the plastic only to have it blown off again and again. Finally, we brought a mattress and placed it against the plastic to keep it in place and pushed the dining table against the mattress to secure it in place. It held through the night, even though the wind seemed determined to push it off in an extremely noisy fashion.

The mattress and table stayed in place for another week until they fixed the glass.

Everything in the chalet was wet from the cloud and the open window all week, and we could not use the beds. We hung blankets on chairs in front of the fire until they were dry enough and then slept on the floor in front of the fire place.

Ironically, we went through all this when there was still not enough snow to really ski, as the season of winter of 1981-1982 started real slow. Snow was usually enough for skiing in early December, but that year, the weather was warmer and dryer than usual. Whatever little snow accumulated lasted about a day before turning into a muddy mush, and we would have to wait a week or so before another meager snow fall allowed us a few hours of skiing. The snow was thin enough for us to scrape it off while skiing.

But, hope reigns eternal. We had to be there just in case there was the chance we could get an hour or two of skiing on thin snow, and we did. That treacherous cloud had deposited enough snow on the mountain to ski on. We hit the slopes first thing in the morning and we were the only ones there. No one else seemed to have wanted to challenge the dense fog.

We got half a day of skiing, partially scraping rocks and dirt and kept moving around in search of unmolested snow. By mid-day, we had turned the whole mountain into a brown mixture of snow and dirt and were starting destroying our skis so we decided to stop.

By then more people were arriving at the resort as the weather had turned really nice. We spent the rest of the weekend partying and lamenting the lack of snow.

INDOMITABLE SPIRIT

BLIZZARD OF '82

Lousy ski conditions lasted through most of January 1982. In early February we had a few days of study period before the final exams of the fall-winter semester at collage, where back then the Fall Semester started early October and ended in Mid-February. We decided to retreat to our chalet in the mountains to study in peace, and maybe get lucky enough for a little snow and a few hours of skiing.

There were eight of us in the chalet. Each had their own courses and studies, but we kept each other company during breaks.

We spent all Wednesday studying and Thursday we woke up to about 30 centimeters of fresh snow and could not resist the slopes. We headed out and plowed through the thin layer of powder, which lasted through mid-day before we were skiing on more mud than snow. It was fun while it lasted, especially since we were the only people on the slopes. It was a Thursday and no one had expected snow.

It was time to hit the books again.

By mid-afternoon we received a telephone call from Mansour the owner of the local restaurant/store. The owner whom we knew well was calling to warn us that a major blizzard was about to hit. He advised that we either leave the mountain immediately, or stack up on supplies for a few days, since we will not be going anywhere for a while.

This was of course before we had 24-hour weather reports. We looked out the window, and found relatively cloudy skies with a few flakes, but nothing that looked like a blizzard. We discount the warning, joking that Mansour wanted to sell his stock and had no other customers at the time.

We return to studying, totally ignoring the warning.

By late morning on Friday, I was laying on my bed studying when I heard screams from down below. One of the guys looked up and shrieked like I had never heard him before. He began to yell for us to come and see. "Millions!!!" "Millions!" he kept repeating, referring to the amount of falling snow.

On a clear day we could see all the way to the coast, but not that afternoon. The sliding glass door might as well be painted white. It was a complete white-out. Snowflakes hitting the sliding door were larger than anything I had ever seen. Some were more than 5 centimeters in diameter, hitting the glass with a huge slush. The deck already had half a meter of snow – including what was there before - and building fast

Obviously, the locals knew what was coming. Mansour was not pulling our chain or trying to sell us his goods. He was honestly being a concerned friend with some really timely advice. If only we had listened.

We scrambled to collect our stuff to rush off the mountain. We had to, since our final exams started on Monday, and we could not afford to be stuck on the mountain. A storm as Mansour had described would lock us in for days.

By the time we got out the front door, there was almost a meter of fresh snow on the ground – in less than an hour - and it was still coming at the same rate with some flakes more than ten centimeters across by then.

The sky was falling.

The cars were already buried in snow and we did not even have any chains on the tires, since we came up clear roads. Upon opening the trunk to remove the chains and place our bags, tons of fresh snow fell in the trunks, which would turn into water by the time we reached Beirut and mess up our bags.

We were fast being buried in snow ourselves as we dug through the accumulation and crouched to place the chains on the tires. The snow would partially melt on our warm cloths and then quickly freeze again, forming a thick layer of ice that was woven into the cloth and could not be removed until it melted after we sat in the car for a while.

The roads were already impassible and we were informed that snow ploughs would lead convoys down the mountain. We would assemble in lines of twenty cars behind each plough and drive in close formation. The snow was falling at such a rate that the road would close up within minutes of clearing it.

I had not driven my car to the mountain on that trip, so on the way down I drove the car of one of the girls who was with us and did not feel comfortable driving in those conditions. I was the next to last car in line, and I did not see any asphalt as the snow was already more than twenty centimeters deep in such a short distance behind the plough.

The snow was fresh and the road beneath it was iced solid from the ploughs and cars that went before us. The car stayed straight as long as it was moving. Yet, whenever we slowed down or stopped, the front of the car – no chains – would drift to the lower side of the road, often almost drifting off the road.

The owner of the car sitting next to me was shrieking all the way down. She was sure we were not going to make it. It was hard enough keeping the car on the road without the constant dire predictions of imminent death. It took almost an hour to descend to the village at the bottom of the mountain when it normally required less than fifteen minutes. That is where the snow ploughs abandoned us to our fate as they headed back up the mountain to escort the remaining cars.

However, the snow did not end there. This blizzard deposited snow all the way down almost to the coast – a rare, but not an unusual occurrence. What was exceptional was the shear amount of snow accumulating at lower altitudes and the rate of snowfall. The sky was really falling on us. We were driving in more than a half meter of snow almost half way down the mountain and then lesser amount further down.

At these altitudes people do not usually have snow chains and most are not adept at driving in deep snow. Yet, people had to make it home and they tried the best they could. Needless to say, conditions were seriously messy. Cars would spin out of control all over the place, and abandoned cars and accidents littered the length of the road.

It was late at night when we made it into Beirut. We were soggy from all the ice on our cloths that melted in the car, cold and exhausted. There was barely a trace of snow in the city by the shore, and the ground was warm enough to prevent any icing or accumulation.

White-out conditions lasted through the weekend with additional snow falling over the next few days, albeit at a lesser rate than what we drove through. All said, that blizzard placed four to six meters of snow foundation on the maintain and allowed us to ski through early May that year.

We finish studying at home over the weekend, and then three days of final exams, all the time dreaming of skiing the massive snow that finally covered the mountain. We could see the mountain from Beirut and the sight of it was driving us crazy.

By the time we finished our final exams and headed back up the mountain the next Thursday, blue skies dominated. We had the most favorable skiing conditions one could hope for –thick fresh snow and sunny skies.

Getting into our chalet was, however, a challenge. We had arrived just as the locals finished clearing the roads, but the maintenance people at our chalet complex had not yet had a chance to clear paths to the entrance doors.

As our Chalet was in the building that sat back from the road and downhill on the edge of the cliff, several meters of snow completely covered the first floor. We literally walked straight towards the balcony of the second-floor bedrooms.

We managed to work our way through the sliding door and into the chalet, only to discover that the storm had disrupted the electric power, which would not be restored until Saturday morning. No power meant no heat, except the wood burning fireplace.

We could easily sleep all cozied up in front of the fireplace. Cozying up with a girl in front of a warm fire is never a problem, and the fire and candles provided all the light we needed. The problem we faced was the lack of hot water and heat for showers. A full day of extreme skiing meant a lot of sweating inside our ski clothes, and we certainly needed that shower.

By the end of Friday, after two days of intensive skiing, we were starting to feel gamy and I decided to hit the showers even without heat. That was spring water straight from the mountain, which at that time of year was freshly melting snow and barely above freezing. The water actually felt more painful than cold. It felt like I was showering with ice cubes.

I am not sure how I managed to finish the shower, but the extreme cold water made the freezing temperature in the chalet feel warm and cozy in comparison. I stepped out of the shower in shorts and no shirt and felt perfectly comfortable – for a while – when the rest of the crew were all wrapped up in their ski jackets.

They shivered at the sight of me and insisted I get dressed quickly before they freeze to death looking to me. I was the only one willing to try the cold shower and the rest of the crew decided to drive down to Beirut for a warm shower, so we all headed down. They showered and we spent the night on the town and came back late at night for the remainder of the weekend.

Everyone still remembers that day and never tire of telling people how I took a cold shower in mountain freezing temperatures. Well at least this is one legacy that I can react to with pride, having the endurance and strength to tolerate such conditions.

With the semester ending we had a one-week break, great weather and a massive amount of snow to ski. We had the best semester break we could wish for.

AUDITORIUM EXPLOSION

On a Friday Evening, later that winter, we had just finished with a play rehearsal and were getting ready to head out to the ski resort, as we always did Friday night. We had no nigh plans in Beirut, but the other auditorium was having a final dress rehearsal of a professional play directed by a school professor, so we decided to catch the last portion of the rehearsal before heading out.

The building was I-shaped with a narrow middle, which allowed for two exterior side doors for the auditorium just in front of the stage, as well as two doors that opened into the building at the top of aisles. The side doors were massive solid wood double doors, about two and a half meters high and one and a half meters across for each leaf, topped by solid glass for lighting all the way to the high ceiling. The glass was at least two centimeters thick and several meters high above the doors.

We entered the auditorium from a back, and just watched the rehearsal from the back. As they finished, the actors headed back stage to change their clothes, while a host of their young children played just in front of the stage along with a spattering of adults waiting on the actors. We lingered for moment discussing our plans.

I had my back turned to the stage talking to one male and two female friends who were with me, when I notice a terrified glare from all of them towards the stage. It is amazing how slow time passes when going through an incident like that, the mind races so fast that everything appears slow. The movies do not exaggerate when they turn the film into slow motion allowing the viewer to see every little detail.

I had time to notice the terrified glare on my friend's faces and turn around to look before the doors completed their dislocation from their hinges. As I turned the two leaves of the door were bowed into the auditorium, relaxing slightly back into position before flying out of place. It was almost as if the doors were taking a practice push before going off, but it was really due to a smaller explosion that set off the larger one.

Luckily someone had walked through the door seconds before the explosion, and since the doors open outwards, he pushed the bomb slightly away from the door. We found out later that he noticed the bomb in a brown paper bag and took off running and calling for help. He got just far enough to save his life but was still thrown off his feet by the explosion, even though he had descended down a long flight of stairs.

Nonetheless, pushing the bomb away from the door reduced the effect of the explosion, but there was still enough force in it to do massive damage. One of the door leaves flew straight across the auditorium hitting the opposing doors with such force that it took both leaves of the door straight to the outside, broken into bits of course.

The other leaf had a man leaning against it, who must have had a guardian angel looking over him as he was actually in full contact with the door. Thus, instead of slamming into him and causing a lot of damage, the door lifted him with it and landed in the middle of the auditorium half way up the seating rows. The sight of that man, pinned to the door and flying towards us is one of those images that would never leave my mind.

The glass above the doors shattered and turned into mini projectiles that got imbedded into the stage, seats, walls and trees outside.

What we witnessed was a slow-motion whirlwind of debris flying across the auditorium and swirling all over. There was no sound, as the sound of an explosion is that of the displaced air clapping back together at the end, and as we were that close to the explosion center the air actually clapped right upon us. We felt the oppressive pressure, but did not hear anything, except for the never-ending whine in our ears that lasts for days. Again. the silence of explosions in the movies is accurate.

The two girls we were with darted out the back doors and kept on running, and they even forgot they had a car, which they left behind. They got a hold of another friend hopped in the car hysterically and asked for a ride home. They had to return to get their car the next day.

My friend and I ran towards the front of the auditorium, where a large number of children were crying and dazed, and quickly began to clear them out of the theater, lifting them above the broken glass and other debris. We were the only adults available and capable of moving for what appeared to be a very long time, even though others fairly quick. The time warp of an acute situation allowed for very fast action in what appeared to be a very slow-moving world.

We must have cleared more than 20 kids from the place before their parents began to arrive from around the building. They had exited through the back door of the backstage area and came around the building looking for their children.

Amazingly, none of the children had a scratch on them, even with the massive amount of broken sharp pieces of glass that had fallen all around them. The glass was thick enough and heavy enough to hurt badly, especially when hitting a little child, yet, none were hit by any of it. Maybe it is true the kids are protected by guardian angels. Maybe they were too innocent to suffer.

With the kids safely in their parents' hands we returned inside, and I headed straight for the flying man who landed in the middle of the seats, who was still laying beneath the door and not moving. Upon lifting the door, I was certain the man was dead, as he laid in what appeared to be a very twisted manner with one leg hooked between the backs of two seats and one arm dangling between two other seats, his eyes half open but not moving and covered in dust and wood chips.

I had not had a chance to examine him further before I heard thundering voices screaming his name. They arrived like a storm, jumping over seats like circus performers, lifted him up like a rag, placed him on the door that brought him to that position and ran out. One of them brought a large American car around, which had windows that open completely, leaving no bar between the back and the front windows. They slid the door with the guy on it into the car and sped away to the hospital. By that time, he was coming around, and clearly not dead.

The next Monday I saw him limping on campus with a common friend who had helped take him to the hospital, and could not believe my eyes. I would have sworn he would be in the hospital for a long time, at least with broken bones, but, instead, he only had a sprained ankle. It just was not his time to go. He was to live to see another day.

Most others walked away with minor scratches, except for one unlucky driver of one of the actors. He had been sitting just in front of the blown door and had a large piece of the door tear through his right leg. It took six months of operations to mend his leg so he could walk again, an, he still limps badly.

I can still remember the face of every kid I lifted to safety, although I have no idea who they were, except one. I can, also, still see the faces of the screaming terrified parents looking for their children. Some images just get imprinted in memory.

I did not know the kids or pay much attention to their parents at that time, but the parents knew who saved their children and were grateful for it. Some of them continue to thank me for saving their lives to this day. Honestly, I did not save their lives, as the explosion was over when I got to them, and they were in no danger of dying at that point. However, for a parent, and I now know what that means, helping their children in any way is always dearly appreciated.

Once all were safe or on their way to a hospital, and the proper people were on hand to handle the building, we proceeded to head towards the ski resort. Yes, ski resort. This was life in a war zone. We dealt with any emergency situation and then returned to our regularly scheduled programming. The show went on.

However, having to deal with all this, we were more than two hours late picking up our friends on the way to the ski resort. This was before cell phones, and we had no way of informing them of our delay – not that we gave it much thought as we handled the post-explosion mayhem. As expected, she began to chew us out for being so late, until we told her what happened, and she calmed down, glad that we were still alive and kicking.

Staying alive was an accomplishment in its own right when living in a war zone. That is why so many Lebanese had gotten into the habit of responding to questions about how they are doing with a simple "Alive" or "Surviving". That was the most critical issue. All else could be replaced.

I could barely sleep that night. It was not the stress of the event as we had gotten immune to that, but the wringing in my ears was deafening. It was trauma to the inner ear that could not be turned off, and it kept me awake all night. I never appreciated loud noises as much as I did the next day, as the noises drowned out the ringing and helped you forget them. It got a little better the next day but took almost a week to go away.

Aside from the ringing in our ears, we put the whole thing behind us and spent the weekend skiing and partying. We were not dead, and not maimed in the hospital. All was good.

The party went on.

KILLER JOE

There were too many people in this crowded little joint in the mountains. It was the type of place where people were literally jammed against each other, with no distinction between the various groups in there. It did not really matter any way since many knew each other, whether they came in together or not. The atmosphere was boisterous and happy, the food was mediocre, the music too loud and the drinks flowed freely.

Past midnight a tall young man walks through the door and just stood there, with a long black overcoat and a red bandana around his neck, and absolutely no emotions or any expression on his face. He stood out like a sore thumb and clearly did not belong there.

I was facing the door when he walked in and could not help but stare at him at length and was absolutely sure I knew him from another life. Someone noticed me staring quietly – I was rarely quite – and turned to see what I was looking at. He quickly turned back and said "Please do not stare at him. We want to get home alive tonight."

He sure looked like bad news from hell, but I could not take my eyes off of him. Deep down I was sure I knew him. Finally, I turned to my friend and said "Joe!!!"

"yes Joe." He said, "Now stop staring at him.

"Joseph Maalouf?" I confirmed.

"Where do you know him from!" another exclaimed, as if it was not expected.

"We were classmates and best friends before the war. He was a great guy."

"Well, not anymore." They both state, emphatically.

INDOMITABLE SPIRIT

Seven years had passed, and we are now grown nineteen-year-old men, not the thirteen-year-old kids in middle school, but I could still recognize an old friend. More accurately, it was a ghost of an old friend. This man was barely human and made everyone's skin crawl.

By then, he had noticed me staring at him and stared right back at me. It actually felt like he was staring through me, with absolute stone-like emotionless face. My friends started to panic that he may get upset about my staring, so I got up and walked towards him, breaking free from those who tried to stop me.

I had to climb over a few chairs and make my way through the crowd, while he still looked on. I got to him smiling as an old friend would and said "Joe! It has been a long time" and reach out to put my hand on his shoulder, but he did not react at all.

I said "Don't you remember me? We were best of friends in IC." He gave a barely noticeable nod of agreement as he looked straight into my eyes, with glassy eyes without a hint of life.

I glared at those black eyes for a few seconds trying to find my old friend somewhere behind the lifeless façade. I swore I could see a small glint in his eyes that said he remembered, but that life was long gone. I tried to hug him, hoping I might break the ice, however, he placed the palm of his hand on my chest and backed away as he firmly pushed be back. With a mixture of anger and sadness – or so it appeared to me – he turned and walked out the door.

Someone grabbed my shoulder and said "You are brave sole. Thank you for getting him out of hear." I did not respond to that as I looked at him. My mind was still with Joe, or what remained of him. What could possible cause such a transformation, I wondered.

I made my way back to my seat over all the hurdles and squeezed in between two ladies, trying to get back in party mood. This was not the time to ask what happened to turn a cheerful fun loving young kid into that – whatever that was.

A couple of shots of vodka, beautiful women and a fun group of people took my mind of the subject for the rest of the night. We enjoy ourselves, with everyone acting like I just got a new lease on life. It turned out those who knew him, or more accurately knew about him, in his current condition were seriously concerned that my intrusion into his space could have gotten me killed.

Next day, sober and quiet, I got to inquire about him. He had stopped coming to school after the first day of fighting and we just assumed that, like everyone else who lived across the divide, he found another school. That was the farthest from the truth.

He lived on a street that became the dividing line on the southern outskirts of the city. One single street divided the two side in that area, and that was where he lived when the war began with Palestinians on one side attacking the Christians on the other.

Palestinians entered his building, before any demarcation lines and fortifications had been established, and kill everyone in it, including his whole family. They raped and dismembered his sisters and mother right in front of him, killed and mutilated his father, cut his throat and left him bleeding to death. Under the bandana lay a huge scar from ear to ear.

This type of barbarity had taken place all over at the beginning of the war and was designed to terrorize the population into segregating along sectarian lines to facilitate what came next. We all heard about it and knew someone who had witnessed it, but not like this. This kid had died that day but kept on walking.

Somehow he did not completely bleed to death. The psychological scars, however, were clearly much deeper than those of the blade, and he would never recover mentally. Maybe the extensive bleeding and starving the brain from oxygen contributed to that? Not sure. However, from that point on, he lived for one purpose - revenge.

He had been on a bloody trail ever since that day. and became known and "Aboul Mout." Mr. Death. He would seek Palestinians, any Palestinians and kill them, and became the go to man to interrogate, torture and then kill any Palestinian captured.

The more he killed the more he died inside. The blood thirst became impossible to quench, and all humanity had eventually bled out of him. He may as well be a robot. Maybe robots had more emotions.

He was not the only kid who was turned into a murdering monster by the brutality of the war. However, we usually came across those people after they had been transformed. The monster was all we knew.

This had been my good friend, and I could not stop thinking about the thirteen-year-old who was full of life and aspirations. He was a brilliant student whom everyone turned to for help and provided it with a pleasure.

A kid who once gave life meaning, had turned into the grim reaper, and was now spending his time ending lives.

I never saw Joe again. Maybe it was for the best. It was not like we were going to become friends again. It would have just been a painful reminder of what had been lost in the horrible hell that beset Lebanon.

We constantly tried to look past those tragedies and focus on the positive. Focusing at all who eluded such fate and striving to shine through the darkness.

SKI RACE IN THE CEDARS

In late winter of 1982, the national ski competition was at the Cedars Mountain ski resort. The resort is the highest in Lebanon and has some of the best snow. However, the division of the country made it a much less accessible and a much less desirable destination for people in Beirut and the central part of the country where most of the affluent population resides.

It was not just a longer trip from Beirut to the Cedars, but the trip required crossing numerous check points that made the trip simply too long for regular weekend fun. As such, the majority of the skiers spent their time in the central mountain resorts of Faraya, Faqra and Qanat Bakish. Yet, competitions were distributed on all resorts.

This particular competition was to be held on Sunday, and many of us had agreed to meet in Junieh late Saturday to share rides and travel in a convoy to the Cedars. We planned to spend the night partying, and then hit the slopes early rather than drive up in pre-dawn hours, as we had done the time before. Some were coming from Faraya where we were skiing Saturday, while others were meeting us straight from Beirut.

The Way Up

Upon conglomerating in Jounieh, one guy, who had come from Beirut, realized he had not brought his skis from Faraya the weekend before, and had to go get them, but he was not driving. Since we shared a Chalet, it fell upon me to make the 60-kilometer round trip up the mountain with him to get his gear.

The rest proceeded to the Cedars, as there was no point in everyone waiting more than an hour for us to return. However, since I had a large American car, while many others had small European cars the luggage of the ladies who were supposed to be in my car, as well as another, remained in my trunk. We also agreed to pick up a girl who was with family in Tripoli, which would have allowed the large convoy to proceed directly to the resort without having to detour through the city.

When we finally got to Tripoli at around 6 pm, there was no one to pick up. The others had decided to get some sweets that Tripoli is famous for and enter the city anyway, at which point they also picked her up while there.

As we turned to leave the city, steam started blowing through the hood of my car. We pulled up at a Gas station to check it, and found we had a leak in the radiator. It had to be fixed before we made the trip up the mountain, as there was no way to make it all the way up with water leaking.

We were told that the only place to fix it was Bab-et-Tibbanneh, the most nefarious neighborhood in the city. People are afraid to enter the area in mid-day, and here we were going there after dark. My friend began to panic, insisting we were going to die. I told him that he was the Sunni Moslem, like the people of Bab-et-Tibbanneh, although not a nefarious character himself, and I should be looking to him for protection – right!! Eventually I started yelling at him to calm down and not attract attention since it would be me they would kill, as I was the Christian whom they would consider an outsider.

Having gotten used to be in the wrong place more times than I cared to remember, I managed to have enough composure for both of us and made it through alive.

When we got to the mechanic shops, most were in the process of closing. I caught the first guy I found and pleaded with him to remain open a few more minutes to look at my car, which by now was engulfed in steam. He took mercy on me when he knew I had to make it to the cedars that night and called his neighbor, who specialized in welding. The problem was simple enough and he managed to weld the crack at the top of the radiator quickly.

We paid both for their help, thanked them profusely and proceeded on our way.

I had never driven to the Cedars before, and the last time I had been up that mountain was eight years earlier, when I was a kid. Needless to say, I was not familiar with the roads, but I knew enough about geography to have a general idea.

At the southern edge of the city was a road through the town of Behsas that leads to the Cedars, which I wanted to take. However, my friend, who had driven to the cedars many times, insisted that we proceed further south and take the main exit to the Cedars, because he "knew that road well" and did not want to take a chance on getting lost. Thus, we drove another 15 kilometers south along the coast and turned inland.

As we drive up, he was giving directions on which way to turn at every fork in the road. I followed his directions, even though I disagreed with him at some point, and had a very strong feeling that he was lost.

It was night and extremely cloudy that we had no geographical reference as to which direction the mountain was. And the road also wound around so much that one could lose any sense of direction. Furthermore, this was one of the few places in Lebanon where there are relative flat lands near the sea before starting a steep ascent up the mountains. Thus, we did not even have the benefit of knowing whether we were headed up or down.

Eventually I came to a sign that says "Welcome to Behsas". Behsas was where I wanted to turn inland to start with, and I turned to him and say" You moron, you just took us in a circle." He replied that Behsas was big and this was the other edge of it and told me to turn left at that intersection.

I was not buying that BS. If we were to cut through it anyway, why on earth did we just drive thirty kilometers. It could not possibly be that big.

Nonetheless, as we turned left and past the first building, I could see all the fishing boats in the sea. We had made a full circle and back on the coast. I asked him to look over to his right and tell me what he saw. He squinted hard out the window and with all honesty asked, "Besharri?" For that he got heavy smacked hard over the head. Besharri was a mile high and the last town before the Cedars. We had not ascended a mountain yet, and he somehow believed we miraculously arrived at the top.

By then, I was seriously pissed. It was 8:30 and we were still in Tripoli. I turned around and went back up the way I wanted to go from the beginning, telling him to zip it as he clearly does not know the way. About half a kilometer up the road we came to a Syrian road block, where the soldier asks "did you not just go through here a minute ago?" There was not a lot of traffic on the road. Confirming that, he asked us where we were headed, and I told him. He then said "You should have said so, I would have told you, you are going in the wrong direction." I contained myself until we pulled away from the soldier, at which time my friend got two hard smacks on the head. "The Syrian soldier is going to tell us which way the mountain lies!"

So, finally, up we go, hairpin curve after another and one Syrian check point after the other, past Besharri, and onto the last leg of the trip. This is where the road got real narrow, much steeper and more winding as we ascended the shear face of the mountain. The temperature was well below freezing and the wind was hauling.

We came around a curve and there sat a temporary Syrian road block with a very irate soldier, who, apparently, did not appreciate standing in the blowing freezing wind. He began to yell at us immediately "Pull over to the side, Wla." "Get out." "Open the trunk." I could not blame him for hating standing on the road in that weather, but it was not my fault for him to take it out on me.

He asked what I had in the bags, and I told him cloths. He unzipped one of the bags and reached in, removing a bra from one of the girl's bags. That confused and infuriated him. "SHOU HAD WLA" (What is this) he yelled, stepping back from me while holding the bra out like it was about to bite him. I tried to explain that I had other people's bags with me, but he was not listening. Of course, the second bag he opened also had women's clothing which set him into a rage, and he tore through the bags scattering cloths all over the trunk.

Finally, he abandoned the trunk, and ordered me to leave. He was yelling almost chasing me away as if I was intruding on him. I truly wonder what he was smoking before we came upon him. I was not done collecting the cloths into the bags yet but did not want to test my luck any further.

Meantime, the other soldier was quizzing my friend, who was still in his seat. He pointed to the Audio Cassette case and asks "Shou Had Wla" (What is this). He showed him the cassettes, the soldier snatched the case and began to go through the titles losing his temper as he found no Arabic music, which he could steel. He yelled, "Don't you have any Arabic music?" My friend said "Sorry, it is not my music." He then threw the open case at him scattering the cassettes all over the car.

By the time I got in, there were cassettes on my seat and under my feet. I looked at my friend, and he just said "Do not ask. Just get us out of here while we still can." I pulled out with cassettes under my butt and between my legs, until I cleared two hairpin curves and out of sight of the soldiers, then pulled over to clean things up.

We collected the cassettes and returned the cloths to the bags and proceeded. I had crushed two cassettes with the clutch in the process, but at least the irate Syrian soldiers did not shoot us.

By the time we made it to the Hotel in the Cedars, it was almost 10 pm, and everyone was worried sick that we had not yet arrived. Someone had called the Lebanese Army to request a search party, as they were sure something bad had happened.

We headed out and told the army that we were ok, and no need to search for us. They laughed and said "Where would we search anyway?" The guys had told them we were somewhere between Faraya and Cedars with a possible stop in Tripoli. That is a lot of mountains and coastal roads to search.

All was fine and we spent the rest of the evening and most of the night enjoying good company, good food and drinks. We had none of the standard athlete's behavior of going to bed early and refraining from alcohol and all that. Weekends, as usual, were one long party that included skiing and long nights, leaving little time for sleep and rest. We could always sleep during the week, including naps in classrooms.

Our group was more than 40 people. Only a few competing in the races, but a lot of leisure skiers and supporter. We took up half the hotel and filled the restaurant/bar at night. We ate, drank, danced and had a blast into the early hours of the morning.

The Race

We hit the slopes early to prepare for the race. It was my first, as I had not been skiing long, and I certainly did not feel qualified to race these guys who had been skiing and racing most of their lives. I did not even have the proper skis for racing, but everyone insisted that I participate, arguing that my fearless – reckless is more accurate - approach to the slopes gave me the edge I needed.

I figured I had nothing to lose. If I bummed out, it would be no big deal since no one was expecting me to win anyway, and, if I did well, I would have accomplished something. I had watched enough races and sat in on enough discussions that I knew the basics of tackling the course. However, I had never actually run a slalom course before - Not even a practice run.

We had the opportunity to ski alongside the race course to assess it and define our strategy. My friends spent the time instructing me how to take each gate and were to slow down and were to speed up. Clearly, they studied the course in depth while doing this.

When race time came, the course was iced up, as usual, to prevent excessive gouging of the snow at turns, but it got too icy. The early runners – top rated – had to tackle very slippery slopes, which caused many to miss gates or crash and burn. Nonetheless, they eventually managed to create serious ruts in the slopes.

When my turn came at the tail end of the race, the ruts were half a meter deep in places, which professionals deem a handicap, as they interfere with their style and their own turning plans. However, I was not a pro, and the ruts were my best friends, as I used them like banks to assist in turning into the gates, which meant less edges and more speed. I went down the course like a luge, following the curves established by others

To everyone's amazement, I finished the race in fifth place, and no one, not even I, could believe it. The amazement led to celebrating my accomplishment more than that of the winners. Their winning was expected, but clearly no one expected me to make it that far up the ranks. Many did not even expect me to finish. I was in it for fun and giggles.

With three of the top five men and two of the top five women coming from within our close circle of friends, the situation called for celebratory lunch, with lots of alcohol. Alcohol helped keep us warm on the slopes, but also made us believe we could do more than we actually could. We were young and fearless, and thought ourselves indestructible.

In the afternoon, some in the group decided they wanted ski the Ainata slope. That was not an official part of the resort, and is called that because it hangs over the road from the Cedars over the mountain to Ainata on the other side in the Bekaa valley. The road is often buried in snow and closed during winter.

INDOMITABLE SPIRIT

We took the highest lift to the top of the mountain then traversed along the top of an extremely steep drop for half a kilometer. The drop is so steep that snow does not accumulate on some parts, leaving exposed rocks - Slipping was not an option.

Then we skied a gentle slope to get to the Ainata run. When we pull to a stop, I could not see the actual slope due to the angle of the mountain. One guy pulled past me and made a quick stop that kicked up a small chunk of the virgin snow and rolled it downwards. It disappeared past the short portion of the slop that I could see and then a few seconds later appeared all the way at the bottom as a much larger snowball.

"We are going down this wall?" I asked.

Those who had skied that before, proceeded to explain the slope without even addressing my question. Just shut up and listen, was the attitude. They explained where there are rocks to avoid. Then they cautioned that the road cut through the slope and we needed to be careful with sudden flatness in the middle of a 60 to 70-degree slope.

We had done some crazy things before, but a 70-degree slope on my crappy skis, was pushing it.

"What alternative do I have?" I asked, and by then some of the others are questioning their sanity also.

The only alternative was to climb back up the slope we just skied, traverse back over the rocks and go down the other side. A couple of people decided to take that alternative, but not me. My pride would not allow me to do so.

So, off I went into the ride from hell. The snow was deep and soft, with a thin crust on top. This meant the skis would break through the crust and sink into the soft snow, getting trapped under the crust, which was at knee level. Lifting skis risked disengaging the ski from the boot, which, on such a slope, would result in tumbling my way down the whole mountain. Turning beneath the crust was a seriously arduous task that made the experience so much harder. Yet, somehow, I made it to the bottom in one piece, avoiding the rocks and all.

The Drive Back

We finish day on the regular slopes, which were steep, but within reason, and without the crusty snow and rocks. By four in the afternoon the slopes were closing, and we took our last after closing run as usual and headed to the hotel to collect our stuff and drive off to Beirut. It was Sunday evening and everyone had classes or work on Monday.

However, that weekend was far from over.

We would need to go through ten Syrian Army check points, before reaching the Lebanese Army check point at Madfoun, and then through the Lebanese Forces checkpoint to enter the Christian heartland. Further down the road we would cross from East to West Beirut, where most of us resided. It was going to be a long drive, and it was already dark.

By the time we get to the eighth Syrian check point we came across what must be the stupidest soldier ever. I was in the lead with skis tied to the top of my car, and the soldier freaked out and screamed at me to pull over, pointing at the skis and asking "MISSILES!!!!" I pulled over and tried to explain that those were skis to not avail. He insisted they are missiles, confiscates our IDs and called his commanding officer.

The commanding officers showed up ready to inspect the missiles we were transporting and found four pairs of skis instead. He began to yell at the soldier for being stupid and told him those are skis. The soldier still insisted, so the officer slapped him hard enough to knock him to the ground, turned to us apologizing for the idiotic behavior, handed us our IDs and sent us on our way.

On the way down, I still had the guy who rode up with me and the two girls that were supposed to ride in my car on the way up. He had a light complexion with reddish hair and was seated in the back. At the ninth check point, the Syrian soldier made the assumption that he was a foreigner and while asking for our IDs, he pointed at him and said "Passport."

As it happened, he had lost his ID card, and was using his passport for identification all the while. So, he handed him the Lebanese passport, which really irritated the soldier who assumed he was being mocked for requesting a passport. Again, we were pulled to the side and had the pleasure of meeting the commanding officer to inquire about the offensive mocking.

We made it through that check point also and as we approached the tenth check point, I heard my friend squealing in the back that he could not find his passport. "The son of a bitch has kept my passport.". It was panic time. If he could not produce identification, we may have a serious problem, and would be at the mercy of the mood of the men at the check point. They may be kind enough to accept the rest of us vouching for him and let us go, however, there was always the possibility of some bastard in a bad mood who could decide to keep him until we could bring identification.

Being kept by the Syrian army was not to be taken lightly, particularly that it would take hours to go get him some form of identification or get a hold of the right people to get him out. Luckily, the tenth check point just waived us through, and we did not have to find out.

The Lebanese army check point was a breeze, as they recognized we were in the ski competition, asked how we did, congratulated us on winning, and sent us on our way.

The Lebanese Forces check point was generally feared by most outsiders, as it was deemed by the forces as their main gateway and could be hard on anyone remotely suspicious. Our group included people of all religions and different parts of the country, and stood a good chance of being scrutinized.

However, the check point was in my hometown, and I knew most of the people manning it as they mostly resided in our town – although not from there – for the past four years. I told everyone to line up the 15 cars behind me, where I would speak to the men at the check point, tell them that all were with me, and we would all zip through without question. That should have been simple enough, except for one driver did not seem to care and pulled off around all of us.

We slowed down upon the last stretch, turned off the head lights and turned on the inside lights, as usual, so the men can see the people inside the cars - A standard process at this check point that bordered on paranoia in their behavior.

Confiscated Car

As I pulled through the check point, I saw our courageous driver, who had sped ahead of us, on the side of the road surrounded by several angry looking guys. These were not people you want to get upset. Nice guys under normal conditions, and I had spent some time with them, but when things got serious, they were lethal.

I stopped in the middle of the road and hopped out of the car, calling on them before things got out of hand. The whole convoy stopped behind me, but no one moved, as they did not know these people and interfering stood the chance of only making things worse. I was on hugging and kissing basis with some of them.

As it was, he came into the check point too fast and without following the lighting protocol, which already put the men in an aggressive state and pulled him over to the side. He was driving a Renault 17, but the registration looked like it had a modified 12. They asked him to step out of the car and he climbed out the window, which was tied in place after the wind in the Cedars blew his door hard enough to break a hinge. Thus, they assumed the car was stolen and were in the process of incarcerating him when I showed up.

Having a good rapport with these people prevented his incarceration after explaining everything, but they told me they had already reported the car to the headquarters and needed to get their agreement to release it. This was not what I hoped for to end the weekend.

We did the shuffle and got the three people from my car with their luggage into the other cars and send them on their way. They picked up my sister from my grandfather's house a few hundred meters down the road, whom I was supposed to pick up and headed to Beirut.

I had the task of releasing his car before it disappeared forever. We headed to one of my mother's cousins who was well connected to the militia and knew who to call. He called in another person via walkie-Talkie, who was an old friend of mine, eager to help, and showed up minutes later.

Three hours and many calls and visits later, the car was released, but now it was past 11 pm, and with this guy being an outsider and already acting idiotic, it was best to stay the night and head into Beirut in the morning.

We needed to call our parents and tell them so they do not stay awake fretting all night, and the only working phones, we were told, were at the Military Police office in Byblos. The man in charge and on location at the time, was a childhood friend of mine, and received me with his usual boisterous hugs and kisses. He offered us coffee and food while we made the call, and, naturally, when the boss receives you like a prince all the underlings treat you like a king.

We got back to my village house after midnight, and the next morning, we headed to Beirut, each in his own car.

By mid-afternoon, as I sat in my usual place in front of the fine arts building enjoying good company, a friend walked over and exclaimed with concern: "What have you done!!!"

I had no idea what he was talking about, so he proceeded to tell me that he just came from AUB and the other guy was in front of West Hall just feigning about how I got him out of his jam. He was telling everyone how I knew everyone in the Lebanese Forces and had them all wrapped around my little finger.

The man I helped did not know any of the people we met from Adam, and could be excused for assuming what he did, rather than realizing that these people were relatives and old friends, and their actions had nothing to do with any position I held in the militia. However, West Hall was the heart of AUB that was teaming with Palestinians and Leftist activists who hated the Lebanese Forces with a passion. Hearing how connected I was, would certainly not be good for my health in West Beirut.

I was immediately on my feet and heading straight down to AUB a kilometer away to shut him up before he got me killed. Several people who were connected on the west side of the divide headed down with me, as they could protect me and set things straight in case I was too late.

We got to West Hall to find him sitting on the main stairs, and I just slapped him right off the steps. As he scurried down a few steps to hold himself he was bewildered at my aggression. I screamed at him: "What the hell do you think you are doing telling all these stories!!!"

He replied with all innocence "I was telling them how much you did for me." "I am talking good about you."

His naivety was worse than his offense. The guys with me pulled me back before I killed him and proceeded to explain the danger of what he was doing. I yelled "I should have let them keep you."

Those Palestinians listening to him began to laugh at the whole situation. Seeing their comrades with me and hearing the explanation made them realize how stupid he was. Some of them knew me from high school and told me I should not have worried, as they knew we all are connected in some way or another.

They tell me "We would have helped you get him out on this side also." "It does not mean you command the PLO."

I said "Thank you." "can you explain it to this idiot."

I continued: "It is never that clear. Do you remember what happened in 1977?" These were some of the people who defending us after we got attacked on the streets, and they knew very well how thigs could be easily misunderstood, and spin out of control

Even so, we eventually laughed it off and went to have a bite to eat at the cafeteria.

One more close call or calls. One more day in the shadow of death. One more victory. We were still alive to face the next ordeal.

SPRING SKIING

In early spring the temperature in the mountains tended to swing substantially between afternoon highs and overnight lows. High temperatures in the afternoon softened the snow to the point that skiers would create deep gouges in the surface, and then the snow froze overnight, creating rugged ice ridges that could be extremely dangerous.

Most skiers treaded carefully in the early hours of the day, and many would wait for the icy conditions to subside under the sun before hitting the slopes. We, however, were not missing a minutes of ski time, regardless of conditions.

My Best Friend's Girlfriend

That was how I met my best friend's girlfriend and eventual wife. He did not ski, but she did and her family had a chalet next to ours. He told me he was going to come visit her at the chalet and asked me to stop by to meet her after skiing.

Earlier that day, however, I came across her on the slopes, but not in the way I was supposed to me his new girlfriend. She was having an issue with the ice early in the day and had stopped at a seriously icy spot. No everyone was allowing the ice to slow them down, and as I came flying over a hump in the mountain, I found her standing sideways right below me.

I had just enough distance to land and veer off to avoid her under normal circumstance, but circumstances were far from normal. I landed and got my left ski locked into a deep, frozen track that pulled me straight towards her. I tried stepping out to avoid her, but there was just not enough distance at the speed I was traveling.

For a split second, I thought I would miss her, and had she stayed standing I would have as my skis ran over the front of hers. However, seeing me approaching like a bat out of hell, she instinctively ducked in fear, which put her upper body right in my path.

Not wishing to tumble on steep icy slopes at high speed, I had but one choice. I leaned forward and rammed her with my left shoulder and elbow out of my way. As I was right on top of her skis when I hit her, I yanked her out of both skis and sent her air born.

As I wobbled and struggled to maintain my balance and avoid falling I heard every curse she must have ever learned. She actually started cursing me before I ran into her and as soon as she realized the collision was a foregone conclusion.

I did not pay any attention to what she looked like and would have never been able to identify her again. I was too focused on surviving to look at anything that was not relevant to my survival. However, my face was etched in her memory as I later learned.

That evening after we were done skiing and relaxed a bit, I walked over to the chalet that my best friend told me was his girlfriends. I knocked at the door and she opened it with a fixated look that was a mixture of surprise and anger. She pointed her finger at me and screamed "IT'S YOU."

I said "Yes, it is me." with some hesitation as her demeanor did not quite indicate that she is identifying her boyfriend's best friend. There was clearly something else that I was not aware of. As I said, I could not remember her. She repeated herself several times with increasing ferocity "IT IS YOU." as my friend approached from behind her. I tried to say hello to him, and she noticed him and turned towards him screaming "IT IS HIM." He started laughing and said "Him? This is the one?" She says "YES. I WOULD NEVER FORGET THIS FACE." Turning to me "YOU are not coming in here". I just stood there dazed and confused.

After my friend had calmed her down, he invited me in, but I still had no idea what she was ranting about, so he told me that she was the one I almost killed on the slopes that morning. Yikes. What a way to make an entrance and meet your best friend's love. Then again, if she was to date my best friend, she would be seeing a lot of me, and might as well get used to the idea of who I was. He was not the least bit surprised, and kept telling her that it sounded like me, and laughing, which she did not appreciate one bit.

As the years unfolded, I would bring tears to her eyes more times than she cared to remember and took pleasure in it. She was a pompous ass and I had absolutely no tolerance for arrogance. I would bring her down every time to she got on her high horse or tried in any way to act as if she was better than others.

Refrigerator Ice

One would think I learned from my mistake and became more careful in spring skiing, but the next weekend, I encountered similar conditions and did not even stop to think.

One of my chalet mates had gotten a job as a ski instructor at Faqra nearby and asked me to come with him. We got there before the lifts opened as he needed to meet his students and I ended up riding up right behind the monitors who were checking the slopes to insure all was well. I did not wait for them to make their rounds, and got in the lift seat just behind them and rode all the way to the top for the steepest run.

We stepped off on solid Ice – refrigerator ice. The surface was so had, the edges of the skis were not catching anything, nor were the poles able to penetrate the surface. I was slipping sideways as I adjusted my goggles and poles. One of the monitors began to ski down the mountain, hooked on a deep track from the slushy afternoon before and began to tumble down the steep hill.

There was nothing to stop him, and he was just bouncing off the ice over and over. The other monitor headed straight down towards him and caught him two thirds of the way down. He just threw himself on the tumbling guy to stop the tumble and create enough friction to stop. He had cleared the steepest stretch of snow and they both came to a stop within a few seconds of skidding.

I was watching this and still sliding sideways no matter how hard I tried to dig my edges into the ice. In fact, the more I pushed on the ice the more I slipped down the mountain. I finally slipped into a deep track cutting across the face of the mountain and managed to stop - the same one that threw the monitor of his skis.

Now what? I was really not interested in duplicating the monitor's descent, so I sat on my skis and lit a cigarette contemplating my next move. I was the only person on the mountain and could see the lift coming to a stop as the monitors had concluded the mountain was too treacherous and decided to delay opening for two hours until the sun softened the snow.

Several other monitors had come to help the tumbling guy off the bottom of the slope. They looked at me and shouted "You need to get off the slope, the resort is closed. It is too icy" Yeah. I really needed that news flash.

A couple of cigarettes later I decided I could not just sit there until the snow softened. I am better off in the restaurant with nice hot chocolate and something to eat than up here on an icy slope, and my butt was beginning to freeze as well.

My skis were locked in twenty-centimeter deep tracks that went sideways and I decided I can roll in them to the other side of the mountain where the slope is gentler. The sun was glaring on the shiny ice and I could not see clearly how far the tracks went, and they did not go far before they turned down hill and took me with them. Ice on a slope steeper than forty-five degrees resulted in super acceleration that drove me down that mountain at hyper speed. Images of the tumbling monitor played in my head and I was sure I would face the same end.

I struggled to angle my descent to the left towards the gentler slope, yet, by the time I made it over the hump to the other side, I had run the full length of the steep run and must have been moving faster than a hundred kilometers per hour on solid ice.

It took the remaining quarter kilometer of gentle run just to bring my speed down – not stop. I was scraping ice with my edges rattling my teeth trying to bring some control to my speed. Finally, at a somewhat reasonable speed and approaching the end of the run, and an impending parking lot, I just laid down and skid flat the rest of the way. At that point, I was on almost flat ground and lying flat created enough friction to stop me before hopping into parked cars. Yet, I skidded another fifty meters before stopping.

The monitors where watching all this and making bets on when I would fall. Towards the end they were betting if I would land in the parking lot or kiss the restaurant deck. They were disappointed by my survival, but glad I was in one piece.

The ski school had naturally been delayed for two hours also, so we had breakfast and hot chocolate while we waited – a rare event for us on the slopes.

INDOMITABLE SPIRIT

RALLY PAPER

In the spring of 1982 BUC decided to put on a Rally Paper - a race combined with riddles. At each stop we would be handed a riddle that needed to be solved to find the next stop, where another riddle is handed to us and so forth.

It was not supposed to be a real speed race as much as a test of intelligence in figuring out where the next station was. However, given our predisposition to excess speeding, it became a formula 1 race, and we were flying through Beirut and the countryside like our lives depended on it.

The Rally started at the West Beirut Campus of BUC and terminated at the New Campus in the mountains north of Beirut with a lot of detours up and down the mountains and coast. Only the start and the first stop where in West Beirut and then the clues sent us across the green line. We rode four to a car to work on deciphering riddles.

The first riddle was fairly easy and many cars were still clustered together headed towards the green line. Some cheated by following those they thought were good at deciphering riddles instead of trying to figure out the answers on their own.

I was the first car as we passed the main police headquarters, to reach our next destination, followed by six others. The road was wide and intersected a wide boulevard right at the police headquarters. We were blaring our horns and flashing our headlights to get people out of our way as we raced ahead.

As I approached the intersection, a car cut into the intersection from the left and stopped upon seeing us coming. I began to swerve right to pass in front of it, when the driver decided to move again to get out of my way, cutting me off. I was too close, moving too fast, and angled right to change directions and pass behind him on the left. I slammed the breaks and turned further hoping to spin and avoid him, but I was too close. I struck him at the rear wheel and spun around him, minimizing the impact, but still did some damage to that Peugeot.

One man steps out of the Peugeot and before I could get a word in twenty-eight college students started yelling and screaming at him for cutting in front of us, holding him responsible for hesitating and confusing me, etc. He was in civilian clothes and no one paid attention to the gun on his waste. War made guns so normal that we stopped noticing them.

They shoved me back into my car and told me we needed to go, it was his fault and fuck him. There was no real damage to my American car and I was fine with that. We had a rally to finish. We sped away leaving the man standing there in the middle of the street that Saturday.

We spent the next three hours racing all over the place from location to location, one riddle after another. Had a great time and placed third in the final tally. After that, it was off to the beach for the rest of the weekend, as the weather had warmed up enough that time of year. Of course, that included a long night out.

When I walked into our apartment in Beirut on Sunday evening, I found my parents sitting in the living room with a man that looked vaguely familiar. I did not think much of it, said hello and proceeded towards my room but got called back. My father asked me if I knew the man, and I said it looked like I had seen him before but could not remember where.

The man smiled and politely said "There was a lot going on yesterday. Too many screaming friends."

Yesterday! I stared at him silently as I then recognized him as the man whose car I hit. How on earth did he find me? Why was he smiling and not angry? Why is my father so calm about the whole thing?

He interrupted my thoughts saying "I was just telling your father that you came out apologizing before the mob took over and prevented you from doing the right thing." I guess the fact that I stopped and got out, when I could easily have kept moving said a lot, because I never got to actually say much else.

He proceeded to tell me that he was a detective, tapping the gun on his waste and telling me that we did not even notice that he could have brought the whole debate to a quick halt if he wanted to. However, he did not wish to harm anyone and someone could have acted stupid and gotten themselves hurt. His friends at the police headquarters were faulting him for not bringing us all to our knees.

What he did instead was go back inside and run the plate number. He called my father and asked him if he had sold the car recently. When my father said no, he told him "then your son just hit my car." I was clearly not the Dean of the college. My dad offered to pay for the damages and they both decided to meet when I was returning home so I could be there.

I was waiting for this to turn ugly at some point and I could not believe it would end with smiles. Yet, they both proceeded to ask about the rally and whether we won. My father apparently was glad I am ok, and the detective was satisfied that his expenses were going to be paid and was kind enough to understand the craziness of youth.

We did not win. We placed third, which is not bad considering more than thirty participants.

And, we survived another crazy day in a war zone.

INDOMITABLE SPIRIT

A BAR-B-Q AND AN INVASION

It was June 3, 1982, the weekend before final exams. After graduating that June, one of our close friends was about to get married and travel abroad, and a big farewell party was certainly required.

We headed for a Bar-B-Q in the mountains southeast of Beirut, only about 8 kilometers up the road, and overlooking the city. We began to gather at the host's back yard in mid-morning and by noon there was more than a hundred people.

Although officially her farewell party, there was a lot more to it. Several people were either graduating or, like myself, finishing their two years of Dual Degree and would not be returning to the college the following year. Many would be heading out of the country to finish their studies or for work.

It was the last time we would all be together. We knew it and meant to get the most out of that day so we let it all hang out and pulled all the stops, with fantastic food, alcohol, music, dancing and all around fun day. We certainly had a day to remember, although the latter part is not what we aimed for.

Mid-afternoon, as we partied away, oblivious to the world around us, the brother of one of the girls at the party came rushing in. They lived one village over, and they had been watching the news, unlike us. He just began yelling at us to leave immediately and go home, chaotically disrupting the mood. Naturally, everyone was displeased, but anger turned into anxiety as he explained that the Israeli army had crossed the Lebanese border in force and had already reached the outskirts of Tyre. According to the news, the Israelis intended to push all the way to Beirut and put an end to the PLO presence in the country.

The party was over. We turned to the radio for news, and anyone with connections was making calls to ascertain the conditions. More than a hundred thousand Israeli troops were on the move in three columns. One along the coast that had already encircled Tyre, another into the Bekaa Valley in the East and another along the mountain ridge in between. This was serious.

It did not take long for anxiety to quickly turn into panic as Israeli Jets appeared overhead and began pounding the Palestinian camps below us with a vengeance. They came in large formations and kept coming. The camps were literally below us. We were at an altitude of about four hundred meters and directly overlooking the camps, and close enough to see people and vehicles scurrying around and blown up.

It was not that we feared being hit where we were because the offensive was specifically directed at the Palestinian camps and we felt would surely miss us. The panic resulted from the fact that the camps were on the way back home, on the southern outskirts of Beirut, and there was no driving through that. The only way back was a serpentine drive up the mountain and back down crossing quite a few dividing lines between warring territories. In times like those, militias went on full alert and deployed check points everywhere. They are in panic mode and suspicious of everyone. Whether pro- or anti-Palestinian, militias were certainly all out in force. All roads and crossings would now be manned and everyone checked.

It was time for serious planning, as the crowd included people of all religions and political persuasions. Some were active in political parties and some were Palestinians with connections to the PLO. Furthermore, we did not know which roads would even be open when we got to them.

We had no choice but to make the arduous trip and decided to redistribute people in cars regardless of how they arrived at the party. Every car was to have at least one person connected to each faction we were about to encounter on the way back. We also drove in convoy formation – more than 25 cars – for added security.

A person with the proper contacts and credentials would be able to simply get through a check point without the others being checked. The convoy added another layer, in case anyone could not muster the proper pull at the check point, those in other cars could step in.

It took three hours to get back, when it would normally take less than 20 minutes, as we went through one check point after another. First, we had to clear the Druze formations in the neighboring towns, which was relatively easy as the crowd included several locals who knew the militiamen personally, and explained the farewell party thrown for another local.

Then we came across Syrian and Palestinian check points. This is where those with PLO connections as well as the Druze, who are politically allied with them intervened on behalf of everyone.

On to the Lebanese Army Check point that separated the Druze from the Christian militias, which few of us feared, except some Palestinians. We got them through that, but then into the Christian area we entered. The Lebanese Forces were in full agreement with the Israeli invasion and had been at war with the Palestinians for seven long years by now. There was a lot of bad blood, and any Palestinian or politically active Moslem or Leftist was in serious danger.

The convoy line up was rearranged so the most connected to the Lebanese Forces would lead. Those were people related to high ranking political and militia personnel, and had the clout to get everyone through, if anyone could, but it was not to be so simple.

The Israeli invasion was viewed by the Lebanese Forces as a critical battle to finally rid the country from the PLO and hopefully the Syrian occupation all at once. This was not the standard flare up where if you were not directly involved, you were OK.

They insisted on checking everyone and found a couple of people who they wanted to keep. One was the niece of a ranking PLO leader, the other a first cousin of a main Moslem militiaman. It took more than an hour of tense negotiations and calls to finally allow them to pass, but not before a special contingent of fighters dispatched by a militia leader arrived to escort us through the Lebanese Forces territory. That was a welcome development as it guaranteed we would not have to go through the ordeal again.

We wound our way down the mountain and into East Beirut, where a few had homes on that side, and decided to stay. The rest of us had to make it through the Green Line, which was now almost sealed off, as the PLO and its allies took defensive positions in anticipation of a potential Lebanese Forces Offensive in conjunction with the Israeli push north. The Lebanese Forces also were in full battle-ready formation to prevent the PLO and its allies from shifting the fight towards them and preventing possible attempts by the leadership to escape.

Many roads were already impassable, with dirt berms erected along with concrete blocks, etc. However, there was always an open road left for those who absolutely had to cross, and our escorts knew where that was and drove us to it.

Calls were made to the other side to inform them that we were coming. Word went out to the snipers that the convoy was to get through unmolested, as it included important people. It was always good to have "important people" with you.

We found our way around the large embankments in the old city center of half blown out buildings, and the short distance felt a lot longer than at any time, as we all held our breath and hoped that all snipers got the message and would abide by it.

Finally, at the college campus in West Beirut, we could breath. We all drove there as we needed to again rearrange people so they could go home with a driver who lived near them. Some lived in the dorms, and I lived on campus.

We parked and exited the cars. We were safe, but adrenaline was still racing through everyone's vanes. We lingered a while in spite of the chaos that engulfed the city. By now, we knew for sure that we will not be seeing many of the people there for a while at least. Most were already talking about leaving the city for the safety of their hometowns, and many already had travel plans in the coming months, including me.

An era of our lives was coming to an end, and it was hard to let go, particularly under such conditions. We had just undergone one more trial under fire, where we saved each other's lives yet again. That forms bonds with people beyond any other, bonds that last a lifetime and endure the test of time and distance.

Some cultures claim that if you save someone's life, you own it. If that was the case, then we all owned each other many times over.

The tense seriousness gave way to joking and trying to alleviate the stress. We hugged and kissed and said our goodbyes over and over again. Gradually people departed, always in a hesitant "I do not want to go" kind of way.

A hijacking

It was already dark, but the dorm residents and a few who lived in the immediate neighborhood lingered on campus late into the night in spite of the intense bombing.

A friend decided to go home for a few minutes to get something. He lived two minutes away by car, yet, he disappeared for almost three hours. Eventually, we saw his unmistakable silhouette walking towards us in the dark and I made teased him, shouting "Aboulman (his nick name) who got lost on his way home."

He continued to walk towards us silently and then placed his forehead against mine and with serious anger shouted "ABOULMAN WHO WAS HIJACKED AND HIS CAR STOLEN."

We thought he was joking and started to laugh, making further jokes about him, but this usually very lighthearted man was not laughing. He was getting truly annoyed with our attitude, because he was serious about the hijacking.

He had just started to head home when three Palestinian armed men stopped him near the lower gate of the college, made him step out of his car and asked him for ID. Upon checking his ID, one told the others "This is him."

As he was wondering what he had done, they ordered him to get in the back seat of his own car. He tried to resist but had three guns pressed against him, so he relented. They took his wallet and all piled up in the car and sped off towards the Palestinian camps as the Israeli jets pounded the area with ferocity.

As he is prayed not to die and wondered what he had done, on a desolate road under bombardment, they stopped and told him to get out. He stepped out of the car believing he was a dead man, and then they told him "You are lucky we did not add you to the list of martyrs" and sped off with his car.

Instead of defending themselves against the Israeli onslaught, or at least, helping their people under bombardment, these bastards took advantage of the invasion to steel cars. Why they decided to take him with them, rather than simply take his car where they stopped him, no one knows. However, he found himself in the middle of the camps under intense aerial bombardment on foot and began to run towards the college several kilometers away.

When he entered Beirut proper, and away from the camps, he could see some cars and found a service cab to bring him to campus. He was glad to be alive but absolutely livid that they put him through this and took his car.

"The mother fuckers are stealing cars instead of fighting the Israelis." He says. "What fucking heroes!"

INDOMITABLE SPIRIT

Well, after hearing that story, we were also glad he was still alive and worked on easing his angst. The car could always be replaced, but people could not.

He would find his car a year later, ironically driven by a Christian Militiaman in East Beirut. The car thieves had that type of arrangement, where they would send the cars they stole to the other side of the divide to minimize the possibility of the cars being found. They had changed the color and even replaced the VIN number, but there was not that many of his car in Lebanon and he was keeping an eye on every one he saw.

He would thank me later for finding it, as I had marked it for him in ways that would not be altered. I had once burned a hole in his back seat with my cigarette. Furthermore, I once installed snow chains on the car too loosely, and they broke loose, tearing a gash in the plastic above the back tire. Those two marks were still on the car, and he argued to the insurance that there could not be two of his car with the same minor damage. He got his insurance money, thanks to me.

Nevertheless, at that time, we clung onto the last moments together as long as we could. We reminisced about our days in college knowing they were over, as a group at least. We choked on our tears as we questioned when we would reunite again.

This was the last I saw many of these friends. The next day I drove my mother and sisters north to the village, supposedly for a few days as my father stayed behind at the college. This was the week before finals and we were planning on returning and taking our exams. This was Lebanon after all, and life proceeded under any circumstances.

However, the Israelis reached Beirut within a couple of days as the PLO was too busy stealing cars and the city came under a prolonged siege. Final Exams were cancelled and we got whatever grade we had at that time.

I would spend time with a few of those friends that summer before I headed out to the US two months later. I kept in touch with the few that I could after that, as so many moved around, and in pre-internet and email times, it was very easy to lose touch. I have since reconnected to others, in some cases 30 years later.

There are a lot of whom I have not seen since. They remain faces from days gone by, forever etched in our memories.

INDOMITABLE SPIRIT

LAST SUMMER

The Israeli siege of West Beirut lasted several weeks with intermittent fighting while the exit of the PLO from Beirut was negotiated. Summer vacation started early that year, and the battles were both a nuisance and entertainment.

We immediately began searching for each other after exiting West Beirut. Some were easy to find as we knew where they stayed in East Beirut and connected quickly, but others were at unknown locations. All communications were severed with West Beirut using HAM radios as the only means of communicating with anyone caught in the siege.

We soon learned from talking to my father that several of our friends who did not exit before West Beirut was sealed off had taken to serve the refugees. The war had displaced some people from the southern outskirts of the city who took refuge, among other places, in schools and colleges. The empty classroom buildings became make shit shelters.

Several of my friends spent their days taking care of these people until they could eventually get out, yet some never left. They delivered blankets, food and whatever else was needed for families to stay in classrooms and even helped provide security for those families.

Everyone knew where I was, and it was the furthest from the fighting with a nice beach, and perfect June weather. They eventually came to the beach by the dozens, some staying at my house, others camping out near the beach, and some just came and went. Once more we turned the disruption of war into an opportunity to party.

Yarze-Baabda: Into the Fire

A few days into the siege, with disrupted communications, a friend and I headed towards Beirut to find Alya, a friend who lived in Yarze in the hills east of Beirut. We did not find anyone home and headed to another friend's house in Baabda nearby overlooking the Palestinian refugee camps.

Israeli aerial bombardment of the camps was in full swing and we decide to sit on their balcony and watch. Israeli artillery was sending so many fluorescent bombs to light up the place that we could see every detail in the night. Our host brought out some drinks and snacks and we settled in to watch the action below.

We could clearly see every movement in the camps, as equipment and personnel scurried around, and watched the jets dive in and take them out. The jets would come low over the water farther out, pop up over the camps, drop their bombs and swing back over the sea. They would turn right in front of us so close we could feel the heat of the engines.

It was an action movie on steroids, and we did not give the risk of being so close to the action any attention. The PLO, for whom we had developed a serious dislike, was being pulverized and we were cheering for what we believed to be the end of a long hegemony over parts of Lebanon.

However, a massive amount of anti-aircraft fire was coming from the camps, particularly fifty caliber guns. Those tended to follow the aircraft after their bombing raids, which would aim them in our direction as the jets swung past us. Yet, we enjoyed our beer, vodka and snacks, and cheered on.

By midnight, her parents came home to find us relaxed on the balcony in a war zone. Let us just say they were not amused. They tossed us out with a few expletives and sent us home. She came to the beach a couple of days later and told us they spent half an hour chastising her for being that stupid. They used the standard, "if your friends are idiots, you do not need to go along". Well, we were not stupid. We were defiant and refused to let the war tame us.

The next day, we tried again to find the friend we had not found the previous day. She lived in a beautiful villa with an iron fence around the property further up the mountain from the balcony we sat on, but the back of the villa overlooked the camps as well.

When we get there, all was quiet but the electricity was gone. We could see candlelight inside, and thought we were in luck, so we parked, walked over and knocked on the door. I had to knock several times before her mother opened the door crouched on the floor, she pulled me in and shut the door.

"Are you OK?" She asked with a high level of anxiety. "What are you doing here?"

"Yeah, I am fine." I told her trying to stay standing as she pulled me down. "We thought we would pick up your daughter to spend some time with us at the beach."

"You drove all the way here just to pick her up!" she barks at me. "Are you crazy!"

At this stage I am thinking the woman had lost her mind. I could hear the Israeli bombardment of the camps below, but there was nothing happening around us, yet she was acting as if the gates of hell were open. Also, why was she so insistent on me crouching down with her? I finally obliged her and crouched down trying to lessen her anxiety and asked if her daughter was around.

"Alya is in Jounieh. It is not safe here. I will tell her to follow you to Monsef. Now get out and leave while you still can." She said as she opened the door and pushed me out.

I told her we could pick Alya up on the way if she told me where she was.

INDOMITABLE SPIRIT

"HURRY." She yelled "No time for explanations."

My friend was still standing outside and watched the whole exchange at the door. He opened his arms at me with a gesture that said, "what the fuck just happened"? As we walked to my car outside the yard fence, I told him she had lost her mind and explained that her daughter, who was in Jounieh, would follow us.

We had barely cleared the villa from our rearview mirror when the gates of hell she was fearing opened up. The Palestinians had decided to vent their frustration in the only direction they could, against the Christians they accused of siding with the Israelis. They had been bombarding the area all day, and we just happened to arrive when they took a brief pose. Maybe they had been letting their artillery guns cool off.

Now they were at it again and bombs were crashing into the area at the rate of more than one per second. Explosions were all around, and I was the only car on the road. I had to drive down the mountain to East Beirut, even closer to the camps, and then turn north to get to Monsef.

We managed to avoid getting hit by any of the artillery but came pretty close on several occasions as shells hit the road a few meters away from the car. Yet, even with all this, we did not go straight home, but stopped on the way and join some friends who were hanging out at a nice bar in Jounieh. The joint was in an arched stone basement and relatively safe from the bombardment, which by then had reached Jounieh.

The music was loud enough to drown out the sound of artillery explosions outside, and we partied late into the night defying the war as usual. Then off to a late-night swim with those camped out at the beach.

The next morning, our Yarze friend showed up at my door in Monsef to spend a few days. With a big laugh, she told me how crazy her mother thought I was. "Did she just figure this out?", I replied. Of course her Momma had warned her to stay in Monsef away from the fighting and not go out at night. Yeah, like that was happening. During the time she spent with us, we hit all the party joints in Byblos and Jounieh and had a blast, once again, against the odds.

LOSING MY BEST CHILDHOOD FRIEND

My closest childhood friend, also from Monsef, had plans to head to California in mid-June. He had volunteered at a summer camp and as a guitar player was dreaming of trying to meet Eric Clapton, who was his idol. He could not stop talking about it, and really believed he could arrange a meeting with Clapton.

The original plan called for a charter plane to take several scout leaders from Beirut to Los Angeles. The siege on Beirut made a change of plans necessary, and the charter plane would thus leave from Cyprus. That required a boat ride from Jounieh to Cyprus, which had become standard during the war as so many in the Christian area could not make it to the airport south of Beirut in a Palestinian controlled area.

However, the Israeli invasion killed that plan as well, as the Lebanese Forces had banned any able-bodied man between the age of eighteen and forty-five from leaving. They were anticipating joining the battle against the Palestinians and potentially the Syrians, and wanted to keep in the country, all the men they could call on.

After a few calls he managed to locate a cargo ship that would take him on board and was leaving from Tripoli in the north. He could not leave through the port but could drive northwards and out of the Lebanese Forces territory and then he could get on the boat in Tripoli.

His mother was adamant that he should not go. She just had such a bad feeling about his trip that she convinced his father not to drive him to Tripoli. As much as he explained to her that he was leaving the war zone, not entering it, she would not listen. In fact, most people were seriously concerned about any movement across dividing lines, but we were not like most people.

Thus, I offered to take him if he really wanted to go. I thought I was being a good friend and helping him out in his time of need. In hind sight, I cannot count how many times I had wished I had not been such a good friend on that day. Maybe he would still be with us. Yet, then I think that maybe it was his time to go, if not that way, it would have been some other way.

The day of the trip his mother dropped to her knees begging him not to go. She clung to his feet and kissed them, weeping as if it was to be the last time she would ever see him. Maybe it was mother's intuition? Maybe she knew what we did not? She certainly felt it was going to be over.

He broke away in tears and I drove him to the port of Tripoli where I found the captain who also had a son about our age taking the voyage with a friend. Before leaving, my friend asked me for some cash and wrote me an American Express traveler's check in return. I still carry that in my wallet, as this signature (as far as I know) was the last thing he ever wrote.

I arrived home late that afternoon and we gathered to watch the football world cup. I still remember Algeria beat Germany 2-1, and we were joking that my friend the die-hard German fan would die if he knew that. We believed he could have watched the game on the boat.

The captain said he did. He watched the game in his quarters with the captain's son and friend. As the story was told, upon exiting the room after the game an explosion ripped through the room tossing his body overboard. However, we heard that later and had no knowledge of it that evening.

The next day a sizeable group of about twenty men and women had planned a trip up Nahr Ibrahim to spend the day at a spring halfway up the river. We drove up to an old hydroelectric power plant and from there hiked a couple of kilometers along the river and veered right.

There was a spring that came out into a small waterfall, which over time had carved out a nice little swimming pool in the rocks.

It was heavenly. We had the place to ourselves except for a brief visit by four people looking to enjoy the same beauty. They arrived as we were finishing lunch and enjoying some fruits. One of the girls in their group reached for a peach from our basket and said it just looked so good she had to have it. We did not mind but her own friends did. One guy from her group tried to pry the peach out of her hand and ended up wrestling her on the rocks for the peach.

We tried to stay out of an argument between friends, but the poor girl was being pulverized by this guy. We intervened and pulled him off of her and told him we wanted her to have the peach, and it was really not worth all that. He backed off, but then they decided to head out all upset and leave the place all for us again.

The water was freezing but exhilarating after a long time in June sun, and we all swam in this tiny crystal-clear pond. We were having the time of our lives when our day was interrupted by very bad news.

My friend's brother and a couple of others followed us up the river to inform us about the explosion aboard the ship. Everyone there knew him well and some were closely related to him. Screams of joy turned into tears of sorrow.

We could not believe he was gone. We did not want to believe it. We kept telling his brother that since they have not found a body, he may still be alive. We argued that he was a good swimmer and if he had jumped overboard he could swim to shore, as the boat was less than two kilometers out at sea when it happened. Wishful thinking, trying to deny a reality we did not want to accept, but, deep down, we knew he was gone.

Either way, the fun was over. We all headed back as his brother argued he wanted to go rent a boat and search for him. We could not convince him that it was not possible. There was a war going on and a boat with strangers roaming along the coast was a formula for getting shot. The Lebanese Army and Coast Guard was searching for him and two others who were missing, and if they were to be found they would find them.

The wait was excruciating as hours turned into days with no news of our friend. Everyone kept telling me that his mother was asking for me. Everyone had been over to console her except me, and she could not believe that I had not gone to see her yet, but I could not bring myself to go to their home.

I had been having nightmares for some time in which he would die in an explosion. I could not remember the whole dream when I woke up, but I remembered the ending. It always ended in me walking into their house and his mother turning and pointing at me while saying "You took him". That is when I woke up in a sweat. She was always in the same spot in the middle of the long couch and in every one of those nasty dreams, she was wearing the same dress.

As the dreams kept coming back to me, I dreaded going to their home more and more. I felt a deep sense of guilt that I actually took him against her most desperate pleas and felt a deep sense of responsibility for his death.

Eventually, we got news that they found a body that matched his description, and two older men headed out to identify the body and managed to confirm his clothing and his wallet. However, having spent six days in the sea the body was badly disfigured, and they decided to seal him in the casket before bringing him home.

It was now funeral time, and there was no avoiding his home. I headed over, and as I entered the living room, his mother was sitting in the middle of the long couch waring the same dress in my dreams. She turned towards me, pointed at me and said "You took him." It was just too much to take. I had been strong and stern until then, but this just knocked me over. The sight of this devastated mother holding me responsible for the loss of her son, just like my nightmares, and rightfully so, felt like a knife through the heart. I turned around and walked outside. I could not make it to hug and kiss her just yet.

The anger I felt for being responsible for his death overshadowed my sadness of losing my closest friend. Had I not driven him there, he would not have died, I kept telling myself. If I could only turn the clock back and refuse to take him. But, tears did not come to my eyes yet. I almost turned into stone.

We helped in all the funeral arrangements and serving all the people that came to present their condolences. That was as much our house as any. We had spent so much time there.

The next day was the church funeral service and then burial behind the church. We carried the casket of our fallen friend in solemn silence. I was still struggling with the notion that I would never see him again, and images of all we had been through together flashed in my head. The whole funeral process was nothing but a blur.

As the crowd thinned, we broke away and walked towards a nearby house of a relative. The third man in the trio that included our lost friend slung his hand over my shoulder and said "Mahatma is gone." We had nicknamed him mahatma due to his thin and extremely flexible body, and joked that he looked like a yogi guru.

With that phrase, we finally broke down and cried. It was the first tears either one of us had shed. However, now we could not stop. We entered the house and sat down still clinging to each other and weeping like babies. Three girls had come along trying to console us, but they cried harder than we did. He was their life-long friend also.

We let it all out. A week of sternness turned into torrential tears. I kept harping on the fact that I was responsible, and they kept weeping and trying to convince me I was not. I needed to believe in fate. I needed to believe that his time was up and would have died anyway by some other means. It would keep me sane. Yet, it did not reduce the pain of loss one bit, and it did not reduce the frustration that I was accomplice to his ending.

A couple of days later a common friend told us we should stop morning him as he was in a better place. That was standard to say, as if it made things better, but she had a different twist. She told us she saw him in a dream carrying a small baby, and he told her to stop crying, because all was fine. He was in a much better place and would be waiting for us, however, for a long time.

In her dream she asked him who the baby was and he told her it was the daughter of someone in the village. It was only the next day that we heard that the women had lost her baby close to full term. The conveyor of the dream did not know about the loss of the baby that night, yet, in her dream our friend was holding the baby in the afterlife.

With that, we believed her and began to think of him in a better place while we still confronted this nasty-world we lived in. Maybe we needed to believe her? It certainly made it easier to accept the reality, but it did not ease the pain of not having him around. We still missed him dearly.

Till this day, I have his picture in my living room. Our other friend named his oldest son after him. He lives on in our hearts and our memories, along with all the others we lost in that dastardly war.

A FINAL FAREWELL

The siege of Beirut dragged on with regular bombardment occurring back and forth all summer. We got over our loss and soon returned to our boisterous behavior defying the war and playing amongst the bombs.

I had dreamt about heading to the US for years, and having been born in Atlanta, I felt I was coming home. I dreamt of the freedom of living on my own in an idealized version of the US, and all these years spent the time feeling that I could not wait.

However, as we approached July of 1982 which was less than a month from my planned trip, I began to feel anxious, as it all became real. As much as I looked forward to my new life in the US, I became acutely aware of what I was leaving behind.

A lifetime of memories. A family that raised me, cared for me and loved me unconditionally. A hoard of dear friends with whom I have been to hell and back more times than I could remember. An endless barrage of places and venues that had become an integral part of who I was. All that would be left behind for good. My departure was not a vacation. In fact, I was leaving to finish my studies, and would be gone for a long time. I began to wonder if any of my past would still be there when I returned, or, would everyone else have moved on as well? We would all certainly grow up, graduate and start working. I knew a certain era of my life was ending and would never come back.

The anxiety of losing all that made me cling even tighter to it all while I still could. I needed to get as much of that life as I could before I let go of it for good. I sometimes found myself staring endlessly at the sea just watching the moonlight dancing on the waves and listening to the waves make their music on the rocks. That was something I would not hear in Texas where I was headed. Suddenly, I would snap out of it and live a little more of that life. There was no time to waste. Time was running out. What else did I need to do before I left?

All those feelings gave new meaning to my last month in Lebanon, and I was not alone in this state. Many others were also about to leave, and even those staying felt the anxiety of the group break up. It is never the same when half the group departs.

There would be no chalet 70 the next winter. There would be no beach house where we all gathered and slept on the floors. There would be no one with the keys to all doors on campus. It certainly would not be the same. Plus, no one knew where the Israeli siege would lead. Would there be any of what we had left by the time the fighting ceased?

We partied tirelessly that July. There were no summer classes for anyone and nothing to interfere with a twenty-four-hour party day. A lot of people, escaping the siege of Beirut, joined us in Monsef, and we lived it up.

We hit every joint we ever knew and could get to that month. We hiked the mountains and travelled the riverbeds. We camped all over the place, but especially on the beach. I could not get enough of that beach. Unlike most of the others, that beach was my whole life. Those rocks were as much a part of me as any of my body parts. I was running and playing on those rocks from the time I could remember. I had every little detail of the rocks memorized and could swim in pitch dark and avoid every underwater rock. I had also left enough skin and flesh on those rocks over the years to make several more of me.

Now I was flying away and would not get to see these rocks, hear the waves or smell the salt water in the morning. I would stand on the shore and take as deep a breath as I could take as if trying to store it for the future and take it with me.

The people where even more important. All those friends who had become more family than friends. We had defied the devil and cheated death together for so long that we had come to depend on each other's presence, and soon we would not be together anymore.

A small consolation was the knowledge that three close friends who grew up with me on that beach were already in Texas and I would be with them. However, the beach would not be with us. Neither would anything else from Lebanon. Yet, such was life. All good things had to come to an end. It is strange to most to hear about life in a war zone as good, but those years were the best of our lives. We lived more in those years than all the remaining years combined. The death machine created a deeper appreciation of life, and we defied the war and lived life by resisting death.

It came time for me I to leave, and the port was still closed to all eighteen to forty-five-year old men. As usual the Lebanese always found a way around any obstacle. My plans shifted to include a long drive to fly from Damascus as there were buses carrying people there.

My father finally came from Beirut to say goodbye to me and bring the stuff I needed to take with me. I had left the city supposedly for a few days in summer, but now I was leaving for good and needed all my clothes, including winter clothes, books, etc. I teased him that I had forced him to leave the city just before it got completely sealed off for the next month. He could not get back into the city as the final push to remove the PLO was underway. My trip got him out and allowed him to relax on the beach with family rather than spend the month in a bomb shelter.

I was to depart at five in the morning to catch the bus, and we did not sleep that night. All my friends came for one last beach party. We partied hard, and I kept going in the water for a night swim, trying to get it out of my system before I left, but I never could. We tried our best to be our usual joyful selves, laughing in the face of anything. We partially succeeded, but there was a lot of angst in the air for me. Every girl I danced with reminded me that it would be the last time we did that. We would kiss and stare endlessly at each other as if making sure we would not forget what we looked like. Everyone wanted to share one more drink, one more swim, one more dance, one more laugh. But it was not enough. It would never be enough.

Eventually as the night changed into morning, I had to shower and get dressed. Everyone waited for me to get out and said their final goodbyes before I got in the car. We hugged so hard we almost crushed each other's chests, and I kissed the girls over and over again.

I did not want to leave but I had to. I stared into the faces of dozens of my closest friends waving goodbye as the car pulled out and I was hit with a massive sinking feeling of loss like I had never felt before. If I had to leave, I wished I could pack them all in suitcases and take them with me.

Under relentless bombardment I boarded the bus in Jounieh, and then it headed north, as the road to Damascus was a front line between the Israelis and the Syrians. We had to drive eight hours north to Tripoli and then Homs and then back south to Damascus, so the bus passed through Monsef, and I got one final look at my beach as I left it all behind.

I would spend five days in Paris with my older sister who was doing an internship there. Some of my friends were already in Paris and we spent time partying and enjoying the city before heading to my new life in Texas.

True, I physically left it all behind but carried it all in my heart. Every moment, every laugh, every smiling face and every tearful eye remained with me. I could take myself out of Lebanon but could never take Lebanon out of me.

I had great times in college in Texas and Atlanta, and beyond college, but, somehow, it would not compare. The danger zone that bound us together was not there. Life was strangely too easy. We had gotten used to doing everything the hard way and against the odds. That adrenaline rush was not present in the US. We could not even get a rush from crazy driving, as the police would throw us in jail.

Maybe it was for the best. Maybe it was time to grow up. Maybe it was meant to ensure that those memories remain unique and special.

Life in the shadow of death was livelier than any I have experienced since.

We resisted evil and maintained our humanity and civility against a world determined to rob us of it all.

We went on to finish college, with a large number acquiring post graduate degrees, and excelled in the business and scientific world. Many who left the country returned to rebuild it.

All the evil of this world could not tame us. It could not destroy us or hinder our progress.

Our indomitable spirit defied death and lived to tell a wonderful story.

WE WON.

www.ingramcontent.com/pod-product-compliance
Lightning Source LLC
Chambersburg PA
CBHW020633230426
43665CB00008B/154